T0159250

RECIPES FROM MY
ITALIAN GRANDMOTHER

RECIPES FROM MY
ITALIAN GRANDMOTHER

A guide to ingredients, techniques and 100 traditional dishes,
handed down from mothers to daughters for generations

KATE WHITEMAN, JENI WRIGHT
AND ANGELA BOGGIANO

LORENZ BOOKS

This edition is published by Lorenz Books, an imprint of Anness Publishing Ltd,
Blaby Road, Wigston, Leicestershire LE18 4SE; info@anness.com
www.lorenzbooks.com; www.annesspublishing.com

If you like the images in this book and would like to investigate using them for publishing,
promotions or advertising, please visit our website www.practicalpictures.com for more information.

Publisher: Joanna Lorenz
Senior Editor: Linda Fraser
Designer: Siân Keogh
Photographers: William Adams-Lingwood
and Janine Hosegood (cut-outs)
Stylist: Marian Price

A CIP catalogue record for this book is available from the British Library.

Previously published as part of a larger volume, *The Italian Ingredients Cookbook*

PUBLISHER'S NOTE
Although the advice and information in this book are believed to be accurate and true at the time of
going to press, neither the authors nor the publisher can accept any legal responsibility or liability for
any errors or omissions that may have been made nor for any inaccuracies nor for any loss, harm or
injury that comes about from following instructions or advice in this book.

NOTES
Bracketed terms are intended for American readers.
For all recipes, quantities are given in both metric and imperial measures and, where appropriate,
in standard cups and spoons. Follow one set of measures, but not a mixture, because they
are not interchangeable. Standard spoon and cup measures are level.
1 tsp = 5ml, 1 tbsp = 15ml, 1 cup = 250ml/8fl oz.
Australian standard tablespoons are 20ml.
Australian readers should use 3 tsp in place of 1 tbsp for measuring small quantities.
American pints are 16fl oz/2 cups. American readers should use 20fl oz/2.5 cups
in place of 1 pint when measuring liquids.
Electric oven temperatures in this book are for conventional ovens. When using a fan oven, the
temperature will probably need to be reduced by about 10–20°C/20–40°F. Since ovens vary, you
should check with your manufacturer's instruction book for guidance.
Medium (US large) eggs are used unless otherwise stated.

Contents

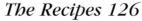

Introduction

···

Italian cooking reflects the fact that the country was unified only in 1861. Until then, each region produced its own characteristic cuisine, relying exclusively on ingredients that could be gathered, cultivated or reared locally. Nowadays, of course, regional produce can be easily transported all over the country, but Italians still prefer to base their cooking on local ingredients, because they regard quality and freshness as more important than diversity and innovation. So the most flavoursome sun–ripened tomatoes, aubergines (eggplants) and (bell) peppers are still found in the south, the freshest shellfish is on offer along the coast, the finest hams come from the area where the pigs are raised, and so on. *La cucina italiana* remains distinctly regional; northern Italian cooking, for example, incorporates ingredients that are simply never found in the recipes of Sicily and Naples, and vice-versa. In the dairy-farming north, butter is used in place of the olive oil so prevalent in the south; bread and polenta are eaten instead of pasta. The only unifying feature is the insistence on high quality ingredients. Good food has always been essential to the Italian way of life. *La cucina italiana* is one of the oldest cooking cultures in the world, dating back to the ancient Greeks and perhaps even earlier.

THIS ITALIAN BUTCHER'S STORE (BELOW) NOT ONLY SELLS THE LOCAL *CINGHIALE* (WILD BOAR), BUT ALSO CURED MEATS, CHEESES AND OTHER ESSENTIAL COOKING INGREDIENTS.

The Romans adored food and often ate and drank to excess; it was they who really laid the foundations of Italian and European cuisine. The early Romans were peasant farmers who ate only the simple, rustic foods they could produce, such as grain, cheeses and olives. For them, meat was an unheard-of luxury; animals were bred to work in the fields and were too precious to eat. Trading links with other parts of the world, however, encouraged Roman farmers to cultivate new vegetables and fruits and, of course, vines, while their trade in salt and exotic spices enabled them to preserve and pickle all kinds of meat, game and fish. Food became a near-obsession and ever more elaborate dishes were devised to be served at the decadent and orgiastic banquets for which the Romans were famed. The decline and fall of the Roman Empire led inevitably to a deterioration in the quality of cooking and a return to simple, basic foods. For centuries, regional cuisine reverted to its original uncomplicated style. With the Renaissance, however, came great wealth and a new interest in elaborate food. Once again, rich families strove to outdo each other with lavish banquets where courses of rich, extravagant foods were served – truffles, song-birds, game, desserts dripping with honey and spices – all washed down with quantities of wine. The poor, of course, continued to subsist

OLIVES (TOP) GROWING IN GROVES ALONG-SIDE GRAPE VINES ON AN UMBRIAN HILLSIDE, AND A SELECTION OF CURED SAUSAGES AND AIR-DRIED *PROSCIUTTO* HANGING IN STORE (ABOVE) ARE JUST TWO OF THE VAST ARRAY OF TRADITIONAL ITALIAN INGREDIENTS THAT ARE NOW EXPORTED AROUND THE WORLD.

ITALIAN COOKS INSIST ON HIGH QUALITY
COOKING INGREDIENTS AND EVEN LOCAL
DELICATESSENS (RIGHT) ARE PACKED FULL OF
FRESH AND PRESERVED INGREDIENTS AND
OTHER FOODS – FRUITY CAKES AND CRISP
COOKIES, SUCH AS *PANFORTE* AND *CANTUCCI*,
DRIED *FAGIOLI* (BEANS), FLAVOURFUL OLIVE
OILS AND VINEGARS, *PROSCIUTTO CRUDO*
(CURED HAMS), TRADITIONAL CHEESES, SUCH
AS *PARMIGIANO REGGIANO,* PICKLES AND
PRESERVES, MARINATED OLIVES, CANNED
TOMATOES AND BOTTLED SAUCES.

THE SUN-DRENCHED SOUTHERN REGIONS OF
ITALY PROVIDE ESSENTIAL STORE CUPBOARD
(PANTRY) INGREDIENTS, SUCH AS FULL-
FLAVOURED GREEN AND BLACK OLIVES AND
DELICIOUS SUN-DRIED TOMATOES.

on the simple foods they had always eaten, but the wealthier middle
classes developed a taste for fine foods and created their own bourgeois
dishes. The finer features of Italian cooking even reached the French,
when Catherine de' Medici went to Paris to marry the future Henri II,
taking 50 of her own cooks with her. They introduced new ingredients
and cooking techniques to France and in return learnt the art of French
cuisine. In those regions of Italy that border France, you can still find
reciprocal influences of French classical cooking, but, generally speaking,
Italians do not like elaborately sauced dishes, preferring to let the natural
flavours of their raw ingredients speak for themselves.

The essence of Italian cooking today is simplicity. The Italian way of
cooking fish is a good example of this. In coastal areas, freshly caught fish
is most often simply chargrilled over hot coals, then served with nothing
more than a splash of extra virgin olive oil, a wedge of lemon and freshly
ground black pepper. Recipes such as *carpaccio di tonno*, in which the
fish is so delicious raw that cooking seems unnecessary, and *branzino al
forno*, where the delicate flavour of fennel is used to compliment rather
than obscure the fresh taste of the fish, are typically simple, as is *grigliata
di calamari*, squid chargrilled with chillies to reflect its robust character.

Italians learn to appreciate good food when they are young children,
and eating is one of the major pleasures of the day, no matter what the day
of the week or time of the year. Witness an Italian family gathered around
the Sunday lunch table in a local restaurant, and consider how the Italian

menu of *antipasto* followed by pasta, rice or gnocchi, then fish, meat and vegetables served in sequence is devised so that each can be savoured separately – both the food and the occasion are to be enjoyed as long as possible. The first course, or *antipasto*, is a unique feature. In restaurants, this can be a vast array of different dishes, both hot and cold, from which diners can choose as few or as many as they wish. At home with the family, it is more likely to be a slice or two of *salami* or *prosciutto crudo* with fresh figs or melon if these are in season. But no matter how humble or grand the setting or the occasion, the *antipasto* is always visually tempting. Dishes such as *bruschetta casalinga* and *peperoni arrostiti con pesto*, which look so attractive, are typical in this way.

The variety and diversity of the Italian ingredients available in super-markets and delicatessens will surely inspire you to concoct any number of delicious meals, from a simple dish of pasta to a full-blown four-course dinner. A plate of *antipasto* followed by pasta or risotto flavoured with seasonal ingredients, then simply-cooked meat or fish and finally a local cheese and fruit make a veritable feast. You could prepare a different meal along these lines every day of the year and almost never repeat the same combination. If you visit Italy, avail yourself of the wonderful local ingredients to prepare a menu full of the flavours of the region. Every area has its own special delights that make cooking a real pleasure.

FRESH INGREDIENTS ARE HIGHLY PRIZED BY ITALIAN COOKS AND ARE OFTEN SOLD FROM THE LOCAL OUTDOOR MARKETS: DOZENS OF *CARCIOFI* (GLOBE ARTICHOKES) ARE TIED READY FOR TRANSPORT TO A LOCAL MARKET (BELOW), AND AN OUTDOOR STALL IS PILED HIGH WITH A TYPICALLY WIDE SELECTION OF HIGH-QUALITY FRESH HERBS AND SALAD LEAVES, VEGETABLES AND FRUITS (BOTTOM).

The Ingredients

*Italian cooks have traditionally relied on local
ingredients – whatever could be gathered, cultivated
or reared locally. Today, our supermarkets and
delicatessens are full of these flavourful, good
quality ingredients. This comprehensive guide
provides essential information on the huge range
of Italian foods and shows you how to prepare and
cook them.*

Pasta

If there is one ingredient that sums up the essence of Italian cooking, it must surely be pasta, that wonderfully simple and nutritious staple that can be formed into an almost infinite variety of shapes and sizes. In Italy, pasta is an essential part of every full meal and does not constitute a meal on its own. Il primo, *as the pasta course is known, is eaten between the* antipasto *(appetizer) and* il secondo *(the main course). Sometimes small pasta shapes are served in soup as* pasta in brodo. *There are two basic types of pasta,* pastasciutta *(dried) and* pasta fresca *(fresh).*

Dried pasta is nowadays factory-made. The dough is made from hard durum wheat, which produces an elastic dough, ideal for shaping into literally hundreds of different forms, from long, thin spaghetti to elaborate spirals and frilly, bow-shaped *farfalle*. Basic pasta dough is made only from durum wheat and water, although it is sometimes enriched with eggs (*pasta all'uovo*), which add an attractive yellow tinge, or coloured and flavoured with ingredients such as spinach (*pasta verde*) or squid ink (*pasta nera*). These traditional flavourings are more successful than modern gimmicky creations such as chocolate-flavoured pasta. (Most Italians would throw up their hands in horror at this unauthentic folly.) Dried pasta has a nutty flavour and should always retain a firm texture when cooked. It is generally used for thinner-textured, more robust sauces.

Fresh pasta is usually made by hand, using superfine plain (all-purpose) white flour enriched with eggs. Unlike dried pasta dough, it can be easily kneaded and is very malleable. Fresh pasta is often wrapped round a stuffing of meat, fish, vegetables or cheese to make ravioli, tortelli or cappelletti, or layered with sauce and meat or vegetables, as in lasagne.

Commercially made fresh pasta is made with durum wheat, water and eggs. The dough is harder than that used for hand-made pasta, but it can be easily kneaded by machine. The flavour and texture of all fresh pasta is very delicate, so it is best suited to more creamy sauces.

HISTORY

The argument about the origins of pasta will probably rage on forever; the Chinese claim that they were the first to discover the art of noodle-making and that pasta was brought to Italy by Marco Polo. The Italians, of course, claim it as their own invention. Historians tell us that the Romans and probably even the ancient Greeks used to eat pasta. Certainly the climate of southern Italy was ideally suited to growing durum wheat, so this theory is quite likely, but the popularity of pasta really spread in Italy in the 14th century, when bakeries in southern Italy started to sell pasta as an alternative to bread.

Then, as now, pasta became the traditional *primo* of the south, although in the poorest areas it constituted a complete meal. Its popularity filtered up to the north of Italy and by the 19th century huge factories had been set up to mass-produce vast quantities of pasta, which became an integral part of all Italian cooking.

BUYING AND STORING

Always buy dried pasta made from Italian durum wheat. Even after the packet has been opened, dried pasta will keep for weeks in an airtight container. Hand-made fresh pasta will only keep for a couple of days, but it can be successfully frozen.

Machine-made fresh pasta is pasteurized and vacuum-packed, so it will keep in the refrigerator for up to two weeks and can be frozen for up to six months. When buying coloured and flavoured pasta, make sure that it has been made with natural ingredients.

COOKING PASTA

Allow about 75g/3oz pasta per serving as a first course. All pasta must be cooked in a large pan filled with plenty of salted, fast-boiling water.

For long shapes such as spaghetti, drop one end of the pasta into the water and, as it softens, push it down gently until it bends in the middle and is completely immersed.

Cooking times vary according to the type, size and shape of the pasta, but, as a general rule, filled pasta takes about 12 minutes, dried pasta needs 8–10 minutes and fresh pasta only 2–3 minutes. All pasta should be cooked al dente, so that it is still resistant to the bite. Always test pasta for doneness just before you think it should be ready; it can easily overcook. To stop the cooking, take the pan off the heat and run a little cold water into it, then drain the pasta.

Preparing Fresh Pasta

1 Allow 1 egg to 90g/3¹/₂oz/³/₄ cup superfine plain (all-purpose) flour (Italian *tipo 00* is best). Sift the flour and a pinch of salt into a mound on a clean work surface and make a well. Break the eggs into the well and gradually work in the flour until completely amalgamated.

2 Knead the dough with floured hands for at least 15 minutes, until it is very smooth, firm and elastic. (If you are short of time or energy, you can do this in a food processor.)

3 Chill the dough for 20 minutes, then roll it to the required thickness and cut it into your desired shape. (You can buy a specially shaped rolling-pin to make the squares for filled pasta.) A pasta machine will make this process much easier. Leave the pasta to dry for at least 1 hour before cooking it.

Pasta Varieties

Pasta shapes can be divided roughly into four categories: long strands and ribbons, flat, short and filled.

The best-known long variety is spaghetti, which comes in a thinner version, spaghettini, and the flatter *linguine*, which means 'little tongues'. *Bucatini* are thicker and hollow – perfect for trapping sauces in the cavity. Ribbon pasta is wider than the strands: fettuccine, *trenette* and tagliatelle all fall into this category. Dried tagliatelle is usually sold folded into nests, which unravel during cooking. A mixture of white and green noodles is known as *paglia e fieno* (straw and hay). Pappardelle are the widest ribbon pasta; they are often served with *sugo alla lepre* (hare sauce). The thinnest pasta strands are vermicelli (little worms) and ultra-fine *capelli d'angelo* (angel's hair).

In Italy, flat fresh pasta is often called *maccheroni*, not to be confused with the short tubes with which we are familiar. Lasagne and cannelloni are larger flat rectangles, used for layering or rolling round a filling; dried cannelloni are already formed into wide tubes. Layered pasta dishes such as this are cooked *al forno* (baked in the oven). Fillings for fresh pasta squares include meat, pumpkin, artichokes, ricotta and spinach, shellfish, chicken and rabbit. There are dozens of names for filled pasta, but the only difference lies in the shape and size. Ravioli are square, tortelli are usually round, while tortellini and *anolini* are ring-shaped.

As for pasta shapes, the list is almost endless and the names wonderfully descriptive. There are *maltagliati* (badly cut), *orecchiette* (little ears) and *cappellacci* (little hats), while from the natural world come penne (quills), *conchiglie* (little shells), *farfalle* (butterflies) and *lumache* (snails).

When choosing the appropriate pasta shape for the sauce, there are no hard and fast rules, but long, thin pasta is best for olive-oil-based and delicate shellfish sauces. Short pasta shapes with wide openings (such as *conchiglie* and penne) will trap meaty or spicy sauces, as will spirals and curls. Almost any pasta is suitable for tomato sauce.

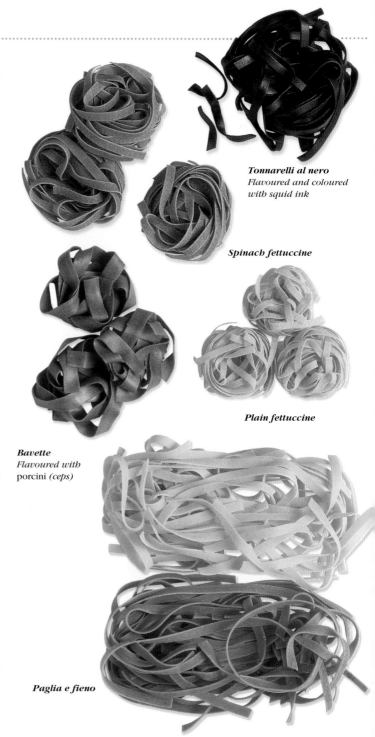

Tonnarelli al nero
Flavoured and coloured with squid ink

Spinach fettuccine

Plain fettuccine

Bavette
Flavoured with porcini *(ceps)*

Paglia e fieno

Long Pasta

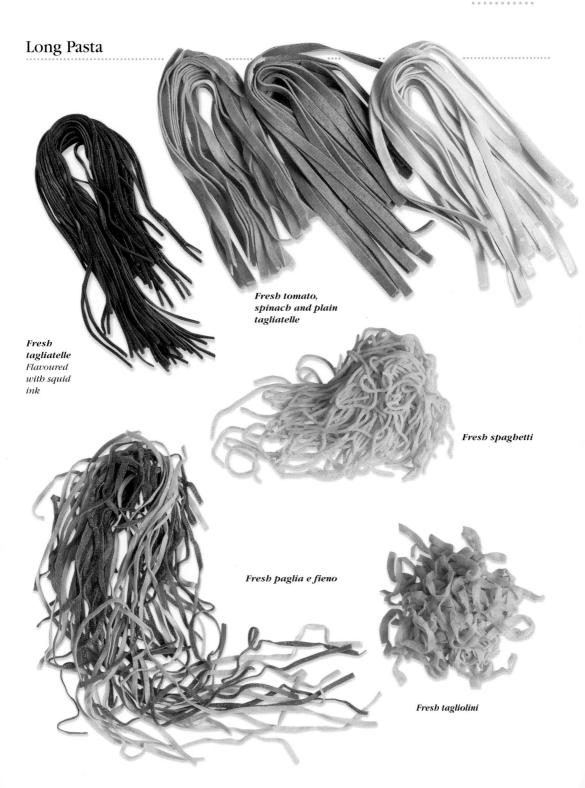

Fresh tomato, spinach and plain tagliatelle

Fresh tagliatelle
Flavoured with squid ink

Fresh spaghetti

Fresh paglia e fieno

Fresh tagliolini

Long Pasta

Wholemeal (whole-wheat) farro

Long, plain spaghetti
Still sometimes sold in the traditional blue paper roll

Spaghetti tricolore
Mixed plain, spinach and tomato spaghetti

Long, plain spaghetti

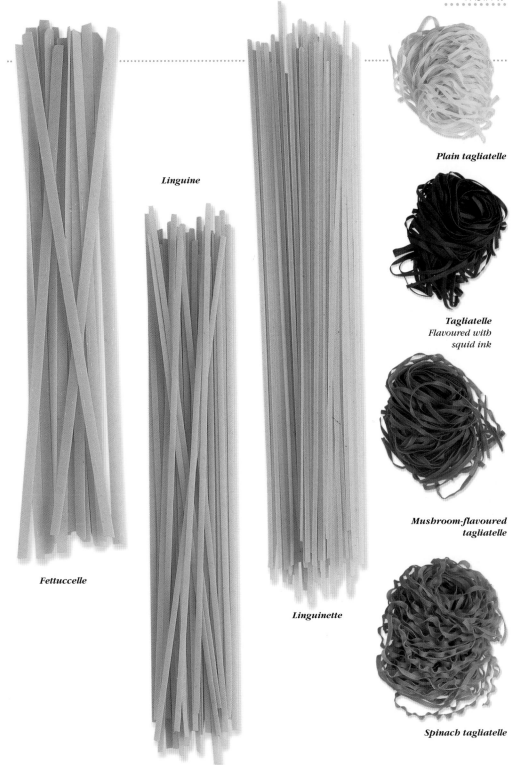

Linguine

Fettuccelle

Linguinette

Plain tagliatelle

Tagliatelle
*Flavoured with
squid ink*

***Mushroom-flavoured
tagliatelle***

Spinach tagliatelle

Long Pasta

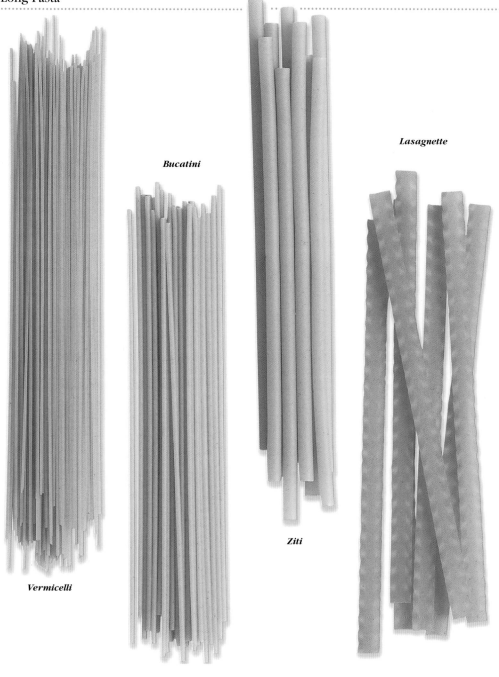

Bucatini

Lasagnette

Vermicelli

Ziti

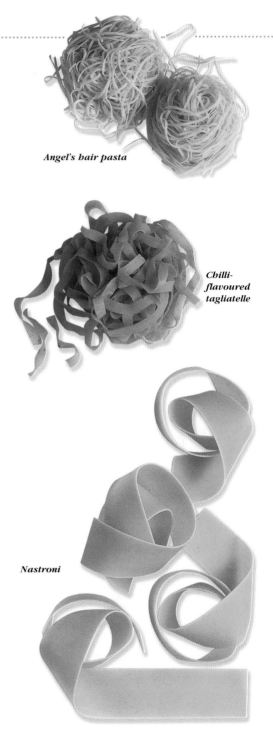

Angel's hair pasta

*Chilli-
flavoured
tagliatelle*

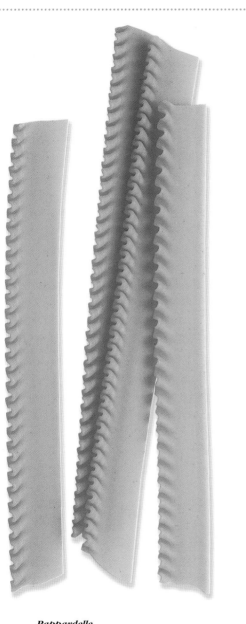

Nastroni

Pappardelle

Short Pasta

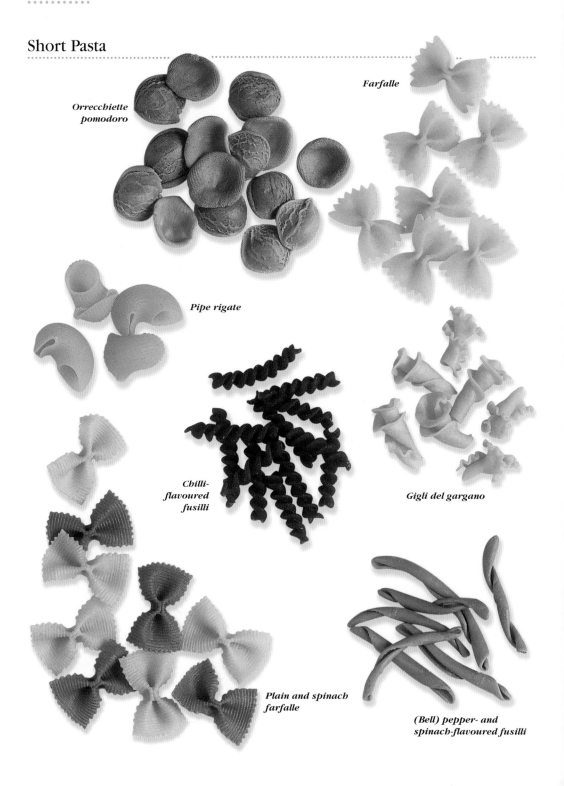

*Orrecchiette
pomodoro*

Farfalle

Pipe rigate

*Chilli-
flavoured
fusilli*

Gigli del gargano

*Plain and spinach
farfalle*

*(Bell) pepper- and
spinach-flavoured fusilli*

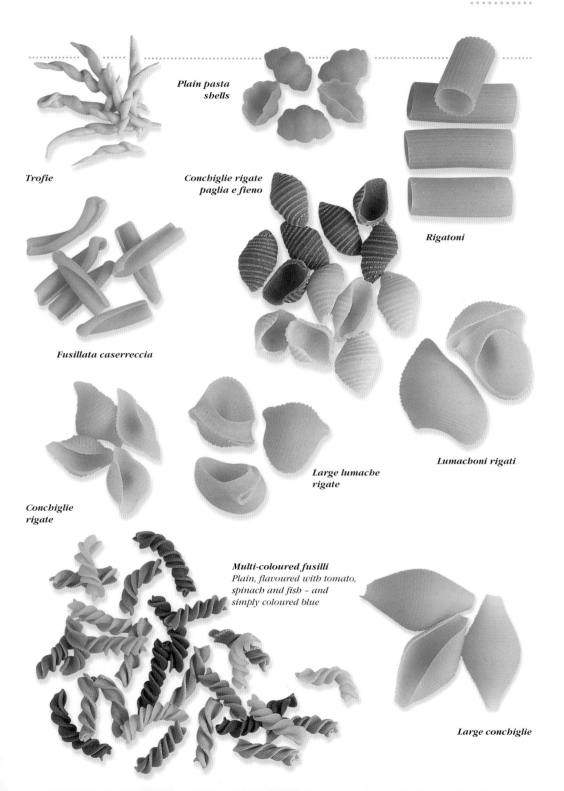

*Plain pasta
shells*

Trofie

*Conchiglie rigate
paglia e fieno*

Rigatoni

Fusillata caserreccia

Lumachoni rigati

*Large lumache
rigate*

*Conchiglie
rigate*

Multi-coloured fusilli
*Plain, flavoured with tomato,
spinach and fish – and
simply coloured blue*

Large conchiglie

Short Pasta

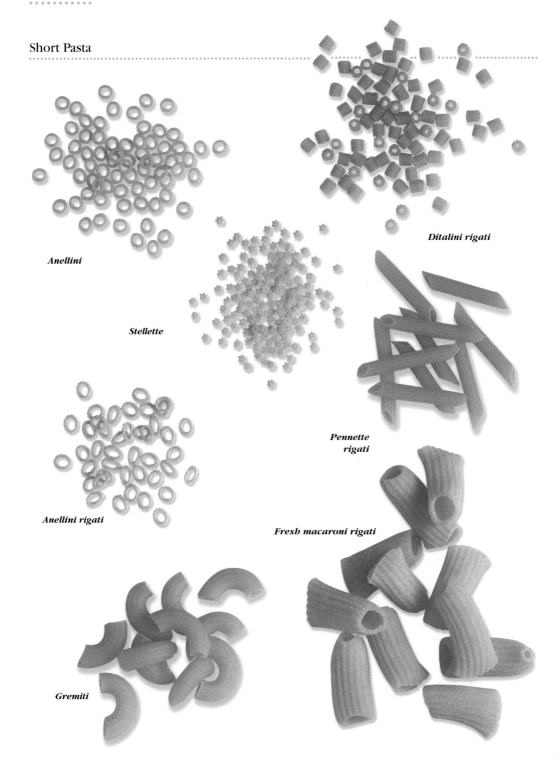

Anellini

Stellette

Ditalini rigati

Pennette rigati

Anellini rigati

Fresh macaroni rigati

Gremiti

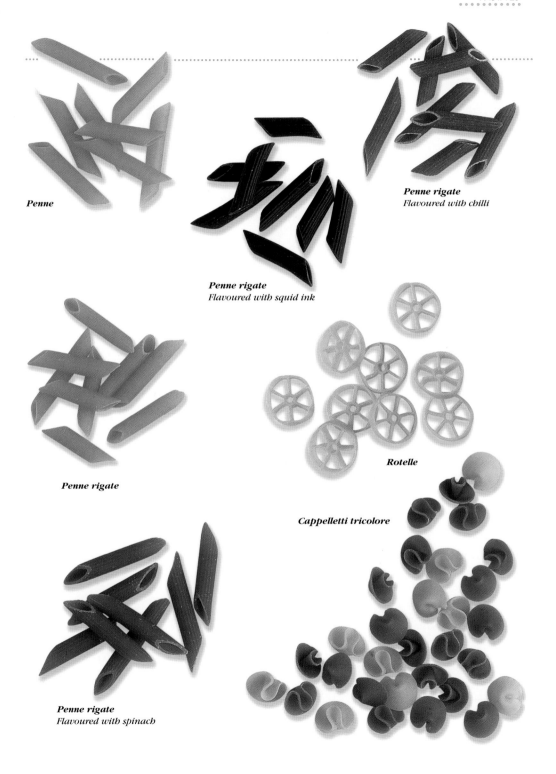

Penne

Penne rigate
Flavoured with squid ink

Penne rigate
Flavoured with chilli

Penne rigate

Rotelle

Cappelletti tricolore

Penne rigate
Flavoured with spinach

Flat Pasta

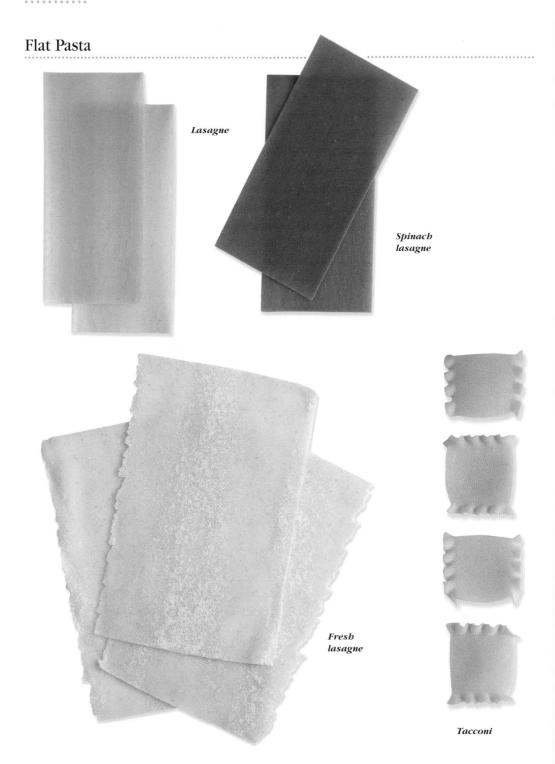

Lasagne

*Spinach
lasagne*

*Fresh
lasagne*

Tacconi

Filled Pasta

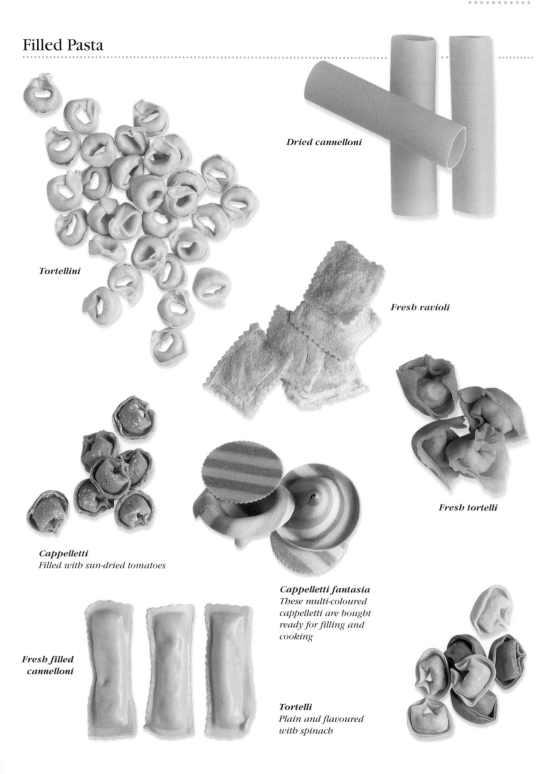

Dried cannelloni

Tortellini

Fresh ravioli

Fresh tortelli

Cappelletti
Filled with sun-dried tomatoes

Cappelletti fantasia
*These multi-coloured
cappelletti are bought
ready for filling and
cooking*

**Fresh filled
cannelloni**

Tortelli
*Plain and flavoured
with spinach*

Gnocchi

Gnocchi fall into a different category from other pasta, being more like small dumplings. They can be made with semolina (milled durum wheat), flour, potatoes or ricotta and spinach and may be shaped like elongated shells, ovals, cylinders or flat discs, or roughly shredded into *strozzapreti* (priest-stranglers); at their worst, store-bought gnocchi resemble large greyish maggots. However they are made, gnocchi should be extremely light and almost melt in the mouth.

CULINARY USES
Gnocchi can be served like any pasta, as a first course, in clear soup or occasionally as an accompaniment to the main course. Almost any pasta sauce is suitable for serving with gnocchi; they are particularly good with a creamy Gorgonzola sauce or they can be served simply, drizzled with olive oil and dredged with freshly grated Parmesan cheese.

BUYING AND STORING
Gnocchi are usually sold loose on delicatessen counters. They are quite sustaining, so a small portion is enough for a first course; allow 115g/4oz per serving. They will keep in a plastic bag in the refrigerator for two or three days. Home-made gnocchi dough will also keep for a couple of days before cooking.

COOKING GNOCCHI

With the exception of oven-baked gnocchi alla romana, all other types of gnocchi should be poached in a pan of lightly salted, barely simmering water.

Drop the gnocchi into the water in batches and cook for about 5 minutes; they will rise to the surface when they are done. Scoop out the cooked gnocchi with a slotted spoon and transfer them to a plate: keep them warm while you cook the rest.

Fresh plain gnocchi

Fresh potato gnocchi

Gnocchi di patate

The best-known type of gnocchi are those from northern Italy made with potatoes and a little flour. To make 4 servings, peel 500g/1¼lb floury potatoes and boil until very tender. Drain and mash until smooth, then mix in 1 large (US extra large) egg and season with salt and pepper. Add 90-115g/3½-4oz/¾-1 cup plain (all-purpose) flour, a little at a time, stirring well with a wooden spoon until you have a smooth, sticky dough that forms a ball on the spoon (you may not need all the flour). Turn out the dough on to a floured surface and knead for about 3 minutes, until soft and smooth. Cut the dough into six equal pieces and, with floured hands, roll these into sausage shapes about 2cm/¾in in diameter. Slice the dough into 2cm/¾in discs. Hold a fork in your left hand and press the discs against the tines just hard enough to make ridges, then flip them downwards off the fork so that they curl up into elongated shell shapes. Poach them as above.

*Fresh spinach and
ricotta gnocchi*

*Fresh gnocchi made
with semolina*

Spinach and Parmesan gnocchi

Spinach and ricotta gnocchi

These attractive green gnocchi originated in Tuscany where, confusingly, they were known as ravioli. For 4 servings, you need:
350g/12oz cooked spinach, well drained and finely chopped
225g/8oz ricotta cheese, mashed until smooth
2 eggs
100g/3 1/2oz/1 cup freshly grated Parmesan cheese
40g/1 1/2oz/3 tbsp plain (all-purpose) flour
65g/2 1/2oz/5 tbsp butter, melted
salt, pepper and nutmeg

1 Put the spinach, ricotta and seasoning in a pan and cook gently, stirring constantly, for 5 minutes. Off the heat, beat in the eggs, 40g/1 1/2oz/3 tbsp of the Parmesan and the flour. Chill for at least 4 hours. Lightly shape into small cylinders and roll them in a very little flour. Poach them as described, left.

2 Preheat the oven to 180°C/350°F/Gas 4. Pour a little melted butter into a serving dish and put in the cooked gnocchi. Sprinkle with some of the remaining Parmesan and place in the oven.

3 Add the rest of the gnocchi as they are cooked and anoint them with melted butter and Parmesan. Replace the dish in the oven for another 5 minutes before serving.

Gnocchi alla romana

These substantial gnocchi from Lazio are made with semolina milled from durum wheat.
For 4–6 servings, you need:
1 litre/1 3/4 pints/4 cups milk
225g/8oz semolina
75g/3oz/scant 1 cup freshly grated Parmesan cheese
2 eggs, plus an extra yolk, eaten
60g/2 1/2oz/5 tbsp butter
salt, pepper and nutmeg

1 Bring the milk to the boil, season with salt, pepper and nutmeg, then add the semolina in a steady stream, whisking for about 15 minutes, until the mixture is very thick. Off the heat, stir in half the Parmesan and the beaten eggs.

2 Pour the mixture into a greased baking tray to a thickness of about 1cm/1/2in, or spread it over a dampened work surface. Leave to cool completely, then cut out 3cm/1 1/4in discs with a plain or fluted pastry cutter.

3 Preheat the oven to 230°C/350°F/Gas 8. Layer the semolina discs in a buttered baking dish, dotting each layer with flakes of butter and a sprinkling of grated Parmesan, finishing with the cheese. Bake the gnocchi in the hot oven for about 15 minutes, until browned on top.

Rice, Grains, Beans & Lentils

Almost as important as pasta in Italian cooking are rice, polenta, beans, peas and lentils, which appear as primi piatti *(first courses) in various guises. Like all basically agricultural countries, Italy relied heavily on these protein-rich ingredients when luxuries like meat were in short supply, and a host of wholesome and delicious recipes were developed using these modest ingredients.*

Riso (Rice)

Italy produces more rice and a greater variety of rice than anywhere else in Europe. Most of it is grown in the Po Valley in Piedmont, where conditions are perfect for cultivating the short-grain Carnaroli, Arborio and *Vialone Nano* rice, which make the best risotto. Italian rice is classified by size, ranging from the shortest, roundest *ordinario* (used for desserts) to *semifino* (for soups and salads), then *fino* and finally the longer grains of the finest risotto rice, *superfino. Superfino* rice swells to at least three times its original size during cooking, enabling it to absorb all the cooking liquid while still retaining its shape and firm al dente texture combined with a creamy smoothness.

HISTORY

The Saracens first introduced rice to Italy as long ago as the 11th century (some believe even earlier), but it only became popular in the 16th century, when it began to be cultivated on a large scale in the Po Valley.

Traditionally, rice has played a much greater part in the cooking of northern Italy than in the south, particularly in the Veneto, where the famous dish of *risi e bisi* (Venetian dialect for 'rice and peas') opened the banquet served every year by the Doges to honour their patron Saint Mark.

***Superfino Carnaroli rice* (left and above)**
This short-grained variety is one of the finest Italian rices. Its ability to absorb liquid and cook to a creamy smoothness while still retaining its shape makes it perfect for risotto

Arborio rice

Superfino Arborio rice

Vialone Nano rice

PREPARING RISOTTO

The most famous of all Italian rice dishes is risotto, which was invented in Milan in the 16th century. A good risotto can be made only with superfine rice. All risotti are basically prepared in the same way, although they can be flavoured with an almost endless variety of ingredients. The rice is coated in butter or oil, then simmering stock is added, one ladleful at a time, and the rice is stirred over a low heat until all the liquid has been completely absorbed.

Only then is more stock added and the risotto is cooked in this way for about 20 minutes until the rice is tender and creamy. The final touch is called mantecatura; *off the heat, a knob (pat) of butter or a few spoons of olive oil and some freshly grated Parmesan cheese are stirred into the risotto to make it very creamy.*

Leftover cold risotto can be rolled into balls enclosing a piece of mozzarella, coated in fine breadcrumbs and deep-fried to make supplì al telefono *or the Sicilian equivalent,* arancini.

Riso (Rice)

Rice is often used in Italian soups; it combines well with almost all vegetables and makes a substantial addition to minestrone. Baked rice dishes are also popular. Cooked rice is layered in a buttered ovenproof dish with meatballs, vegetables or poultry and cheese, then topped with breadcrumbs and baked in the oven until the top is crispy and brown. The Italians never serve main dishes on a bed of rice, but prefer to serve plain boiled rice on its own with plenty of butter and cheese stirred in.

BUYING AND STORING
Buy only special superfine risotto rice for use in Italian cooking. Shorter grain *semifino* is best for soups, and *ordinario* for desserts (try *riso nero*, a rice denser topped with melted chocolate). Once you have opened the packet, reseal it tightly; you can then keep the rice in a dry place for several months.

Semifino rice

Brown semifino rice

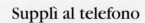

Supplì al telefono

These rice croquettes contain mozzarella cheese, which, when cooked, melts into strings that resemble "telephone wires". For 4 servings, you will need:

2 eggs, lightly beaten
225g/8oz cold, cooked risotto
50g/2oz Parma ham (prosciutto), cut into 1cm/¹⁄₂in dice
115g/4oz Mozzarella cheese, cut into 1cm/¹⁄₂in dice
fine dried breadcrumbs, for coating
oil, for deep-frying
salt and freshly ground black pepper

1 Mix the eggs into the cold risotto and season to taste with plenty of salt and pepper.

2 Form the rice mixture into balls about the size of a small orange and make a hollow in each one. Fill this with a cube of ham and one of cheese, then roll each ball in your hand to enclose the ham and cheese completely, adding a little more rice if necessary.

3 Spread out the breadcrumbs in a shallow tray or plate and roll the rice balls in the breadcrumbs to coat them lightly.

4 Heat the oil in a deep, heavy pan and deep-fry the rice balls in batches for 3–5 minutes until golden brown. Drain on kitchen paper and keep warm while you cook the remaining balls. Serve piping hot.

Farro

This is the Tuscan name for spelt, a hard brown wheat with pointed grains, which is very little used in other parts of Italy. Farro is much harder than other wheat and therefore takes longer to process and cook, but it will grow even in poor soil. In Tuscany it is used to make *gran farro*, a delicious and nourishing soup, which is served as a first course instead of pasta.

CULINARY USES
Farro is used mainly as an ingredient for soups, but in remoter country areas of Italy it is sometimes used to make bread.

COOK'S TIP

When cooking rice, a good rule of thumb is: the better the rice, the longer the cooking time required, so ordinario *will need only 10 - 12 minutes' cooking compared with up to 20 minutes for* superfino.

COOK'S TIP

Farro is a very hard grain and must be boiled for up to 3 hours to make it digestible before adding to other recipes. It can also be simply cooked and served with olive oil and freshly ground black pepper.

Farro

Ordinario rice

Gran farro

This Tuscan soup is often served as a first course instead of pasta. For 4 servings, you will need:

225g/8oz/1¼ cups dried borlotti or
  cannellini beans, soaked overnight,
  then drained
1 onion, chopped
2 garlic cloves, chopped
100g/3½oz finely
  chopped pancetta
4 sage leaves
a pinch of chopped fresh oregano
45ml/3 tbsp olive oil
225g/8oz chopped fresh tomatoes
150g/5oz prepared farro
salt, freshly ground black pepper
  and grated nutmeg

1 Cook the beans in fresh water until tender (reserve the cooking water). Rub the beans through a vegetable mill. Gently cook the onion, garlic, pancetta and herbs in the olive oil until pale golden brown. Add the tomatoes, season with salt, pepper and nutmeg, then simmer for 10 minutes.

2 Add the bean purée (paste) and enough of the cooking water to make a thick soup. Stir in the farro and simmer for 45 minutes, adding more water if the soup becomes too thick. Serve with some extra virgin olive oil to trickle into it.

Polenta

For centuries, polenta has been a staple food of the north of Italy, particularly around Friuli and the Veneto. This grainy yellow flour is a type of cornmeal made from ground maize, which is cooked into a kind of porridge with a wide variety of uses. Polenta is sometimes branded according to the type of maize from which it is made. *Granturco* and *Fioretto* are the two most common types.

In Italy, polenta is available ground to various degrees of coarseness to suit different dishes, but there are two main types – coarse and fine. Coarse polenta has a more interesting texture but takes longer to cook.

HISTORY

The Romans made a savoury porridge they called *puls* using *farro*, a kind of spelt, and the tradition continued in northern Italy, where gruels were prepared from local cereals such as buckwheat, barley and oats. Maize or corn was only introduced into Italy from the New World in the 17th century; soon it was being grown in all the north-eastern regions, where cornmeal overtook all other types of grain in popularity, because it combined so well with the local dairy products. Traditionally, polenta was cooked in a *polaio*, a special copper pot that hung in the fireplace; here, it was stirred for at least an hour, to be served for breakfast, lunch or dinner (sometimes all three).

CULINARY USES

Polenta is extraordinarily versatile and can be used for any number of recipes, ranging from rustic to sophisticated. Although it is most often served as a first course, it can also be used as a vegetable dish or main course and even made into cookies and cakes. Plain boiled polenta can be served on its own, or enriched with butter and cheese to make a very satisfying dish. It goes wonderfully well with all meats, sausages and game, helping to cut the richness and mop up the sauce. It can be cooled and cut into squares, then fried, grilled (broiled) or baked and served with a topping or filling of mushrooms, meat, vegetables or cheese. Fried or grilled squares of polenta form the basis of *crostini*, which are served as an *antipasto*.

Fine polenta

FRIED OR BAKED POLENTA

Pour the cooked polenta on to a wooden board and spread it to a thickness of about 2.5cm/1in. Leave it to cool and harden, then cut into squares.

Fry in hot vegetable oil until crunchy and golden, then drain on kitchen paper or grill (broil) until golden brown on both sides.

To make a pasticciata *(layered baked dish) of polenta, cut the cold polenta horizontally into 1cm/¹/₂in slices and layer it in a buttered baking dish with your chosen sauce, mushrooms, cheeses etc. Bake in a hot oven for about 15 minutes, or until the top is lightly browned.*

BUYING AND STORING

It is possible to buy quick-cooking polenta, which can be prepared in only 5 minutes. However, if you can spare the 20 minutes or so that it takes to cook traditional polenta, it is best to buy this for its superior texture and flavour. Whether you choose coarse or fine meal is a matter of personal preference; for soft polenta or sweet dishes, fine-ground is better, while course-ground meal is better for frying. Once you have opened the bag, put the remaining polenta in an airtight container; it will keep for at least a month.

Coarse polenta

Recipe for Basic Polenta

To make a basic polenta for 4–6 people, bring to the boil 1.5 litres/2½ pints/6 cups salted water or stock.

Gradually add 300g/11oz/2 cups polenta in a steady stream, stirring constantly with a wooden spoon.

Continue cooking, stirring all the time, until the polenta comes away from the sides of the pan. This will take 20–30 minutes (5 minutes for quick-cooking polenta).

One alternative, foolproof (though unauthentic) method is to put the polenta meal into a pan, add salt, then stir in the cold water, bring the mixture slowly to the boil and simmer gently for about 20 minutes, stirring occasionally.

Another is to cook the polenta for 5 minutes, then finish cooking it in the oven for about an hour.

Pour the cooked polenta into a serving dish, season with pepper and stir in abundant quantities of butter and a strong-flavoured cheese – Parmesan, Fontina, Bel Paese and Gorgonzola are all delicious with piping hot polenta.

COOK'S TIP
Polenta can be cooked in water, stock or a mixture of water and milk. Whichever liquid you use, cook the polenta very slowly and steadily so that it does not go lumpy. Allow 50–75 g/2–3 oz/½ cup polenta meal per person.

Beans, Peas and Lentils

Fagioli (haricot (navy) beans)

Haricot beans are another staple of Tuscan cooking; indeed, the Tuscans are sometimes nicknamed 'the bean-eaters', although haricot beans are eaten all over Italy. The most popular varieties include the pretty red-and-cream speckled borlotti, the small white cannellini (a kind of kidney bean), the larger *toscanelli* and *fagioli coll'occhio* (black-eyed beans (peas)). All these are eaten as hearty stews, with pasta and in soups, and cannellini are often served as a side dish simply anointed with extra virgin olive oil. *Ceci* (chickpeas) and *fave* (broad (fava) beans) are also popular.

HISTORY

Beans were a staple of the Roman and Greek diet, and several recipes for bean stews survive from that period. Many of the beans were brought to Italy from the Middle East, but some, like *fave*, were indigenous and were used as ritual offerings to the dead at Roman funerals. Haricot beans have always been a popular peasant food, but, during the Renaissance, Catherine de Medici attempted to refine Italian cuisine, and beans fell out of favour with the nobility and sophisticated urban dwellers. Thanks to their highly nutritious and economical qualities, however, beans, peas and lentils have once again become an important element in Italian cooking.

CULINARY USES

Haricot beans can be made into any number of nutritious soups and stews, or served as the basis of a substantial salad such as *tonno e fagioli* (tuna and beans). A popular Tuscan dish is *fagioli all'uccelletto* (beans cooked like little birds). Cooked cannellini beans are combined with chopped garlic, fresh sage leaves and tomatoes and simmered for about 15 minutes until tender and fragrant. This dish is delicious served with some fried or grilled (broiled) coarse country sausages.

Dried red borlotti beans

Dried cannellini beans

Dried borlotti beans

Dried cannellini beans

Canned borlotti beans

BUYING AND STORING

During the summer and early autumn in Italy, you may find fresh haricot beans, sometimes still in the pod. Borlotti beans come in an attractive speckled pod, cannellini in a slim yellowish pod. The pods represent a high proportion of the weight, so allow at least 300g/11oz per serving. Most haricot beans, however, are sold dried. Try to buy these from a store with a quick turnover, or they may become wizened and very hard. Prepacked beans will have a 'best before' date on the packet. Loose beans will keep for several weeks in a cool dry place, but are at their best soon after purchase.

If you haven't the time to prepare dried beans, canned varieties make an acceptable substitute, but you cannot control the texture and they are sometimes too mushy. They are, however, fine for recipes that call for puréed beans. Bear in mind, though, that they are an expensive alternative to dried beans.

Canned haricot (navy) beans

COOKING BEANS

All dried beans should be soaked for about 8 hours in cold water or 4 hours in boiling water before cooking (this is not necessary for fresh beans). Discard the soaking water before cooking the beans.

Cook the beans in plenty of unsalted boiling water. Boil briskly for 10 minutes (this is essential to kill off the toxins, which may cause severe stomach upsets), then simmer for 1–2 hours, depending on the size and freshness of the beans.

You can add whatever flavourings you wish to the cooking liquid, but never add salt or any acidic ingredients, such as tomatoes or vinegar, until the beans are cooked, or they will never become tender however long you cook them. To make a hearty stew, after the initial boiling, the beans can be mixed with pancetta, garlic and herbs and cooked very slowly in the oven.

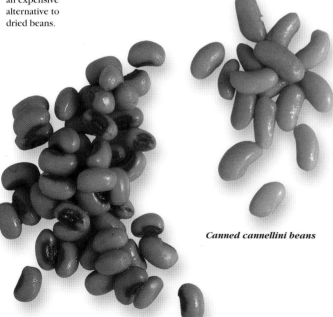

Canned black-eyed beans (peas)

Canned cannellini beans

Beans, peas and lentils

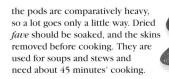

Fave (broad (fava) beans)

Broad beans are nicest eaten fresh from the fat green pod in late spring and early summer when they are very small and tender with a bittersweet flavour. They are particularly popular in the area around Rome, where they are eaten raw with *prosciutto crudo*, salami or Pecorino cheese. Later in the season, they should be cooked and skinned (hold the hot beans under cold running water; the skin will slip off quite easily). Cooked *fave* have a milder flavour than raw and are excellent with ham and *pancetta*. When buying fresh *fave* in the pod, allow about 350g/12oz per person; it may seem a lot, but the pods are comparatively heavy, so a lot goes only a little way. Dried *fave* should be soaked, and the skins removed before cooking. They are used for soups and stews and need about 45 minutes' cooking.

Chickpeas
These round golden peas can be bought dried (above), or canned and ready to use (left)

Ceci (chickpeas)

These round golden peas are shaped rather like hazelnuts and have a distinctive, nutty flavour. They are the oldest of all known beans, peas and lentils and, though not indigenous to Italy, have become very popular in Italian country cooking.

CULINARY USES

Chickpeas are cooked and used in the same way as haricot (navy) beans and are an essential ingredient of *tuoni e lampo* (thunder and lightning), a sustaining dish of pasta and chickpeas served with tomato sauce and Parmesan. They can also be served cold, dressed with lemon juice, chopped fresh herbs and olive oil, to make a substantial salad.

Broad (fava) beans
Dried fave *need to be soaked overnight before cooking*

Canned broad (fava) beans
The canned beans (right) are ready to use

> #### COOK'S TIP
> *Chickpeas can be very hard, so it is best to soak them for at least 12 hours, then cook them in plenty of boiling water for up to 2 hours.*

Lenticchie (lentils)

Although lentils grow in pods, they are always sold podded and dried. Italian lentils are the small brown variety, which are grown in the area around Umbria; they do not break up during cooking and are often mixed with small pasta shapes or rice for a contrast of flavours and textures. They make the perfect bed for cooked sausage, such as *zampone* or *cotechino*, and are delicious served cold dressed with olive oil. The ultimate Italian pulse feast must surely be *imbrecciata*, a nutritious and sustaining soup from Umbria made with chickpeas, haricot beans and lentils.

Brown lentils
These are available in different sizes, large (below) and small (above)

COOK'S TIP
Lentils will absorb the flavours of whatever aromatics they are cooked with, so add any appropriate herbs or spices to the cooking liquid.

Cheeses

Italy has an even greater variety of cheeses than France, ranging from fresh, mild creations such as mozzarella to aged, hard cheeses with a very mature (sharp) flavour, such as Parmesan. All types of milk are used, including ewe's, goat's and buffalo's, which produces the best mozzarella, and some cheeses are made from a mixture of milks. As in France, the Italians eat their cheese after the main course, either accompanied or followed by fresh fruit. You will not, however, find the large selection of cheeses offered on a French menu; Italian restaurants serve only one or two types of cheese and rarely have a cheeseboard.

Many of the cheeses made in Italy are suitable for cooking. What would a pizza be without its delicious, stringy topping of melted mozzarella, or a pasta dish without a grating of fresh Parmesan?

HISTORY

Fresh, rindless cheeses were first introduced to Italy by the ancient Greeks, who taught the Etruscans their cheese-making skills. They in turn refined the craft, developing the first long-matured cheeses with hard rinds, which could last for many months and would travel. Today's Parmesan and Pecorino cheeses are probably very similar to those produced 2,500 years ago.

In ancient days, the milk was left to curdle naturally before being made into cheese. The Romans discovered that rennet would speed up this process. Originally, they probably used rennet made from wild artichokes (this is still used in remoter parts of Italy), but later they began to use animal rennet. The process used to make farmhouse cheeses today has changed very little since Roman times.

Italian cheeses can be divided into four categories: hard, semi-soft, soft and fresh. Some cheeses have an enormously high fat content; others are low in fat and suitable for dieters. Many Italian cheeses are eaten at different stages of maturity; a cheese that has been matured for about a year is known as *vecchio*; after 18 months, it becomes *stravecchio* and tends to have a very powerful flavour. Almost all Italian cheeses can be eaten on their own and used for cooking, making them an extremely versatile ingredient.

Hard Cheeses

Asiago

This cheese from the Veneto region develops different characteristics as it ages. The large round cheeses with reddish-brown rinds each weigh 10–12kg/22–55lb. They are made from partially skimmed cow's milk and have a fat content of only 30 per cent. Asiago starts life as a pale straw-coloured dessert cheese, pitted with tiny holes, with a mild, almost bland flavour. After six months, the semi-matured cheese (*Asiago da taglio*) develops a more piquant, saltier flavour, but can still be eaten on its own. Once it has matured for 12 to 18 months, the *stravecchio* cheese becomes grainy and sharp-tasting, resembling an inferior Grana Padano, and is really only suitable for grating and cooking.

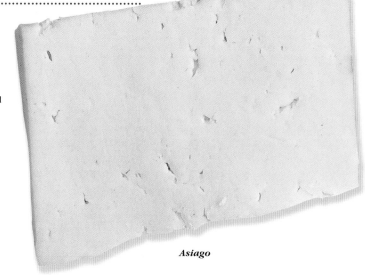

Asiago

Parmesan

Parmesan is by far the best-known and most important of the Italian hard cheeses. There are two basic types – Parmigiano Reggiano and Grana Padano – but the former is infinitely superior to the latter.

PARMIGIANO REGGIANO

Parmigiano Reggiano can be made only in a strictly defined zone, which lies between Parma, Modena, Reggio-Emilia, Bologna and Mantua. Farmers from this area claim that the cheese has been made there for over 2,000 years; certainly it appears to be almost identical to that produced by the Etruscans and the methods of production have scarcely changed. The milk comes only from local cows, which graze on the area's rich pastureland.

It takes about 600 litres/132 gallons of milk to make one 30–35kg/ 70–80lb wheel of Parmigiano Reggiano. The milk is partially skimmed and some of the whey from the previous day's cheese-making is added, then the mixture is carefully heated before rennet is added to encourage curdling. (The rest of the whey is fed to local pigs destined to become Parma hams (prosciutto).) The curds are poured into wheel-shaped

forms and the cheese is then aged for a minimum of two years; a really fine Parmesan may be aged for up to seven years. During this time, it is nurtured like fine wine, until it becomes pale golden with a slightly granular flaky texture and a nutty, mildly salty flavour. Authentic Parmigiano Reggiano has the word "Reggiano" stamped on the rind.

GRANA PADANO

This cheese is similar to Parmigiano Reggiano, but is inferior in flavour and texture. Although it is made in the same way, the milk used comes from other regions and the cheese is matured for no more than 18 months, so it does not have the crumbly texture of Reggiano and its flavour is sharper and saltier. Its grainy texture (hence the name "grana") makes it fine for grating and it can be used for cooking in the same way as Reggiano.

CULINARY USES

A really good Parmigiano Reggiano can be eaten on its own, cut into chunks or slivers; it is delicious served with ripe pears and a good red wine. But Parmesan, both Reggiano and grana, really comes into its own when used for cooking. Unlike other cheeses, it does not become stringy or rubbery when exposed to heat, so it can be grated over any number of hot dishes, from pasta, polenta and risotto to minestrone, or layered with aubergines (eggplants) or truffles and baked in the oven. Slivers of fresh Parmesan are also excellent with asparagus or in a crisp salad. Don't throw away the rind from Parmesan; use it to add extra flavour to soups and vegetable stocks.

Parmigiano Reggiano

BUYING AND STORING

If possible, buy Parmigiano Reggiano, which is easily recognizable by the imprint 'Reggiano' in pinpricks on the rind. Whether you buy Reggiano or grana, always buy it in a piece cut from a whole wheel and grate it freshly when you need it; if possible, avoid pre-packed pieces and never buy ready-grated Parmesan cheese, which is tasteless. Tightly wrapped in foil, a hunk of Parmesan will keep in the refrigerator for at least a month.

Grana Padano

Hard Cheeses

Pecorino

All Italian cheeses made from ewe's milk are known as Pecorino, but they vary enormously in texture and flavour, from soft and mild to dry and strong. The best-known hard Pecorino cheeses are *romano* from Lazio and *sardo* from Sardinia; both are medium-fat, salty-tasting cheeses with a sharp flavour, which becomes sharper the longer the cheeses are matured. The milder *sardo* is usually aged for only a few weeks; the *romano* for up to 18 months. Hard Pecorino is a pale, creamy colour with a firm granular texture with tiny holes like Parmesan cheese. Sicilian *Pecorino pepato* is studded with whole black peppercorns, which add a very piquant note.

Fresh Pecorino comes from Tuscany and is sometimes known as *caciotta*. This semi-hard cheese has a delicious mild, creamy flavour, but is not easy to find outside Italy, as it keeps for a very short time.

HISTORY
Pecorino romano is probably the oldest Italian cheese, dating back to Roman times. Then, as now, the cheeses were shaped and laid on *canestri* (rush mats, rather like hammocks) to be air-dried. Sicilian Pecorino is still called *canestro* after these rush mats.

CULINARY USES
Hard Pecorino cheese can be grated and used exactly like Parmesan cheese. It has a more pungent flavour, which is suited to spicy pasta dishes, such as *penne all'arrabiata*, but it is too strong for more delicate dishes such as risotto or creamy chicken dishes. *Caciotta* can be cubed and marinated in olive oil for about 2 hours, then served with a grinding of black pepper to make a delicious and unusual *antipasto*.

BUYING AND STORING
Fresh or semi-hard Pecorino cheese should be eaten the day you buy it, but well-matured Pecorino cheese will keep in the fridge for several weeks wrapped tightly in foil.

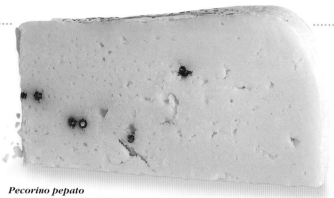

Pecorino pepato
This cheese is studded with whole black peppercorns

Pecorino sardo
A milder version that is aged for only a few weeks

Caciotta
A semi-hard cheese with a mild, creamy flavour

Provolone

A southern Italian cheese, straw-white in colour with a smooth, supple texture and an oval or cylindrical shape, Provolone cheese comes in many different sizes (some enormous) and can often be found hanging from the ceiling in Italian delicatessens. Provolone can be made from different types of milk and rennet; the strongest versions use goat rennet, which gives them a distinctively spicy flavour. In the south of Italy, buffalo milk is often used, and the cheeses are sometimes smoked to make *provolone affumicato*. The cheese is made by the *pasta filata* (layering) process, which gives it a smooth, silky texture; the curds are left to solidify, then they are cut into strips before being pressed together into a sausage shape. This is salted in brine for 6 to 12 hours, then the cheese is shaped and left to mature.

Variations on Provolone include *caciocavallo*, a smooth smoky cheese made from a mixture of cow's and goat's or ewe's milk, which develops a sharp flavour that becomes sharper as it matures. It takes its name from the way the oval cheeses are tied up in pairs and hung up to dry over a wooden pole, as though on horseback. (One fallacious theory is that the cheese was originally made from mare's milk; another is that the cheeses were stamped with a horse, which is the symbol of Naples.) In Calabria, a version called *burrino* is made enclosing a lump of unsalted butter in the centre of the cheese, so that when it is sliced, it resembles a hard-boiled egg.

Provolone burrino
There is a lump of butter buried in the centre of this cheese, so that when cut it resembles a hard-boiled egg yolk

CULINARY USES

Milder fresh Provolone cheese can be eaten on its own or in a sandwich with mortadella or ham. Once it becomes strong, it should only be used for cooking; its stringy texture when melted makes it ideal for pizzas and pasta dishes.

BUYING AND STORING

Enclosed in their wax rinds, Provolone and similar cheeses will keep for months. Once they have been opened, they should be eaten within a week. Provolone cheese can be used for cooking in the same way as Parmigiano Reggiano.

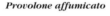

Provolone affumicato

Provolone
The stringy texture when melted makes this cheese particularly good for pizzas

Provolone

Semi-hard Cheeses

Bel Paese

This cheese, poetically named 'beautiful country', is a baby among Italian cheeses, having been created by the Galbani family from Lombardy early last century. Made from cow's milk, it contains over 50 per cent fat, which makes it very creamy. It is the colour of buttermilk, with a very mild flavour, and is wrapped in pale yellow wax to preserve its freshness. A whole Bel Paese weighs about 2kg/4¹/₄lb, but it is often sold ready-packed in wedges.

Culinary Uses

Bel Paese can be eaten on its own; its mild creaminess makes it popular with almost everyone. It is also excellent for cooking, with a good melting quality, and can be used as a substitute for mozzarella cheese, but because it is rather bland it will not add much flavour to a dish.

Buying and Storing

Like most cheeses, it is best to buy a wedge of Bel Paese cut from a whole cheese; pre-packed pieces tend to be soggy and tasteless, although they are fine to use in cooking. Use freshly cut cheese as soon as possible after purchase, although wrapped in foil or clear film (plastic wrap) it will keep in the refrigerator for two or three days.

Fontina

The only genuine Fontina comes from the Val d'Aosta in the Italian Alps, although there are plenty of poor imitations. True Fontina is made from the rich unpasteurized milk of Valdostana cows and has a fat content of 45 per cent. Although Fontina is nowadays produced on a large scale, the methods are strictly controlled and the cows are grazed only on alpine grass and herbs. Because it is matured for only about four months, the cheese has a mild, almost sweet, nutty flavour and a creamy texture, with tiny holes. Longer-matured Fontina develops a much fuller flavour and is best used for cooking. A whole Fontina weighs about 15–20kg/33–44lb; the cheese is pale golden and the soft rind is orangey-brown. The rind of authentic Fontina has the words 'Fontina dal Val d'Aosta' inscribed in white writing.

History

Fontina has been made for at least 500 years; it is mentioned in the 'dairy bible' *La Summa Lacticiniorum* of 1477. Its name probably comes from the mountain peak Fontin.

Culinary Uses

Fontina cheese is delicious eaten on its own, and because it melts beautifully and does not become stringy, it can be used instead of mozzarella cheese in a wide variety of dishes. It is also perfect for making a *fonduta*, the Italian equivalent of a Swiss cheese fondue.

Bel Paese
This creamy, mild-flavoured cheese can also be eaten on its own, and it is excellent for cooking, too

Soft Cheeses

Taleggio

A square creamy cheese from Lombardy with a fat content of almost 50 per cent, Taleggio has a mild, salty-sweet flavour, which can become pungent if it is left to age for too long (it reaches maturity after only six weeks). The cheeses are dipped in brine for about 14 hours before maturing, which gives them a slightly salty tang. Each cheese with its soft edible rind weighs about 2kg/4¹/₄lb. If you intend to eat the rind, remove the paper from the top!

CULINARY USES

Taleggio cheese is perfect eaten on its own as a cheese course. Like Fontina cheese, it melts into a velvety smoothness when cooked and does not become stringy, so it can be used in any cooked dish that requires a good melting consistency.

BUYING AND STORING

Both Fontina and Taleggio cheeses should be eaten as soon as possible after purchase. If necessary, they can be tightly wrapped in waxed paper or clear film and kept in the refrigerator for a day or two.

Stracchino

Stracchino cheese is made from very creamy milk and matured for only about ten days, and never longer than two months. The smooth rindless cheese with a fat content of about 50 per cent is reminiscent of Taleggio cheese, but softer-textured and with a sweeter flavour. Robiola is a small, square stracchino weighing about 100g/3¹/₂oz. Because these cheeses are so delicate, they are wrapped in plasticized paper to preserve their freshness.

HISTORY

The name Stracchino comes from the Lombardian dialect word meaning 'tired'. It does not reflect on the quality of the cheeses, but merely indicates that they were traditionally made in the winter months when the cows were tired from their long trek down from the mountains to their winter quarters on the plain of Lombardy. Some farmhouse-produced Stracchini are still made only in winter, but most are now produced all year round.

CULINARY USES

Stracchino should only be eaten as a dessert cheese; it is not suitable for cooking. On Christmas Eve in Lombardy, Robiola is served as a special delicacy with the spicy candied fruit relish, *mostarda di Cremona*.

Stracchino
A soft-textured cheese with a sweet flavour

Taleggio
Perfect to eat on its own, taleggio has a mild, sweet flavour

Robiola
This is a small square stracchino and is always wrapped in paper to preserve its freshness

Soft Cheeses

Gorgonzola

The proper name for this famous blue-veined cheese is Stracchino Gorgonzola, because it is made from the curds of stracchino. Originally made only in the town of Gorgonzola, the cheese is now produced all over Lombardy. Gorgonzola is prepared by making alternate layers of hot and cold curds. The difference in temperature causes the layers to separate, leaving air pockets in which the mould (*penicillium glaucum*) will grow. The best Gorgonzola cheeses are left until the mould forms naturally, but more commonly copper wires are inserted into the cheese to encourage the growth. The cheeses are matured from three to five months; the longer the ageing, the stronger the flavour.

Gorgonzola is a very creamy cheese, the colour of buttermilk, with greenish-blue veining and a fat content of 48 per cent. Its flavour can range from very mild (*dolce*) to extremely powerful (*piccante*). The best-known mild version outside Italy is Dolcelatte (sweet milk), which is exceptionally creamy and delicately flavoured. Another version, *torta*, consists of Gorgonzola and mascarpone arranged in alternate layers like a cake.

History

Gorgonzola has been made in the village of the same name since the 1st century AD, when the cheeses were matured in the chilly caves of the Valsassina.

Culinary Uses

Although it is usually eaten as a cheese course, Gorgonzola is also used in cooking, particularly in creamy sauces for vegetables or pasta or as a filling for pancakes and ravioli. It is delicious stirred into soft polenta, or spread on deep-fried polenta *crostini*. Surprisingly, cooking diminishes the flavour of Gorgonzola, so that it does not dominate a delicate dish.

Buying and Storing

Supermarkets sell vacuum-packed portions of Gorgonzola, which are acceptable but not nearly as good as a wedge cut from a whole, foil-wrapped cheese. If you don't like a very strong flavour, be sure to buy Gorgonzola *dolce* or Dolcelatte. Wrapped in clear film (plastic wrap), the cheese will keep for several days in the refrigerator.

Dolcelatte
An exceptionally creamy, delicately flavoured Gorgonzola

Torta
This striped cheese consists of layers of Gorgonzola and mascarpone

Gorgonzola
The greenish-blue veining is typical of this classic cheese

Fresh Cheeses

Caprini

These little disc-shaped goat's cheeses come from southern Italy. They have a pungent flavour, which becomes even stronger as the cheeses mature. Fresh Caprini do not travel well, so you will rarely find them outside Italy, but they are available bottled in olive oil flavoured with herbs and chillies.

CULINARY USES
Fresh goat's cheeses can be fried and served warm with salad leaves as an appetizer, or crumbled over pizzas to make an unusual topping. Bottled Caprini should be drained and eaten as a cheese course. If you like a spicy kick, trickle over some of the oil from the jar, but beware – it will be very piquant.

Mascarpone

This delicately flavoured triple cream cheese from Lombardy is too rich to be eaten on its own (it contains 90 per cent fat), but can be used in much the same way as whipped or clotted cream and has a similar texture. Mascarpone is made from the cream of curdled cow's milk. It is mildly acidulated and adds a distinctive richness to risottos and creamy pasta sauces. It takes only 24 hours to produce, so it tastes very fresh, with a unique sweetness that makes it ideal for making desserts. A new lighter version called *fiorello light* is now being produced for the health-conscious. While it is useful for those on a diet, it is nothing like as good as the real thing.

CULINARY USES
In Italy, mascarpone is used for savoury dishes as well as desserts. It makes wonderfully creamy sauces for pasta and combines well with walnuts and artichokes. Mascarpone can also enhance the texture and flavour of risottos or a white bean soup. It is most commonly used in desserts, either served with fresh berries, or as a filling for pastries. It is an essential ingredient of tiramisu and can be churned into a rich, velvety ice cream.

BUYING AND STORING
Delicatessens in Italy serve fresh mascarpone by the *etto* (about 100g/3½oz) from large earthenware bowls, but outside Italy it is sold in 250g/9oz or 500g/1¼lb plastic tubs. Although the flavour is not as good, pre-packed cheese will keep for a week in the refrigerator; fresh mascarpone should be eaten immediately.

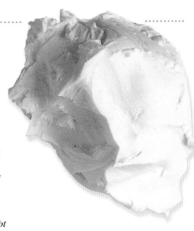

> **COOK'S TIP**
> *To lighten the texture of mascarpone and make it less rich, fold in some beaten egg white.*

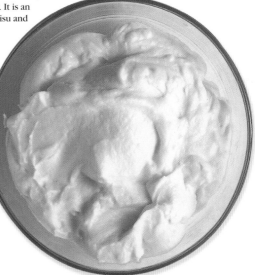

***Mascarpone** (above and below)*
A triple cream cheese that is too rich to eat on its own, but is ideal for desserts. It is an essential ingredient in tiramisu

Caprini
Rarely found fresh outside Italy, these cheeses are usually found bottled in flavoured olive oil

Fresh Cheeses

Cow's milk mozzarella
Known as fior di latte – 'flower of the milk'

Smoked mozzarella
This cheese has a very smooth texture, a rich golden colour and an interesting smoky flavour

Mozzarella
The best is made from buffalo milk

Mozzarella

Italian cooking could hardly exist without mozzarella cheese, the pure white, egg-shaped fresh cheese, whose melting quality makes it perfect for so many dishes. The best mozzarella is made in the area around Naples, using water buffalo's milk. It has a moist, springy texture and a deliciously milky flavour. The cheeses are made by the *pasta filata* (layering) method, where the curds are cut into strips, then covered with boiling water. As they rise to the surface, they are torn into shreds and scrunched into egg-shaped balls each weighing about 200g/7oz. These are placed in light brine for 12 hours, then packed in their own whey inside a paper or plastic wrapping to keep them fresh.

Other types of mozzarella include a cow's milk version called *fior di latte* (flower of the milk) and tiny balls of cheese called *bocconcini* (little mouthfuls). Sometimes, the cheese is wound into plaits (braids) called *treccie*. All these are fresh cheeses, but mozzarella can also be smoked, which gives it a golden-brown colour and an interesting flavour. You will also find in supermarkets a pale yellow semi-hard mozzarella, which is sometimes sold ready-grated. This is the type used in cheap pizzas; it resembles mozzarella only in name and should be avoided.

History

No one is quite sure when water buffaloes were brought to Italy from India. They may have been introduced by the Greeks or the early Christians; certainly by the 16th century they had become a feature of southern Italian agricultural life. At this time, farmers began to use the buffalo milk to make mozzarella. Its popularity soon spread to the northern regions, where cheese-makers started to produce inferior versions made from cow's milk.

Culinary Uses

Fresh mozzarella is delicious served in an *insalata tricolore*, a salad in the colours of Italy, with white mozzarella, red tomatoes and fresh green basil. Smoked mozzarella is good in sandwiches or as part of an *antipasto*. When cooked, mozzarella becomes uniquely stringy, so it is perfect for topping pizzas or filling *mozzarella in carrozza* (mozzarella in a carriage), sandwiches dipped in beaten egg and deep-fried. A favourite Roman dish is *supplì al telefono*: mozzarella wrapped inside balls of cooked rice and fried until it melts to resemble telephone wires.

Buying and Storing

Cow's milk mozzarella is perfectly adequate for cooking, but for a really fine cheese try to buy *mozzarella di bufala*. Unopened, mozzarella will keep in the refrigerator for several days, but once the wrapping has been pierced it should be eaten as soon as possible. Opened mozzarella can be kept for a brief time in a covered bowl containing the whey from the bag or, failing that, skimmed milk or lightly salted water.

Mozzarella bocconcini
The name means 'little mouthfuls'

Ricotta
*Widely used in Italian
cooking, ricotta can
be combined with
spinach for a ravioli
filling, or used in
desserts, such as
cheesecake*

Ricotta salata
*This hard, salted version of the cheese has
a compact, flaky texture and can be used
as a substitute for Parmesan or Pecorino*

Ricotta

Ricotta cheese derives its name
(literally 'recooked') from the process
of reheating the leftover whey from
hard cheeses and adding a little fresh
milk to make a soft white curd cheese
with a rather solid yet granular
consistency and a fat content of only
about 20 per cent. The freshly made
cheeses are traditionally put into
baskets to drain and take their
hemispherical shape and markings
from these *cestelli* (little baskets).

Commercially produced ricotta
cheese is made from cow's milk, but
in rural areas ewe's or goat's milk is
sometimes used.

Ricotta salata is a hard, salted
version of the cheese, made from the
whey of Pecorino. It has a compact,
flaky texture and looks rather like a
hard Pecorino.

CULINARY USES

Ricotta cheese is widely used in Italian
cooking for both savoury and sweet
dishes. It has an excellent texture but
very little intrinsic flavour, so it makes
a perfect vehicle for seasonings such
as black pepper and nutmeg or
chopped fresh herbs. In its best-
known form, it is puréed with cooked
spinach to make a classic filling for
ravioli, cannelloni or lasagne, or
delicious light gnocchi.

It is often used in desserts, such as
baked cheesecakes, or it can be
sweetened and served with fruit.

Hard *ricotta salata* can be grated
and used as a lower-fat substitute for
Parmesan or Pecorino cheeses.

BUYING AND STORING

Fresh ricotta cheese should always
be eaten the day it is bought, as it
quickly develops a sour taste. Most
supermarkets sell a pre-packed version
of the cheese, which has a much
longer keeping time.

Ricotta salata is sometimes sold in
pre-packed wedges, but for a good
flavour and texture you should buy it
freshly cut from a whole cheese.
Tightly wrapped in foil, it will keep in
the refrigerator for up to a month.

Cured Meats & Sausages

Every region of Italy has its own special cured meats and sausages, each differing as widely as the regions themselves. Prosciutto crudo *and* salami *appear in every guise and often constitute an* antipasto *(appetizer) on their own.*

HISTORY

Italy was traditionally an agricultural country, so almost every rural family kept a pig and cured every part of it, from snout to tail, to provide food for the family throughout the year. In any Italian pantry, a range of home-cured hams, sausages and bacon would be found hanging from the ceiling. Nowadays hundreds of different types of hams, cured meats and sausages are commercially produced, many still using the old artisanal methods. Wherever you travel in Italy, you will find regional variations on the same theme.

Most of these cured meats are served as an *antipasto* before a meal. A Tuscan *antipasto* will consist of a selection of thinly sliced *affettati* (sliced ham and *salami*), and it is sometimes served with pickled vegetables, which are designed to whet the appetite.

Prosciutto crudo

Italy is famous for its *prosciutto crudo*, salted and air-dried ham that requires no cooking. The most famous of these hams, *prosciutto di Parma*, comes from the area around Parma, where Parmesan cheese is also made. The pigs in this region are fed partly on the whey from the cheese-making process, which makes their flesh very mild and sweet. Because they are always reared and kept in sheds and never allowed to roam outdoors, they tend to be rather fatty. Parma hams (prosciutto) are made from the pig's hindquarters, which are lightly salted and air-dried for at least one year (and sometimes up to two). The zone of production of Parma ham is restricted by law to the area between the Taro and Baganza rivers, where the air and humidity levels are ideal for drying and curing the hams. In fact, every year thousands of ready-salted hams are sent here from neighbouring regions to be dried and cured in the unique air around Parma.

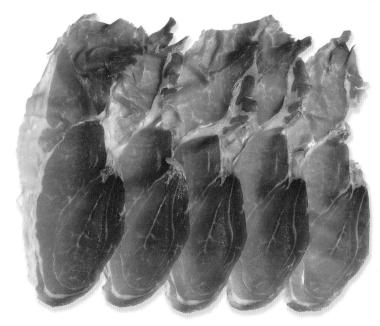

Prosciutto di Parma
The most famous Italian ham comes from the area around Parma, where Parmesan is also made

Prosciutto cotto

Italy also produces a range of cooked hams, usually boiled. They can be flavoured with all sorts of herbs and spices. Cooked ham is sometimes served as an *antipasto* together with raw ham, but it is more often eaten in sandwiches and snacks.

San Daniele

Some people regard these hams from the Friuli region as superior even to Parma ham. San Daniele pigs are kept outside, so their flesh is leaner, and their diet of acorns gives it a distinctive flavour. San Daniele is produced in much smaller quantities than Parma ham, which makes it even more expensive.

Prosciutto cotto
This cooked ham is sometimes
served with sliced cured hams as
an antipasto

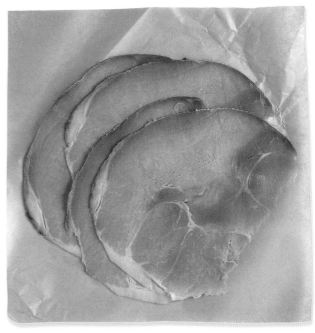

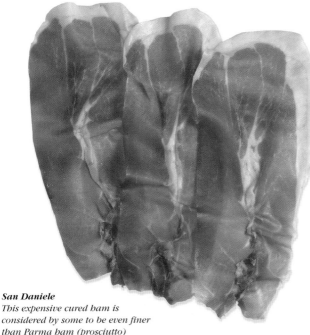

San Daniele
This expensive cured ham is
considered by some to be even finer
than Parma ham (prosciutto)

CULINARY USES

Wafer-thin slices of *prosciutto crudo* are delicious served with melon or fresh figs or, when these are out of season, with little cubes of unsalted butter. If you serve bread with this ham, that too should be unsalted to counterbalance the salty-sweetness of the ham. *Prosciutto crudo* can be rolled up with thin slices of veal and sage leaves and pan-fried in butter and white wine or Marsala to make *saltimbocca alla romana*, finely chopped and added to risotti and pasta sauces, or used as a filling for ravioli.

BUYING AND STORING

The best part of the ham comes from the centre. Avoid buying the end pieces, which are very salty and rather chewy. Because *prosciutto crudo* should be very thinly sliced, buy only what you need at any one time or it may dry out. Ideally you should eat it on the day it is bought, but it will keep in the refrigerator for up to three days.

Cured Meats

Pancetta and Lardo

Pancetta resembles unsmoked bacon, except that it is not sold sliced, but rolled up into a sausage shape. It is made from pork belly, which is cured in salt and spices, to give it a mild flavour. *Lardo* is very similar (but flat) and is generally less readily available.

CULINARY USES

Pancetta can be eaten raw as an *antipasto* (although it is very fatty), but it is usually cut into strips and cooked like bacon. It is an essential ingredient for *spaghetti alla carbonara*.

Pancetta
These round rolled slices of cured pork belly are the Italian equivalent of unsmoked bacon

Smoked pancetta
The smoked version of pancetta *is sold in thin strips rather than being rolled*

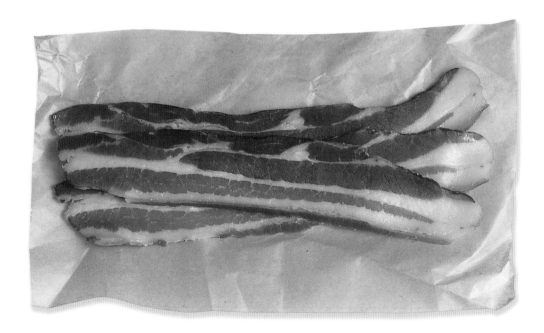

Speck

This fatty bacon is made from pork belly, which is smoke-cured over beechwood with herbs and spices, then air-dried. Sometimes it is covered with peppercorns or dried herbs, which add a distinctive flavour. It comes from the Tyrol, near the Swiss border, which explains its German-sounding name.

Culinary Uses

Speck is too fatty to be eaten raw, but it is used to add flavour to soups, stews and sauces. It is excellent cooked with fresh peas or lentils.

Buying and Storing

Italian bacon is sold in the piece, not sliced. Wrapped in clear film (plastic wrap), *pancetta*, *lardo* and *speck* will keep in the refrigerator for up to one month.

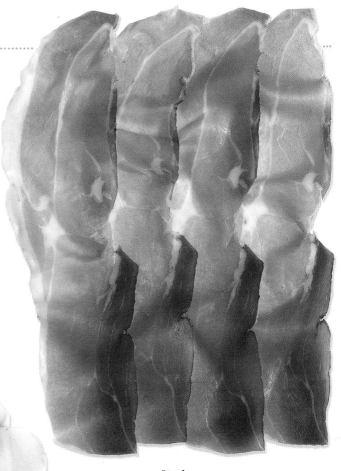

Speck
A fatty ham, smoke-cured over beechwood with herbs and spices, then air-dried

Lardo
An extremely fatty Italian bacon that is always used for cooking

Cured Meats

Bresaola

This cured raw beef is a speciality of Valtellina in Lombardy, but it is eaten and enjoyed all over Italy. It can be made from any cut of beef, but prime fillet (tenderloin) produces the best bresaola. It is first cured in salt, then air-dried for many months before being pressed to produce an intensely dark red meat, which resembles *prosciutto crudo* in flavour, but is more delicate and less salty. Like *prosciutto crudo*, it is always sliced wafer-thin and served in small

quantities, so you don't need to buy very much. Each bresaola weighs 2–3kg/4¼–6¼lb, depending on the size of the original cut of beef.

CULINARY USES

Bresaola is often served as an *antipasto*, sliced very thinly and simply dressed with a drizzle of extra virgin olive oil and a sprinkling of fresh lemon juice. In Lombardy, bresaola is sometimes wrapped around a filling of soft goat's cheese and then rolled up like cannelloni.

BUYING AND STORING

Only buy bresaola made from beef fillet. You can tell the type from the shape; that made from fillet is long with rounded edges, like the original cut of beef, while the cheaper bresaola made from other leg cuts is pressed into an oblong shape. Use it as soon as possible after slicing, preferably the same day, or it will dry out and develop an unpleasantly sharp flavour.

Bresaola
The delicate flavour of this salt-cured beef makes it perfect to serve, thinly sliced, as an antipasto

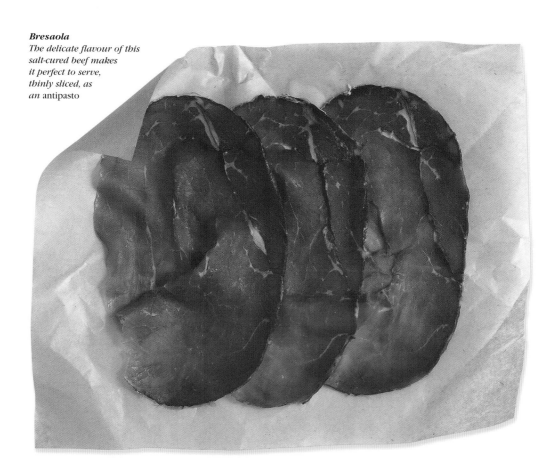

Sausages

Italy boasts almost as many different sausages as there are towns. Practically all are made with pork, although venison and wild boar sausages are popular in country areas. Most sausages and *salami* are factory-produced nowadays, but many towns in Italy still have *salumerie* (sausage shops) selling home-made sausages flavoured with local produce, such as wild mushrooms or herbs and spices. The most famous sausage-producing town is Bologna. Fresh sausages are made from coarsely chopped pork and contain a high proportion of fat for extra flavour. They are usually sold in links, tied together with string. Most Italian sausages, however, are cured and ready to eat.

Luganega

A speciality of northern Italy, luganega is a mild spiced country sausage made from pork, which often contains Parmesan cheese. Sometimes known as *salsiccia a metro*, because it is sold in a long continuous rope, which is coiled up like a snake, and is sold by the metre/yard or whatever length you require. It can be grilled (broiled) or pan-fried with white wine and is often served on a bed of lentils or mashed potatoes. Luganega can also be cut into short lengths and stirred into a hearty risotto.

Cotechino

A large fresh pork sausage weighing about 1kg/2¹/⁴lb, which has been lightly spiced and salted for only a few days. Cotechino is a speciality of Emilia Romagna, Lombardy and the Veneto. It takes its name from *coteca* meaning 'skin'.

COOKING COTECHINO

Cotechino is boiled and served hot, often as part of a bollito misto (mixed boiled meats). Pierce the skin in several places to prevent it from bursting and place the sausage in a large pan. Cover with cold water and bring slowly to the boil, then simmer slowly for 2–3 hours.

Slice the cotechino thickly and serve on a bed of cooked lentils, mashed potatoes or cannellini beans.

Luganega
This mildly spiced sausage, which is coiled up like a snake, is sold by the metre/yard, or whatever length you require

Sausages

Coppa

This salted and dried sausage is made from neck or shoulder of pork, and the casing is made from natural skin. *Coppa* has a roughly rectangular shape and a rich deep red colour. It comes from Lombardy and Emilia Romagna, although, confusingly, in Rome you will find a *coppa* that is a sort of pig's head brawn (this variety is never exported).

Zampone

This speciality sausage from Modena is a pig's trotter stuffed with minced (ground) pork shoulder and other cuts, including some skin. The stuffing has a creamy texture and the skin of the trotter encloses it to retain its original shape, complete with feet. Each zampone weighs up to 2kg/4¹/₄lb.

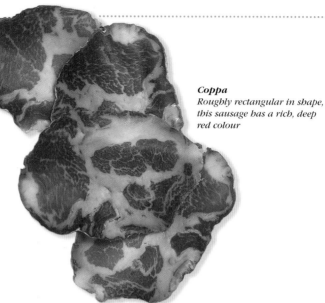

Coppa
Roughly rectangular in shape, this sausage has a rich, deep red colour

Zampone
A part-cooked zampone needs only to be heated through

COOKING ZAMPONE

A raw zampone needs to be boiled for 2–3 hours, depending on the size, although some vacuum-packed varieties are already part-cooked and need only to be heated through. For a fresh zampone, make a couple of incisions in the skin and cook in the same way as cotechino. Zampone is traditionally sliced into rings and served with lentils or mashed potatoes. A bollito misto often contains a zampone.

Mortadella

The most famous of all the sausages from Bologna, mortadella is also the largest, often having a diameter of up to 45cm/18in. Nowadays it is cooked in hot-air ovens to a core temperature of 72°C/140°F, which means that it will keep for several weeks. It is considered to be the finest Italian pork sausage, with its wonderfully smooth texture, although it has a rather bland flavour. Apart from its huge size, mortadella is distinctive for its delicate, pale pink colour studded with cubes of creamy white fat and sometimes pale green pistachios. It is the original *bologna* or 'boloney' so beloved in America.

Buying

Authentic Bolognese mortadella is made only from pure pork, but cheaper varieties may contain all sorts of other ingredients, such as beef, tripe, pig's head, soya flour and artificial colourings.

Beware of mortadella that looks too violently pink and, if you are buying it sliced and pre-packed, check the ingredients on the packet before you buy.

Culinary Uses

Mortadella is usually thinly sliced and eaten cold, either in a sandwich or as part of a plate of assorted cold meats as an *antipasto*. It can also be cubed and stirred into risotti or pasta sauces just before the end of cooking, or finely chopped to make an excellent stuffing for poultry or filled pasta.

Mortadella
Considered to be the finest Italian cooked sausage, mortadella has a wonderfully smooth texture, but a rather bland flavour. It is studded with cubes of creamy fat, and often has pale green pistachios peppered through the meat

Salami

Salami

There are dozens of types of *salami*, whose texture and flavour reflect the character and traditions of the different regions of Italy. Essentially, all *salami* are made from pure pork, but the finished product varies according to the kind of meat used, the proportion of lean meat to fat, how finely it is minced, the seasonings and the period of drying and seasoning.

Salame di Felino

This soft, coarse-cut sausage comes from Felino near Parma and is regarded as one of the finest Italian *salami*. It has a very high proportion of lean pork to fat and is

flavoured with peppercorns, a small amount of garlic and the local white wine. Because it is only very lightly cured, it has a very delicate flavour but does not keep well. You may find it in good Italian delicatessens, where it is easily recognizable by its uneven truncheon shape, which makes it look hand-made. Like its neighbour, Parma ham (prosciutto), *salame di Felino* is very expensive, but well worth the cost.

Salame fiorentina

This large coarse-cut pork sausage from Tuscany is often flavoured with fennel seeds and pepper, when it is known as *finocchiona*. The fennel gives it a very distinctive flavour.

Salame di Felino
*One of the finest Italian salame
– this lightly cured sausage is
flavoured with peppercorns,
garlic and white wine*

Salame fiorentina
*This coarse-cut pork sausage from
Tuscany is often flavoured with
fennel seeds and pepper*

Salame milano

Probably the most commonly found of all *salami*, this Milanese sausage is made from equal quantities of finely minced (ground) pork, fat and beef, seasoned with pepper, garlic and white wine. It is deep red in colour and speckled with grains of fat resembling rice. Also known as *crespone*, it is mass-produced and regarded as inferior to most other *salami*. There is also a small whole *salame milanese*, weighing about 500g/1¼ lb, called *cacciatoro*, which is cured and matured for a much shorter time and has a more delicate flavour and softer texture.

Salame sardo

This fiery red *salame* from Sardinia is a rustic sausage flavoured with red pepper. A similar sausage is *salame napoletano* from Naples, which uses a mixture of black and red pepper for a powerful kick.

Salame ungharese

Despite its name, this *salame* is manufactured in Italy, using a Hungarian recipe. It is made from very finely minced pure pork or pork and beef, and flavoured with paprika, pepper, garlic and white wine. The fat is evenly spread throughout the sausage, giving it a mottled appearance.

BUYING AND STORING

With the exception of *salame di Felino*, almost all *salami* can be bought ready-sliced and vacuum-packed, but taste much better if they are freshly cut from a whole *salame*. A good delicatessen will slice the *salami* to the thickness you require. Ideally, it should be eaten the same day, but it will keep for three or four days in the refrigerator.

Salame ungharese
Made in Italy to a Hungarian recipe

Salame sardo
A fiery salame *flavoured with red (bell) pepper*

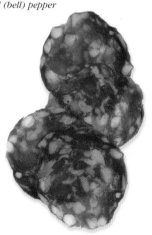

Salame napoletano
Similar to salame sardo, *this* salame *uses a mix of black and red pepper*

Salame milano

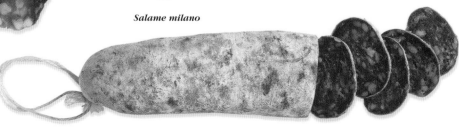

Cacciatoro
This small whole salame milanese *is cured and matured for only a short time*

Meat & Poultry

Until recently, meat did not figure largely in Italian cooking, which relied much more heavily on the peasant staples of pasta, bread, vegetables and, in coastal areas, fish. As the country became more prosperous, however, more people added meat to their daily diet and now animals are farmed all over Italy to provide veal, pork, beef, lamb and kid.

Veal is a favourite meat in Italy and appears in innumerable recipes from every region. The best comes from milk-fed calves that are reared in Piedmont. The area around Rome is famous for its lamb, and spit-roasted suckling lamb and kid are popular specialities of the region. Superb beef cattle are bred in Tuscany, but the beef from other regions comes from working cattle that have reached the end of their useful lives, and is best used for stews and dishes that require long, slow cooking.

Many peasant families in Italy still own a pig, which provides pork as well as a huge variety of hams, sausages and other cured meats. Every part of the pig is eaten in one form or another, from snout to tail. Indeed, Italians never waste any edible part of their meat, so offal of all kinds is used in many dishes. A Tuscan *fritto misto* is composed of a variety of offal (innards) ranging from brains to sweetbreads and lungs, while the Milanese version also includes cockscombs – so, unless you are an offal lover, be warned if you see these dishes on a menu!

Poultry is another popular food. Factory farming does exist in Italy, but many flavoursome free-range birds are still available. Chicken, guinea fowl and turkey appear in a huge variety of simple and delicious dishes, usually filleted for quick cooking. Duck and goose make their appearance, too, often cooked with sharp fruits to counteract the richness of the meat. Many recipes use wild duck, shot by the enthusiastic (some say over-enthusiastic) hunters who abound in every region. Mercifully, the Italian habit of shooting every type of wild bird, whether edible or not, is less prevalent than it was; but hunters are

lax about observing a close season for shooting, so game, both feathered and furred, seems to be available almost all year round.

Abbacchio and agnello (lamb)

Lambs are bred mainly in southern Italy, particularly in the area around Rome. They are slaughtered at different ages, resulting in distinctive flavours and texture. The youngest lamb is *abbacchio*, month-old milk-fed lamb from Lazio, whose pale pinkish flesh is meltingly tender. *Abbachio* is

usually spit-roasted whole. Spring lamb, aged about four months, is often sold as *abbacchio*. It has darker flesh, which is also very tender and can be used for roasting or grilling (broiling). A leg of spring lamb weighs about 1–1.5kg/2¼–3½lb. Older lamb (*agnello*) has a slightly stronger flavour and is suitable for roasting or stewing.

Lamb cutlets
Allow at least three small, succulent lamb cutlets like these per serving

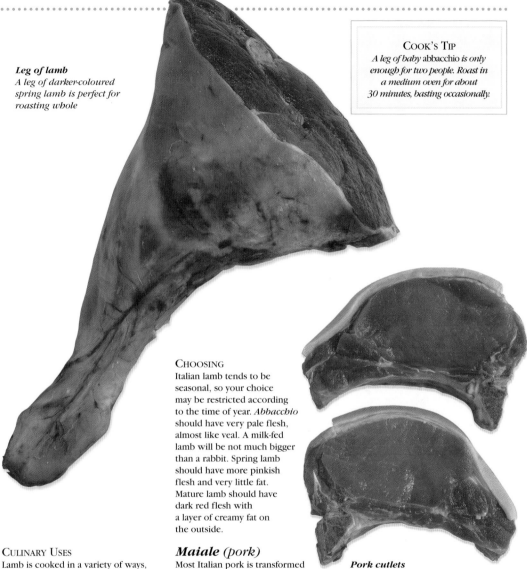

Leg of lamb
A leg of darker-coloured spring lamb is perfect for roasting whole

CHOOSING
Italian lamb tends to be seasonal, so your choice may be restricted according to the time of year. *Abbacchio* should have very pale flesh, almost like veal. A milk-fed lamb will be not much bigger than a rabbit. Spring lamb should have more pinkish flesh and very little fat. Mature lamb should have dark red flesh with a layer of creamy fat on the outside.

Pork cutlets
Tender chops or cutlets can be grilled (broiled) or braised with herbs

CULINARY USES
Lamb is cooked in a variety of ways, from *al forno* (roast) to *costolette alla milanese* (fried breaded cutlets). Roast lamb is the traditional Easter dish. It is not cut into thin slices, but served in large chunks, which should be so tender that they fall off the bone. A favourite recipe for spring lamb is *agnello alla giudea* (Jewish-style lamb), braised in a delicate egg and lemon sauce.

Maiale (pork)
Most Italian pork is transformed into sausages, *salami* and hams, but fresh meat is enjoyed all over Italy, often combined with local herbs such as rosemary, fennel or sage. Different regions eat different parts of the pig; Tuscany is famous for its *arista di maiale alla fiorentina*, (loin of pork roasted with rosemary), while in Naples *il musso* (the snout) is considered a great delicacy.

CULINARY USES
Pork chops or cutlets can be grilled or braised with herbs or artichokes. Loin of pork is deliciously tender braised in milk (*arrosto di maiale al latte*), or it can be roasted with rosemary or sage.

Meat & Poultry

Manzo (beef)

The quality of Italian beef has an unjustifiably poor reputation. It is true that in agricultural areas, particularly the south, beef can be stringy and tough. This is because the cattle are working animals, not bred for the table, and are only eaten towards the end of their hard-working life. This type of beef is only suitable for long, slow-cooked country stews. In Tuscany, however, superb beef cattle from Val di Chiana produce meat that can rival any other world-renowned beef and which provide the magnificent *bistecche alla fiorentina* (T-bone steaks).

CULINARY USES

Thick-cut T-bone steaks (*bistecche alla fiorentina*) from Val di Chiana cattle are grilled (broiled) over wood fires until well-browned on the outside and very rare inside. Rump (round) steaks or fillet steaks (beef tenderloin) are also cooked very rare and sliced on the bias as a *tagliata*. A modern creation is *carpaccio*, wafer-thin slices of raw beef marinated in olive oil and aromatics and served as an *antipasto*. Thinly sliced topside (pot roast) is rolled around a stuffing to make *involtini* (beef olives). A favourite Italian family dish is *bollito misto*, a mixture of boiled meats and offal (innards) including beef. Leftover boiled beef can be sliced and made into a salad.

Less tender cuts of meat are usually braised, stewed or minced (ground) to be used in *ragù* (meat sauce) or *polpettone* (meatballs).

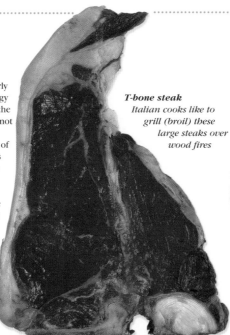

T-bone steak
Italian cooks like to grill (broil) these large steaks over wood fires

Beef olives
Thinly sliced topside (pot roast) beef rolled around a stuffing

Minced (ground) beef
Less tender cuts of beef are minced and used for ragù *(meat sauce) or* polpettone *(meatballs)*

Carpaccio
These wafer-thin slices of raw beef are simply marinated in olive oil and served as an antipasto

Frattaglie (offal (innards))

Nothing is wasted in Italian butchery, so a huge variety of offal is available. Liver is a great favourite; the finest is *fegato di vitello*, tender calf's liver, which is regarded as a luxury. Chicken livers are popular for topping *crostini* or for pasta sauces and pork liver is a speciality of Tuscany. Butchers often sell pig's liver ready-wrapped in natural caul (*rete*), which keeps the liver tender as it cooks. Lamb's and calf's kidneys (*rognoni or rognoncini*), brains (*cervello*) and sweetbreads (*animelle*) are specialities of northern Italy. They are similar in texture and flavour, but sweetbreads arc creamier and more delicate. Every region has its own recipes for tripe (*trippa*); this almost always comes from veal calves rather than other cattle, whose tripe has a coarser texture and flavour. All parts of a veal calf are considered great delicacies. The head is used in *bollito misto* (mixed boiled meats), and the trotters give substance to soups and stews. Oxtail (*coda di bue*) comes from older beef cattle.

Oxtail
Nothing is wasted in Italian butchery – the oxtail is used for wonderful slow-cooked stews and soups

Chicken livers
These rich-tasting livers are a popular topping for crostini

Pig's liver
This is a speciality of Tuscany

Calf's liver
Thinly sliced, this is often simply pan-fried with onions

COOKING OFFAL (INNARDS)

Most offal will benefit from being soaked in milk before cooking to remove any coarseness of flavour. Some types, such as liver and brains, require very little cooking in order to preserve their delicate texture. In Venice, thinly sliced calf's liver is cooked with onions to make *fegato alla veneziana*; this is often served with grilled (broiled) polenta. The Milanese version is coated in egg and breadcrumbs and fried in butter. The simplest and one of the most delicious ways with liver is to sauté it quickly in butter with fresh sage. Brains and sweetbreads can be blanched, then quickly fried in butter, or pounded to a paste and made into croquettes (*crocchette*). Kidneys should be sautéed in butter, or braised with wine and onions or Marsala (*trifolati*). Pre-prepared (dressed) tripe will have been scrubbed, soaked and boiled by the butcher, but it should still be blanched for 30 minutes before cooking. Tripe can be prepared *alla fiorentina* in tomato sauce flavoured with oregano or marjoram; the version from Parma (*alla parmigiana*) is fried in butter and topped with Parmesan cheese, while in Bologna, eggs are added to the mixture.

Meat & Poultry

Vitello (veal)

Veal is the most popular meat in Italy and appears in hundreds of different recipes. Like lamb, calves are slaughtered at different ages to produce different qualities of meat. The best and most expensive veal is *vitello di latte* from Piedmont and Lombardy. The calves are fed only on milk and are slaughtered at just a few weeks old, producing extremely tender, very pale meat with no fat. Older calves, up to nine months old, are known as *vitello*. Their flesh is still tender, but darker in colour than milk-fed veal. *Vitellone* is somewhere between veal and beef. It comes from bullocks aged between one and three years, which have never worked in the fields and whose flesh is therefore still quite tender and lighter in colour than beef.

CULINARY USES

Young, milk-fed veal is ideal for *scaloppine* (escalopes (US scallops)) and *piccate* (thin escalopes), which need very little cooking. *Vitello* can be served as chops, cutlets or a rolled roast. The shin is cut into *osso buco* (literally 'bone with a hole'), complete with bone marrow, or *schinco* (the whole shin), and braised until meltingly tender. An unusual combination that works wonderfully well is *vitello tonnato*, cold roast veal thinly sliced and coated in a rich tuna sauce. *Vitellone* should be treated like tender beef. It can be grilled (broiled), roasted or casseroled, but it is not suitable for escalopes or similar cuts.

CHOOSING

Young veal should have very pale, slightly rosy fine-grained flesh with no trace of fat. *Vitellone* should be pinker and paler than beef, with only a faint marbling of fat, and should feel firm, not flabby. Escalopes and *piccate* must be cut

only from very young veal. They should be sliced across the grain so that they keep their shape and do not shrivel during cooking. If you are buying boned veal, ask the butcher to give you the bones, which make wonderful stock.

Veal escalopes
These are always sliced very thinly across the grain

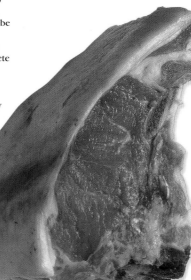

Loin of veal
Usually boned, then roasted with herbs – the bones make the most wonderful stock

Cinghiale (wild boar)

Wild boar are the ancestors of the domestic pig, which used to roam in large numbers in the forests of Tuscany and Sardinia, but which are becoming increasingly rare thanks to the predisposition of some Italians to shoot anything that moves. Baby wild boar are an enchanting sight, with light brown fur striped with horizontal black bands. The adults have coarse, brown coats and fierce-looking tusks. The flesh of a young *cinghiale* is as pale and tender as pork; older animals have very dark flesh, which is tougher but full of flavour.

CULINARY USES

Haunches of wild boar are made into hams, which are displayed in butchers' shops. Young animals can be cooked in the same way as pork. Older boar must be marinated for at least 24 hours to tenderize the meat before roasting or casseroling. The classic sweet and sour sauce, (*agrodolce*), sharpened with red wine vinegar, complements the gamey flavour of the meat.

Coniglio (rabbit) and lepre (hare)

Farmed and wild rabbits often replace chicken or veal in Italian cooking. The meat is very pale and lean and the taste is somewhere between that of good-quality farmhouse chicken and veal. Wild rabbit has a stronger flavour, which combines well with robust flavours; farmed rabbit is very tender and much more delicate.

Hare cannot be farmed, so the only animals available come from the wild. Given the Italian obsession with hunting, it is a miracle that the hare population has not been totally decimated. These wily creatures, however, must sometimes escape the gun, as they continue to breed. A hare weighs about twice as much as a rabbit (2kg/4¼lb is about average). The flesh is a rich, dark brown and has a strong gamey flavour similar to that of wild rabbit.

Hare
This is always wild – the rich brown flesh has a strong gamey flavour

Rabbit
This can be bought either farmed or wild – wild rabbit has a stronger flavour

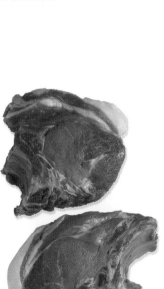

Wild boar
Chops such as these can be cooked in the same way as pork

CULINARY USES

Farmed rabbit can replace poultry in almost any recipe. Wild rabbit can be stewed or braised in white wine or Marsala, or with aubergines (eggplants), bacon and tomatoes. It can be roasted with root vegetables or fresh herbs. In Sicily, rabbit is often cooked with sultanas (golden raisins) and pine nuts in an *agrodolce* (sweet and sour) sauce.

Hare is generally casseroled in red wine or Marsala, cooked *in agrodolce* or made into a sauce for pappardelle or other wide noodles. Both rabbit and hare are often served with polenta or fried bread.

COOKING RABBIT AND HARE

Wild rabbit and hare must be cut into six or eight pieces and marinated in red wine and aromatics for 24 hours before cooking. If you like a sweet and sour flavour (game in agrodolce is very popular in Italy), add plenty of red wine vinegar to the marinade. A rabbit weighing about 1kg/2¼lb when cleaned will need about 1½ hour's braising or stewing; a hare needs about 2 hours.

Meat & Poultry

Fagiano (pheasant)

Occasionally in the Italian countryside, you may still catch a glimpse of a pheasant with its beautiful plumage and long tail feathers. Cock pheasants have bright, iridescent blue and green feathers, while hens are browner and less dramatic-looking. Pheasant farming is still unknown in Italy, and wild pheasants are something of a rarity, so they are regarded as a luxury. They are not hung, but are eaten almost as soon as they are shot, so their flavour is less gamey than in some other countries. Although pheasants are expensive, they are meaty birds for their size, so a cock pheasant will feed three to four people and a hen pheasant two to three.

CULINARY USES

Hen pheasants are smaller than cocks, but their meat is juicier and the flavour is finer. Young hen pheasants can be roasted with or without a stuffing, but cock birds are more suitable for casseroling. Pheasant breast can tend to be dry, so they should be well barded with bacon or thickly smeared with butter before roasting. A good knob (pat) of butter placed inside the cavity will help to keep the flesh moist. For special occasions, pheasants can be stuffed with candied fruits or pomegranate seeds and nuts. Pheasant breasts can be sautéed and served with a wine or balsamic vinegar sauce, but they can sometimes be rather dry.

Pheasant
Usually eaten as soon as they are shot, Italian pheasants are less gamey than in some other countries. Remember that pheasants contain lead shot pellets, so take care not to bite on these!

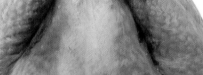

COOKING QUAIL

Quail should be browned in butter until golden all over, then roasted in a hot oven for about 15 minutes. Their flavour is well complemented by the fruit of the vine, so they are often served with a light sauce containing grapes or raisins soaked in grappa. They can also be wrapped in vine leaves before roasting, which keeps them moist and adds a delicious flavour.

Quaglie (quail)

These small migratory birds are found in Italy throughout the summer months. Wild quails have the reputation of being so stupid that they never run away from hunters, but stay rooted to the spot as sitting targets. As a result, they have become very rare, and most of the birds now available are farmed. They are very small (you need two to serve one person) and have a delicate, subtly gamey flavour. Farmed quails have less flavour than the wild birds and benefit from added flavourings, such as grapes.

Quail
These birds have a very delicate, gamey flavour. They are very small, and so you will need to serve two per person

COOKING PHEASANTS

Unless you know for sure that a pheasant is very young, it is best to wrap the breast in streaky (fatty) bacon before roasting to prevent dryness. To roast a pheasant, put a knob (pat) of butter inside the cavity, or make a stuffing, drape bacon over the breast and roast at 200°C/400°F/Gas 6 for about 40 minutes, until tender. Plain roast pheasant is often served with a risotto. Pheasant can also be pot-roasted or casseroled with wine and herbs. If you are serving cock birds, it is worth removing the lower part of the legs after cooking, as they contain hard sinews that are not pleasant to eat.

Faraona *(guinea fowl)*

Guinea fowl are extremely decorative birds with luxuriant grey-and-white spotted plumage. They originated in West Africa, but are now farmed all over Europe, so that, although they are technically game, they are classified as poultry. They taste similar to chicken, but have a firmer texture and a more robust flavour.

COOKING GUINEA FOWL

Although their abundant plumage makes them seem larger, guinea fowl are only about the size of a small spring chicken, so one bird will not feed more than three people. To roast guinea fowl, bard the breasts with bacon rashers (strips) and roast like chicken, basting frequently. A vegetable stuffing will keep the flesh moist. Guinea fowl can be substituted for chicken or turkey in any recipe.

CULINARY USES

Guinea fowl are hugely popular in Italy, where they are served in much the same ways as chicken. The flesh of an adult guinea fowl is firmer than that of a chicken, so it is best to bard it or cover the breasts with bacon rashers (strips) before roasting. The breasts are sometimes sautéed and served with the pan juices mixed with balsamic vinegar, or with a sauce of cream and Marsala. The birds can be roasted or pot-roasted whole, or cut into serving pieces and casseroled with mushrooms (wild mushrooms are especially delicious) or herbs. A favourite autumn dish in Tuscany is guinea fowl braised with chestnuts.

Guinea fowl
These popular birds can be pot-roasted, roasted or casseroled with wild mushrooms

---

Piccione *(pigeon)*

Wood pigeons have dark, gamey flesh and a robust flavour, which the Italians love. They are generally too tough to roast, but they make the most delicious casseroles. Domestic pigeons are also reared for food and you will often see large dovecotes in farmyards. Domestic birds are less likely to be tough than wild ones, but their flavour is less robust.

Wild pigeon
Italians love the rich, robust flavour of these small birds; however, they can be very tough, so cook them very slowly, either by braising or casseroling

---

COOKING PIGEONS

Wild pigeons can be tough, so, unless you are sure that they are young, it is best to casserole them. In Tuscany, they are braised with tomatoes and olives; the classic Venetian way is to stew them with pancetta, ox tongue and fresh green peas. If you desperately want to roast wild pigeons, marinate them in a red wine marinade for three days before cooking, then stuff them with a moist vegetable stuffing. Cover the breasts with streaky (fatty) bacon and roast in a hot oven for about 20 minutes, basting with the marinade every few minutes.

Fish & Shellfish

Italy's extensive coastal waters once teemed with a huge variety of fish and shellfish, many unique to that part of the Adriatic and Mediterranean. Sadly, pollution and over-fishing have taken their toll, and there is no longer the abundance of shellfish there once was, but what remains is of excellent quality. A visit to an Italian fish market will reveal fish and shellfish of every description, some beautiful, some hideous, many unknown outside Italy. Italians like their fish and shellfish very fresh and tend to cook it simply, without elaborate sauces. Large fish are usually grilled (broiled) or baked and dressed with olive oil, or baked in cartoccio *(enclosed in a paper bag). Small fry are deep-fried for a crisp* fritto misto di mare. *Every coastal area has its own version of fish soup, which uses a mixture of local fish and constitutes a meal in itself –* cacciucco *from Livorno, cold* burrida *from Sardinia,* brodetto *from the Adriatic coast – each region claims that its version is the best.*

It is impossible to give a complete list of all the fish that you will find in Italy. Popular favourites include *coda di rospo* (monkfish), *dentice* (dentex – a white-fleshed fish found only in Italy), *sogliola* (sole) and even non-indigenous fish such as salmon.

Freshwater fish – trout, perch, carp and eels – abound in the lakes and rivers and are eaten with gusto. Eels are regarded as a particular delicacy and are cooked in many different ways, from grilling (broiling) to baking, stewing and frying.

Some fish are dried, salted or preserved in oil. The most popular is tuna, which is packed in olive oil and sold by weight from huge cans. *Baccalà* is salted dried cod, which is creamed to a rich paste or made into soups and stews. Anchovies are salted, or packed in olive oil, or preserved in a sweet and sour marinade. Sardines are also very popular and are used to make a Sicilian pasta sauce.

Anchovies
Canned in olive oil (above) or salted (left) – these tiny, strong-tasting fish are used to add flavour to pasta sauces and salads

Salt cod *(baccalà)*
This dried fish is creamed to a paste or made into soups and stews

CHOOSING FRESH FISH

You can almost guarantee that any fish you buy in an Italian early morning market will be ultra-fresh, but in fishmongers and restaurants you should look for pointers. Fish should have bright, slightly bulging eyes and shiny, faintly slimy skin. Open up the gills to check that they are clear red or dark pink and prod the fish lightly to check that the flesh is springy. All fish should have only a faint, pleasant smell; you can tell a stale fish a mile off by its disagreeable odour.

Orata (gilt-head sea bream)

This popular Mediterranean fish takes its name from the crescent-shaped golden mark on its domed head and the gold spots on each cheek. It has beautiful silvery scales and slightly coarse but delicious flaky white flesh. Orate usually weigh between 600g/ 1lb 6 oz and 1kg/2¼lb; a larger fish will serve two greedy people. Orata is best simply grilled, baked *in cartoccio* or barbecued and served with wedges of fresh lemon.

Pesce spada (swordfish)

In Italy, you will occasionally find a whole swordfish on the fishmonger's slab. These huge Mediterranean fish, up to 5m/15ft long and weighing 100–500kg/220–1200lb, are immediately recognizable by their long sword-like upper jaw. Because of their size, they are more usually sold cut into steaks. Their firm, close-grained, almost meaty flesh has given them a nickname of 'steak of the sea'.

Swordfish
Often either baked or grilled (broiled), this firm-fleshed fish needs to be marinated to keep it moist during cooking

> ### COOKING SWORDFISH
>
> *Swordfish tends to be dry, so it should be marinated in oil and lemon juice or wine and herbs before cooking. It is excellent grilled (broiled) or barbecued, or part-cooked in butter or olive oil, then baked in a sauce. Its firm texture makes it ideal for kebabs. It is plentiful in the waters around Sicily, where it is cooked with traditional Mediterranean ingredients such as tomatoes, olives, capers, sultanas (golden raisins) and pine nuts. Another popular Sicilian dish is* bracciole di pesce spada, *thin slices of swordfish rolled around a stuffing of breadcrumbs, mozzarella cheese and herbs and grilled. It is also delicious sliced wafer-thin, marinated in olive oil, lemon juice and herbs and served raw.*

Tuna
Immensely popular throughout Italy, canned tuna in oil is either sold by weight from huge cans or bought in small cans like these

TONNO ALL'OLIO D'OLIVA

NOSTROMO

TONNO
DI PRIMA SCELTA

300 g

Fish

Sarde or sardelle
(sardines)

Fresh sardines probably take their name from Sardinia, where they were once abundant. These small, silvery fish are still found in Mediterranean waters, where they grow to about 13cm/5 in. They are at their best in spring. Allow about four larger sardines or six smaller fish per serving. Sardines have very oily flesh and should only be eaten when extremely fresh. They can also be bought preserved in oil or salt.

Sardines
These fresh fish are at their best in the spring

PREPARING
AND COOKING SARDINES

Sardines should be gutted before cooking. If the fishmonger has not already done this, cut the head almost through to the backbone and pull it off; the gut will come away with the head.

Sardines can be barbecued, grilled (broiled) or baked alla genovese with potatoes, garlic and parsley. Their oily flesh combines well with spices and tart ingredients such as capers and olives. In Sicily they are stuffed with breadcrumbs, pine nuts, sultanas (golden raisins) and anchovies and fried, then finished in the oven (a beccaficcu). Sardines can also be deep-fried, plain or stuffed with mushrooms, herbs and cheese (alla ligure) or with chopped spinach and cream (alla romana).

Spigola or branzino
(sea bass)

The silvery sea bass, which come from Mediterranean waters, are as beautiful to look at as to eat, although their rapacious nature has earned them the nickname of 'sea wolf'. These slim, elegant fish are almost always sold whole and rarely weigh much more than 1kg/2¼lb, so one fish will feed no more than two or three people. Sea bass is prized for its delicate white flesh and lack of irritating small bones. As a result, it is never cheap.

One way of bringing the price down is to farm sea bass, but the flavour of the farmed fish is not so fine as that of wild sea bass, whose predatory habits ensure that their flesh develops a full flavour. So far, farming of these wonderful fish does not seem to have caught on in Italy, where flavour is rarely compromised for cost.

PREPARING AND COOKING SEA BASS

Sea bass should be gutted before cooking. They have quite hard scales, which should be removed before grilling (broiling) or pan-frying. Scale the fish with a de-scaler or blunt knife, working from the tail towards the head. If you are going to poach or bake sea bass, leave the scales on, as they will hold the fragile flesh together.
Sea bass has rather soft flesh, so it is best grilled (broiled), barbecued or pan-fried and dressed with a trickle of olive oil. It can be stuffed with sprigs of fresh herbs (fennel is particularly good) and baked in the oven for 20 – 30 minutes, depending on the size of the fish. For spigola alla livornese, lay the fish in an ovenproof dish on a layer of rich tomato sauce, sprinkle with seasoned breadcrumbs and olive oil and bake.

Triglia (red mullet)

These small Mediterranean fish rarely weigh more than 1kg/2¼lb. They have bright rose-coloured skin and a faint golden streak along their sides. Their flesh is succulent with a distinctive, almost prawn-like (shrimp-like) flavour, quite unlike any other fish. The liver of red mullet is regarded as a great delicacy and is not removed during cooking, which gives the mullet its nickname of 'sea woodcock'. Red mullet are extremely perishable and should be eaten the day they are bought. The skin should always look very bright; dullness is a sure indication that the fish is not fresh.

PREPARING AND COOKING RED MULLET

Larger fish should be scaled before cooking, but be warned - this is a delicate operation, as the skin is very fragile. Scaling is worth the effort, however, as it reveals the wonderful red skin in all its glory. Red mullet combines well with traditional Mediterranean flavours of olive oil, black olives, herbs, garlic, saffron and tomatoes. It can be baked, grilled (broiled) or cooked in cartoccio *with powerful herbs such as rosemary or fennel. For* triglia all'italiana, *place whole red mullet on a bed of finely chopped mushrooms and onions that have been sweated until soft and mixed with fresh breadcrumbs, and bake for 20–30 minutes.*

Red mullet
The flesh of these pretty fish has a distinctive almost prawn-like (shrimp-like) flavour

Sea bass
Prized for their delicate white flesh, these slim, elegant fish are almost always sold whole

Shellfish

Italian coastal waters are host to a huge variety of shellfish and crustaceans, many with wonderfully exotic names such as *datteri di mare* (sea dates; a kind of mussel), *tartufi di mare* (sea truffles; a type of clam) and *fragolino di mare* (sea strawberry; a tiny octopus that turns bright pink when cooked). Almost all shellfish is considered edible, from clams to *cannolichi* (razor-shells), *lumache di mare* (sea snails) and *canestrelli* (small scallops). Shrimps and prawns come in all sizes and colours, from vibrant red to pale grey, while crustaceans range from bright orange crawfish to blue-black lobsters.

> ### COOKING SQUID AND CUTTLEFISH
>
> *Small squid and cuttlefish should be cooked only briefly - just until they turn opaque - or they will become rubbery and tough. Larger specimens need long, slow cooking to make them tender. They can be stuffed with minced (ground) fish or meat, anchovies and seasoned breadcrumbs or rice, and baked with tomatoes and wine sauce until tender, or cut into rings and fried in a light batter, or simply dusted with seasoned plain (all-purpose) flour and deep-fried.*
>
> *Squid and cuttlefish are also delicious stewed in their own ink; seal the molluscs in hot oil with some chopped onions and garlic, add finely chopped fresh parsley and seasoning, then cover with dry white wine and a little water and simmer gently for 15 minutes. Crush the ink sacs, mix the inky liquid with a little cold water and 30-45ml/ 2-3 tbsp plain flour and work to a smooth paste. Add the flour mixture to the pan and cook for another 5-10 minutes to thicken the sauce.*

Squid
Large specimens like this one need long, slow cooking to make them tender - conversely small baby squid should be cooked very quickly or they will become tough

Calamari or totani (squid) and seppie (cuttlefish)

Despite their appearance, squid and cuttlefish are actually molluscs, whose shell is located inside the body. They are indistinguishable in taste, but cuttlefish have a larger head and a wider body with stubbier tentacles. The cuttlebone much beloved of budgerigars and parrots is the bone of the cuttlefish inside the body. Once this has been removed, cuttlefish are very tender. The 'shell' of a squid is nothing more than a long, thin, transparent quill. Both *seppie* and *calamari* have ten tentacles.

Squid and cuttlefish are immensely popular in Italy, cut into rings and served as part of either an *insalata di mare* (shellfish salad) or *fritto misto* (mixed fried fish). Their black ink is used to flavour and colour risotto and fresh pasta.

> ### PREPARING AND COOKING MUSSELS
>
> *Scrub the shells under cold running water. Pull away the 'beard' protruding from the shell. Give any open mussels a sharp tap; they should close immediately. Discard any that do not, as they are probably dead.*
> *The simplest way to cook mussels is alla marinara. For 4 people, finely chop 1 large onion, 2 garlic cloves and 15ml/1 tbsp chopped parsley, put in a large pan with 300ml/10fl oz/2¼ cups white wine and simmer for 5 minutes. Add the scrubbed mussels, cover and steam, shaking the pan from time to time, for 5 minutes, or until the shells have opened. Discard any unopened mussels, sprinkle the rest with extra parsley and serve. For a richer sauce, transfer the mussels to a bowl and reduce the sauce over a high heat. Pour over the shellfish and serve.*

Polipi (octopus)

These are much larger than squid and have only eight tentacles. Their ink sac is not located in the head but in their liver, and the ink has a strong, pungent taste. Octopuses look and taste similar to squid, but need a good deal of preparation. They must be pounded (99 times, some say) to tenderize them before they are subjected to very long, slow cooking.

If you can find very small octopuses, they can be cooked in the same way as squid, but otherwise it is much less trouble to substitute squid or cuttlefish.

Octopus
When small, these can be cooked like squid

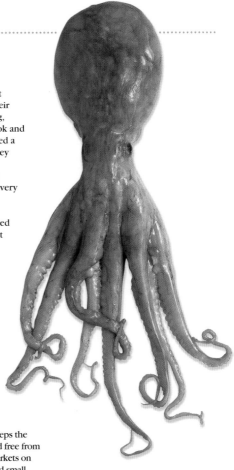

Cozze (mussels)

Mussels, with their smooth texture and sweet flavour, make an attractive addition to many pasta and fish dishes. Pollution in the Mediterranean had threatened the indigenous mussel population, but nowadays most Italian mussels are farmed by the *bouchot* method, on ropes attached to long stakes

set in pure seawater, which keeps the molluscs clean and healthy and free from grit and sand. In Italian fish markets on the Adriatic coast, you may find small sweet local mussels with different names such as *peoci* or *datteri di mare*. These can be prepared in the same way as other mussels.

CHOOSING

Mussels, are sold by the litre in Italy, and are very inexpensive. Because the shells constitute so much of the weight, allow at least 500ml/generous 1 pint/2½ cups mussels per serving. Choose those which feel heavy for their size and discard any with broken shells. Use mussels the day they are gathered or bought.

Mussels
Steamed mussels combine well with black fettuccine or tagliatelle

CULINARY USES

Once mussels have been steamed open, they can be served with a garlicky tomato sauce, or baked on the half shell with garlic butter or a breadcrumb topping. For *cozze gratinate al forno*, lay the mussels on the bottom shells in an ovenproof dish, sprinkle with breadcrumbs seasoned with garlic and parsley and drizzle with olive oil. Bake in a hot oven for 10 minutes.

Shelled cooked mussels are combined with prawns (shrimp) and squid for an *insalata di mare* (shellfish salad), or used as a pizza topping, while mussels in the shell are often mixed with other shellfish and pasta for dishes such as *spaghetti allo scoglio* (spaghetti of the rock).

Shellfish

Gamberetti, gamberelli and gamberoni (shrimps, prawns and scampi)

There are so many different varieties of shrimps and prawns in Italian coastal waters that it is almost impossible to recognize them all. The smallest are the *gamberetti*, small pink or brown shrimps that are usually boiled and served simply dressed with olive oil and lemon juice as part of an *antipasto*. Next in size come the *gamberelli*, pink prawns (shrimp) with a delicate flavour. These are the prawns that are most commonly used in a *fritto misto di mare* (mixed fried seafood). *Gamberi rossi* are the larger variety of prawn, which turn bright red when they are cooked. They are highly prized for their fine, strong flavour, and are eaten plainly cooked and dipped into a bowl of *maionese* (mayonnaise). Best (and most expensive) of all are *gamberoni*, large succulent prawns from the Adriatic, which have a superb flavour and texture. Similar to these is the *cicala*, which resembles a small flattish lobster.

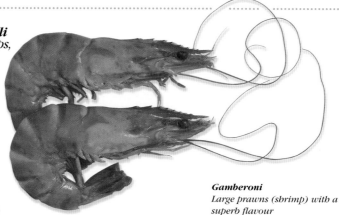

Gamberoni
Large prawns (shrimp) with a superb flavour

COOKING SHRIMPS, PRAWNS AND SCAMPI

Whatever the size, all types of shrimps and prawns can be cooked briefly in boiling salted water (sea water, if possible) until they turn pink. Shrimps will take only 1–2 minutes, large prawns and scampi up to 5 minutes. The robust flavour of prawns makes them ideal for serving in a rich tomato or cream sauce or with rice. Shell them after cooking.
To grill (broil) gamberoni, rub the shells with olive oil and coarse salt and grill over charcoal or on a grilling (broiling) pan, turning them often. When they turn opaque, slit them through the underside and open them out flat like a butterfly. Brush the underside with oil and grill until just cooked. Peeled prawns and scampi can be pan-fried in olive oil flavoured with garlic and/or chilli, parsley and capers; or coated in batter or egg and breadcrumbs and deep-fried.

Gamberi rossi
These large prawns (shrimp) turn bright red when cooked

PREPARING SHRIMPS, PRAWNS AND SCAMPI

Shrimps, prawns and scampi should be de-veined before or after cooking. Pull off the heads, shell the tails and pick out the black thread-like intestine with a knife tip.

CHOOSING

Almost all the shrimps and prawns you buy in Italy are sold uncooked. They should have bright shells that feel firm; if they look limp or smell of ammonia, do not buy them.

CULINARY USES

Shrimps and prawns are extremely versatile and can be used in a wide variety of dishes. Small shrimps are served as *antipasti*, either on their own, or as a stuffing for tomatoes. They can be added to risotto and pasta dishes or shellfish sauces.

Prawns combine well with almost any other shellfish. They are usually included in an *insalata di mare* (shellfish salad) or *fritto misto di mare* (mixed fried shellfish). They make a fine *antipasto* added to an *insalata russa* (Russian salad) or served with haricot (navy) beans dressed with extra virgin olive oil. They combine well with a spicy tomato sauce or mushrooms, and can be used for shellfish casseroles. Large prawns and scampi can be skewered or split and grilled (broiled), or boiled and served with mayonnaise or lemon.

Gamberetti
These small pink shrimps are delicious simply dressed with olive oil and lemon juice

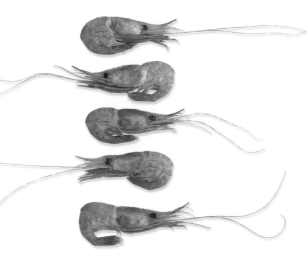

Vongole (clams)

There are almost as many different types of clam as there are regions in Italy, ranging from tiny smooth-shelled *arselle* or *vongole* to long thin razor shells and the large Venus clams with beautiful ridged shells called *tartufi di mare* ('sea truffles'). All have a sweet flavour and a slightly chewy texture. Because they vary so much in size, it is best to ask the fishmonger how many clams you will need for a particular dish.

Clams
These smooth-shelled vongole *are often steamed and served as part of a shellfish salad*

Vegetables

Vegetables have always played a very important role in Italian cooking, particularly in the south of the country, where meat was a luxury that few could afford. They are most often served as dishes in their own right, rather than accompaniments, and the range of imaginative vegetable recipes from all over Italy seems infinite.

One of the great joys of Italy is shopping at the markets, where an astonishing range of seasonal vegetables is on offer, from asparagus, beans and *cavolo nero* from the north to aubergines (eggplants), (bell) peppers and courgettes (zucchini) from Calabria and Sicily. In spring and summer, you will find at least ten different varieties of salad leaves, and you will be overwhelmed by the aroma of freshly picked local tomatoes still on the vine. Italians almost never buy imported or out-of-season vegetables, but prefer to purchase fresh seasonal produce bursting with flavour.

Asparagi *(asparagus)*

Asparagus has been grown commercially in north-eastern Italy for over 300 years and is still highly prized as a luxury vegetable. It has a short growing season from April to early June and is really only worth eating during this period. Both green and white asparagus are cultivated in Italy; the green variety is grown above ground so that the entire spear is bright green. They are harvested when they are about 15cm/6in high. The fat white spears with their pale yellow tips are grown under mounds of soil to protect them from the light, and harvested almost as soon as the tips appear above the soil to retain their pale colour. Both varieties have a delicious, fresh, grassy flavour.

CULINARY USES

In spring, Italians enjoy young asparagus spears simply boiled, steamed or roasted in olive oil and served as a *primo* (first course) with butter and freshly grated Parmesan cheese. For an extra treat, they add a fried egg and dip the asparagus tips into the creamy

White asparagus
This variety is grown under mounds of earth to retain the pale colour

Green asparagus
Enjoyed by Italians, simply boiled or roasted in olive oil

yolk. When served as a vegetable accompaniment, asparagus can be crisply fried in egg and breadcrumbs. The tips also make a luxury addition to risotto.

BUYING AND STORING

Asparagus starts to lose its flavour as soon as it has been cut, so be sure to buy only the freshest spears. The best guide is the tips, which should be firm and tight. If they are drooping and open, the asparagus is past its best. The stalks should be straight and fresh-looking, not yellowed and wizened or very woody at the base. Allow about eight medium spears per serving as a first course and always buy spears of uniform thickness so that they cook evenly. Asparagus will keep in the vegetable drawer of the refrigerator for two or three days.

PREPARING AND COOKING ASPARAGUS

Freshly cut garden asparagus needs no trimming, but cut off at least 2cm/¾in from the bottom of the stalks of bought spears until the exposed end looks fresh and moist. Peel the lower half with a potato peeler. (You need not do this for very thin stalks.)

Boiling asparagus can be problematical, since the stalks take longer to cook than the tips. The ideal solution is to use a special asparagus kettle, so as to immerse the stalks in boiling water while steaming the tips.

Asparagus can equally well be stood upright in a deep pan of boiling water, tented with foil and cooked for 5–8 minutes, until tender but still al dente. Alternatively, steam the spears in a vegetable steamer. Serve with a drizzle of extra virgin olive oil or melted butter.

Asparagus can also be successfully microwaved. Wash the spears and lay them in an oval dish in a single layer with the tips all pointing the same way. You do not need added water. Cover tightly with microwave clear film (plastic wrap) and cook on full power for 5 minutes per 500g/1¼lb. If the spears are not quite done, turn them over and cook for a little longer.

To roast asparagus, heat some olive oil in a roasting pan, turn the spears in the oil, then roast in a hot oven for 5–10 minutes.

To fry, roll the spears in beaten egg and fine dried breadcrumbs, then fry them a few at a time in very hot olive oil until crusty and golden. Drain on kitchen paper and sprinkle with sea salt.

Cardi *(cardoons)*

Cardoons are related to artichokes, but only the leaf-stalks are eaten. They are commercially grown in mounds of soil to keep them creamy white, but in the wild, the stalks are pale green and hairy and can grow to an enormous size. The tough outer stalks are always discarded, and only the inner stalks and hearts are eaten. Cardoons are a popular winter vegetable in Italy and can be found in the markets ready-trimmed.

CULINARY USES

Cardoons can be eaten raw as a salad, or cooked in a variety of ways – fried, puréed or boiled and served with melted butter or a rich cream and Parmesan sauce. They are traditionally used as a vegetable to dip into the hot anchovy and garlic fondue known as *bagna cauda*.

BUYING AND STORING

Cardoons bought in the market will have been trimmed of their outer stalks and are sold with a crown of leaves, rather like large heads of celery. The stalks should be plump and creamy-white and not too hairy. Wrapped in a plastic bag, they will keep in the vegetable drawer of the refrigerator for two or three days.

PREPARING AND COOKING CARDOONS

Cut off the roots and peel the stalks with a potato peeler to remove the stringy fibres. Cut the stalks into 5cm/2½in lengths and the hearts into wedges, and drop into acidulated water to prevent discoloration. Blanch in boiling salted water, then simmer or fry gently in butter until tender. To serve in a sauce, put the blanched cardoons in an ovenproof dish, cover with sauce, sprinkle with grated Parmesan and bake in a very hot oven until browned.

Cardoons
Related to globe artichokes, the tough outer stalks of this vegetable are always discarded

Vegetables

Carciofi (globe artichokes)

As their appearance suggests, artichokes are a type of thistle. Originating from Sicily, where they grow almost wild, they are cultivated throughout Italy and are a particular speciality of Roman cooking. The artichoke itself is actually the flower bud of the large, silvery-leaved plant. There are many different varieties, from tiny purple plants with tapered leaves, which are so tender that they can be eaten raw, to large bright or pale green globes, whose leaves are pulled off one by one and the succulent flesh at the base stripped off with your teeth.

HISTORY

Although artichokes have always grown like weeds in Sicily, they were first cultivated near Naples in the 15th century. Their popularity spread to Florence, where they became a favourite dish of the Medici family. They were believed to have powerful aphrodisiac properties and women were often forbidden to eat them!

CULINARY USES

Tiny tender artichokes can be quartered and eaten raw or braised *alla romana* with olive oil, parsley and garlic. Large specimens can be served boiled with a dressing to dip the leaves into, or stuffed with savoury fillings. They can be cut into wedges, dipped in batter and deep-fried. A favourite Italian dish is the ancient Jewish recipe *carciofi alla giudea*, where the artichokes are flattened out and deep-fried twice, so that the outside is very crisp while the inside remains meltingly moist.

BUYING AND STORING

Artichokes are available almost all year round, but they are at their best in summer. Whichever variety you are buying, look for tightly packed leaves (open leaves indicate that they are too mature) and a very fresh colour. When an artichoke is old, the tips of the leaves will turn brown. If possible, buy artichokes still attached to their stems; they will keep fresher and the peeled,

cooked stems are often as delicious as the artichoke itself.

Artichokes will keep fresh for several days if you place the stalks in water like a bunch of flowers. If they have no stalks, wrap them in clear film (plastic wrap) and keep in the vegetable drawer of the refrigerator for a day or two.

Globe artichokes
These popular vegetables are actually the flower bud of a type of large thistle

Cavolo (cabbage)

Cabbage is an essential ingredient of many Italian hearty winter soups. Three main types are used; *cavolo verza* (curly-leaved Savoy cabbage), which is used in Milanese dishes, *cavolo cappuccio* (round white or red cabbage) and the speciality of Tuscany, *cavolo nero*, a tall leafy cabbage whose name means 'black cabbage', but which is actually dark purplish green.

CULINARY USES

Italians rarely eat cabbage as a vegetable accompaniment, but prefer to include it in hearty soups, such as *ribollita* or minestrone, or to stuff and braise the outer leaves and serve them as a main course.

BUYING AND STORING

Cabbage heads should be solid and firm, with fresh, unyellowed leaves. It is best to buy them complete with their outer leaves; not only are these tasty for cooking, but they protect the hearts and give a good indication of the freshness of the cabbages. A cabbage will keep in the vegetable drawer of the refrigerator for up to a week.

Cavolo nero
The name of this tall leafy cabbage means 'black cabbage'

Red and white cabbage
The red variety is often cooked gently with apples and spices to serve with rich meats, while the white variety is added to soups and stews

Savoy cabbage
This curly-leaved cabbage is used in Milanese dishes

PREPARING AND COOKING CABBAGE

Cut off the outer leaves and stalk, cutting out a cone-shaped section of the stalk from the inside of the cabbage. To use the leaves for stuffing, blanch them in boiling water for about 3 minutes, until malleable. For soups and braised dishes, coarsely shred the cabbage and wash it well.

Cabbage can be cooked in a variety of ways. The simplest cooking method is to toss shredded cabbage in butter or olive oil until just tender. Never overcook cabbage; it should still retain some crunch. Winter cabbages are good shredded and braised with pancetta *and garlic, while cavolo rosso (red cabbage) can be spiced with apples, cinnamon and cloves and stewed in a little white wine to cut the richness of pork, duck or roast goose.*

Vegetables

Cipolle (onions)

Onions are an essential part of Italian cooking. Many varieties are grown, including mild yellow onions, the stronger-flavoured white onions and their baby version, which is used for pickling and sweet-and-sour onions. The best-known Italian onions are the vibrant deep red variety, which are delicious raw (in a tuna and bean salad, for example, or cooked).

CULINARY USES

The best Italian onions are grown in Piedmont, so many classic Piedmontese recipes include these versatile bulbs. Large onions can be stuffed with Fontina or minced (ground) meat and herbs, and baked. Baby white onions are traditionally cooked *in agrodolce*, a sweet-and-sour sauce of sugar and wine vinegar, and served cold as an *antipasto* or hot as a vegetable accompaniment.

BUYING AND STORING

You will often find young fresh onions in Italian markets. These are sold in bunches like large, bulbous spring onions (scallions), complete with their leaves. They have a mild flavour and can be used for pickling or in salads. They will keep in the refrigerator for three or four days; wrap them tightly to stop their smell pervading everything else in the refrigerator. Older onions have thin, almost papery skins that should be unblemished. The onions should feel firm and not be sprouting green leaves. They quickly deteriorate once cut, so it is best to buy assorted sizes, then you can use a small onion when the recipe calls for only a small amount. Stored in a dry, airy place, onions will keep for many weeks.

White onion
This variety is very strongly flavoured

Red onion
This vibrant red variety is now widely available – they are delicious raw

Baby white onions
Traditionally cooked in agrodolce, *a classic Italian sweet-and-sour sauce, and served cold as an* antipasto

Yellow onions
These mild onions are best cooked gently in olive oil

PREPARING AND COOKING ONIONS

Some onions are easier to peel than others. The skins of red and yellow onions can be removed without much difficulty, but white onions may need to be plunged into boiling water for about 30 seconds to make peeling easier.

There are all sorts of old wives' remedies to stop your eyes watering when peeling onions. The most effective method is to hold them as far away from you as possible while you peel! For most cooked dishes, onions should be sliced or chopped, but for salads they are sliced into very thin rings.

The flavour of onions will develop in different ways, according to how you cook them. In Italian cooking, they are rarely browned, which gives them a bitter taste, but are generally sweated gently in olive oil to add a mellow flavour to a multitude of dishes.

Finocchio (fennel)

Originally a medicinal remedy for such disagreeable conditions as flatulence, fennel has become one of the most important of all Italian vegetables. Bulb or Florence fennel (so-called to distinguish it from the feathery green herb) resembles a fat white celery root and has a delicate but distinctive flavour of aniseed and a very crisp, refreshing texture.

CULINARY USES

Fennel is delicious eaten raw, dressed with a vinaigrette or as part of a mixed salad. In southern Italy, raw fennel is served with cheese as a dessert instead of fruit – an excellent aid to digesting a meal.

When cooked, the aniseed flavour becomes more subtle and the texture resembles cooked celery. Braised fennel is particularly good with white fish. Fennel can be cooked in all the same ways as celery or cardoons.

BUYING AND STORING

Fennel is available all year round. If possible, buy it with its topknot of feathery green fronds, which you can chop and use as a herb or garnish in any dish where you would use dill. The bulbs should feel firm and the outer layers should be crisp and white, not wizened and yellowish. It should have a delicate, very fresh scent of aniseed and the crisp texture of green celery. Whole fennel bulbs will keep in the refrigerator for up to a week. Once cut, however, use them immediately, or the cut surfaces will discolour and the texture will soften. Allow a whole bulb per serving.

PREPARING AND COOKING FENNEL

If the outer layer of the fennel bulb seems stringy, peel it with a sharp knife. Cut off the round greenish stalks protruding from the top. For salads, cut the bulb vertically into thin slices. For cooked dishes, quarter the bulb. Any trimmings can be chopped and used for soups or sauces for fish.

Fennel can be sautéed, baked or braised. For all cooked fennel recipes, blanch the quartered bulbs in a large pan of salted boiling water until it is just tender.

To sauté, heat about 25g/ 1oz butter per bulb with some chopped garlic, drain the fennel and fry it gently in the butter until very tender. To enhance the flavour, add a teaspoon of Pernod or other aniseed-flavoured alcohol.

Braised fennel should be cooked in a little olive oil using a covered frying pan.

To bake fennel, lay the blanched bulbs in a buttered ovenproof dish, season, dot with butter and sprinkle a generous quantity of freshly grated Parmesan cheese over the top. Bake in the oven at 200°C/ 400°F/Gas 6 for 20–30 minutes, or until the top is bubbling and golden brown.

Fennel
The distinctive aniseed flavour makes this vegetable a perfect partner for white fish

Vegetables

Melanzane (aubergines (eggplants))

The versatile aubergine plays an important role in the cooking of southern Italy and Sicily, possibly because its dense, satisfying texture makes a good substitute for meat. You will find many different aubergines in Italian markets, the two main types being the familiar deep purple elongated variety and the rotund paler mauve type, which has a thinner skin. Some are small, some huge, but they all taste similar and can be used in the same way for any recipe.

PREPARING AUBERGINES (EGGPLANTS)

Some people believe that aubergines should be sliced and salted for 30 minutes before cooking to draw out the bitter juices; others deem this unnecessary. Salting does stop the aubergine soaking up large quantities of oil during cooking.

Slice or dice the aubergines, place them in a colander, sprinkle with 15ml/1 tbsp salt per 1kg/2¼lb. Place a dish on the aubergines and weight it down. Leave for 30 minutes. Rinse the aubergines and dry with kitchen paper.

If aubergines have a very tough skin, it is best to peel them (unless you are stuffing them and need the skin as a container). Otherwise, leave the skin on, as its colour will enhance the appearance of the finished dish.

BUYING AND STORING

Shape and size are not important when choosing aubergines; the essentials are tight, glossy skins and a fairly firm texture. Do not buy aubergines with wrinkled or damaged skins. They should feel heavy for their size; a light aubergine will probably be spongy inside and contain a lot of seeds. They will keep in the refrigerator for up to a week.

Aubergines (eggplants)
The familiar deep purple variety plays an important role in the cooking of southern Italy

HISTORY

Aubergines originated in Asia. They were cultivated in Europe in the Middle Ages, but only very rarely featured in Italian cooking at the time, since they were regarded with suspicion; indeed, the name *melanzane* comes from the Latin *melum insanum* (unhealthy apple). This mistrust had been overcome by the Renaissance, and aubergines began to be grown and used extensively in the south of Italy.

CULINARY USES

Aubergines are extremely versatile vegetables and add a wonderful depth of flavour and substance to any dish in which they appear. They can be grilled (broiled), baked, stuffed, stewed and sautéed, on their own or with other ingredients, such as tomatoes, cheese or creamy or meat sauces. The rich colour of their skins enhances the appearance of many different Italian dishes.

COOKING AUBERGINES (EGGPLANTS)

The simplest way of cooking aubergines is to slice and fry them in very hot olive oil. For a more substantial dish, coat them in light batter, then fine breadcrumbs, and fry until golden brown.

To bake them, halve the aubergines lengthways, removing the calyx and stalk. Make slashes in the flesh and rub it with a cut garlic clove. Drizzle some olive oil over the top, cover with foil and bake in a hot oven for about 1 hour, until very soft. Season with salt and pepper and add lemon juice to taste.

Probably the most famous Italian aubergine dish is melanzane alla parmigiana, where the aubergines are layered with rich tomato sauce and Parmesan and baked in the oven. A favourite Sicilian dish, caponata, combines them with celery and a piquant sweet-and-sour sauce enlivened with olives and sometimes capers.

Peperoni (sweet (bell) peppers)

Generically known as capsicums, the shape of these sweet peppers gives them the alternative name of 'bell peppers'. Although they come in a range of colours – green (these are unripe red peppers), red, yellow, orange and even purplish-black – all peppers have much the same sweetish flavour and crunchy texture, and are interchangeable in recipes. They are a healthy food, being rich in vitamin C. The locally grown peppers you will see in the markets in Italy are much larger and more misshapen than the uniformly perfect, hydroponically grown specimens found elsewhere, but their flavour is sweet and delicious.

CULINARY USES

Each region of Italy has its own specialities using peppers. They can be used raw or lightly roasted in salads or as an *antipasto* and can be cooked in a variety of ways – roasted and dressed with olive oil or vinaigrette dressing and capers, stewed (as in *peperonata*), or stuffed and baked. Peppers have a great affinity with other Mediterranean ingredients, such as olives, capers, aubergines, tomatoes and anchovies.

BUYING AND STORING

Choose firm peppers with unwrinkled, shiny skins. Size does not matter unless you plan to stuff the peppers, in which case choose roundish shapes of uniform size. The skin of green peppers may be mottled with patches of orange or red; this indicates that the pepper is ripening, and as long as the pepper is unblemished, there is no reason not to buy it. Peppers can be stored in the refrigerator for up to two weeks.

COOKING (BELL) PEPPERS

To make a classic Italian peperonata, sweat sliced onions and garlic in olive oil, add sliced peppers, cover the pan and cook gently until just tender. Add an equal quantity of peeled, deseeded and chopped tomatoes, a splash of wine vinegar and seasoning and cook, uncovered, until meltingly tender. For peperonata alla romana, stir in some capers at the end.

(Bell) peppers
Locally grown Italian peppers are often larger and more misshapen than the uniformly perfect varieties grown in hot-houses

Vegetables

Place the peppers under a very hot grill (broiler) or hold them over a gas flame and turn them until the skin blackens and blisters. Put them in a plastic bag, seal and leave until the peppers are cool enough to handle. The skin will peel off.

To slice peppers, halve them lengthways, cut away the calyx and stem and pull out the core, seeds and white membranes. Cut the flesh into strips.

To stuff peppers, cut off the stalk end and remove the seeds and membranes. Fill the pepper with your chosen stuffing (rice, vegetables, meat – what you will) and replace the stalk end. Arrange the peppers in a shallow ovenproof dish, drizzle over some olive oil and pour in enough water to come about 2cm/³⁄₄in up the sides of the peppers. Bake at 200°C/400°F/Gas 6 for about 1 hour.

For baked peppers alla piemontese, *halve the peppers lengthways and fill each with a chopped tomato, a chopped anchovy fillet and a little chopped garlic. Arrange the peppers on a baking tray, rounded side down. Drizzle over some olive oil and bake at 200°C/400°F/Gas 6 for about 30 minutes.*

Pomodori *(tomatoes)*

It is impossible to imagine Italian cooking without tomatoes, which seem to be a vital ingredient in almost every recipe. But these 'golden apples' were unknown in Italy until the 16th century, when they were brought from Mexico. At first they were grown only in the south, but as their popularity spread, tomatoes were cultivated all over Italy and were incorporated into the cooking of every region. Italians grow an enormous variety of tomatoes, from plum tomatoes (San Marzano are the best) to ridged, pumpkin-shaped, green-tinged salad tomatoes, bright red fruits bursting with aroma and flavour, and tiny *pomodorini* (cherry tomatoes).

CULINARY USES

Tomatoes are used in so many different ways that it is hard to know where to begin. They can be eaten raw, sliced and served with a trickle of extra virgin olive oil and some torn basil leaves (basil and tomatoes have an extraordinary affinity). They are the red component of an *insalata tricolore*, partnering white mozzarella cheese and green basil to make up the colours of the Italian flag. Raw ripe tomatoes

Cherry tomatoes
Bright red and bursting with flavour, these tiny tomatoes can be used to add colour and flavour to any dish

Plum tomatoes
San Marzano are the best variety of these smooth-skinned tomatoes

can be chopped with herbs and garlic to make a fresh-tasting pasta sauce, or made into a topping for *bruschetta*.

Tomatoes can be grilled (broiled), fried, baked, stuffed, stewed and made into sauces and soups. They add colour and flavour to almost any savoury dish.

BUYING AND STORING

Tomatoes are at their best in summer, when they have ripened naturally in the sun. Choose your tomatoes according to how you wish to prepare them. Salad tomatoes should be very firm and easy to slice. The best tomatoes for cooking are the plum tomatoes, which hold their shape well and should have a fine flavour. Tomatoes will only ripen properly if left for long enough on the vine, so try to buy 'vine-ripened' varieties. If you can find only unripe tomatoes, you can ripen

them by putting them in a brown paper bag with a ripe tomato or leaving them in a fruit bowl with a banana; the gases the ripe fruits give off will ripen the tomatoes, but, alas, they cannot improve the flavour.

Try to buy tomatoes loose so that you can smell them. They should have a wonderful aroma. If the flavour is not all it should be, add a good pinch of sugar to enhance it. For cooked recipes, if you cannot find really flavourful tomatoes, use canned instead. The best are San Marzano plum tomatoes, which are grown near Salerno. In Italy, you will often find large knobbly green tomatoes, which are sold as *pomodori insalata*. Although you can allow them to ripen in the usual way, Italians prefer to slice these tomatoes thinly and eat them in their unripe state as a crunchy and refreshing salad.

Large tomatoes
Not always as smooth as these, locally grown Italian tomatoes bought from a market can be very ridged and almost pumpkin-shaped

PEELING TOMATOES

It is easy to remove the skin from tomatoes. Prick the tomatoes with the point of a sharp knife, plunge them into a bowl of boiling water for about 30 seconds, then refresh in cold water. Peel away the skins, cut the tomatoes into quarters or halves and remove the seeds using a teaspoon.

Vine-ripened tomatoes
Tomatoes sold on the vine are likely to have a far better flavour than those sold loose

Vegetables

Spinaci (spinach)

Spinach and its close relatives, *bietola* (Swiss chard) and *biete* (spinach beet), are dark green leafy vegetables, rich in minerals (especially iron) and vitamins. Unlike many other vegetables, they are often served in Italy as an accompaniment to a main course, although they appear in numerous composite dishes as well. All spinach, whether flat-leafed or curly-leafed, has a distinctive metallic flavour, which people either love or loathe. The latter should avoid dishes *alla fiorentina*, which use spinach in large quantities.

Curly-leaf spinach is a summer variety with very dark green leaves. Winter spinach has flat, smooth leaves, but tastes very similar. Usually, only the leaves are eaten and the stalks are discarded. Spinach has a delicate, melting quality and should be cooked only very briefly.

The coarser *bietola* contains less iron and has a less pronounced flavour than spinach. The leaves have broad, tender creamy or pale green midribs, and both the leaves and stalks are eaten, but are cooked in different ways. *Bietola* is available all year round, but is particularly popular in autumn and winter, when more delicate spinach is not available. No one is quite sure why it is called Swiss chard; the Swiss certainly eat it, but in much smaller quantities than the French or Italians.

Biete (spinach beet) has a much smaller stalk and more closely resembles spinach. The stalks are usually left attached to the leaves for cooking. The coarser texture of *biete* makes it more suitable than spinach for recipes that require more than the briefest cooking. Balls of ready-cooked *biete* are often sold in Italian delicatessens.

History

Spinach was originally cultivated in Persia in the 6th century and was brought to Europe by Arab traders some thousand years later. It had become very popular in France, Spain and England by the 16th century, when it was used for both sweet and savoury dishes, but it did not reach Italy until the 18th century.

Culinary Uses

Tender young spinach leaves can be eaten raw in salads or cooked and served cold with a dressing of olive oil and lemon. Cooked spinach is used to make gnocchi and is often combined with ricotta to make fillings for pasta and *crespoline* (pancakes). Florentine-style recipes usually contain spinach, and it is a classic partner for eggs, fish, poultry and white meats. Spinach, *biete* and *bietola* are all used in savoury tarts, such as *torta alla pasqualina*, an Easter speciality. They make excellent soups and soufflés. *Bietola* stalks are delicious sautéed in butter and baked in a white sauce sprinkled with Parmesan cheese.

Spinach
The tender young leaves can be eaten raw; larger leaves need to be cooked

Spinach beet
The coarse texture of biete *makes it more suitable than spinach for slower-cooked recipes*

BUYING AND STORING

All types of spinach should look very fresh and green, with no signs of wilting. The leaves should be unblemished and the stalks crisp. Spinach and spinach beets contain a very high proportion of water and wilt down to about half their weight during cooking, so always buy far more than you think you will need – at least 250g/9oz per serving. Loose spinach should be used as soon as possible after buying. Packed loosely into a plastic bag, it will keep in the refrigerator for a couple of days. Unopened bags of pre-packed spinach will keep for up to a week.

Bietola *(Swiss chard)*

Pull off the green leaves from the stems. Snap the veins and leafstalks and remove the stringy parts (do not cut with a knife, or the strings will not come away). Wash as for spinach and cut the stalks into 6–8cm/ 2½–3½in lengths.

Swiss chard
Available all year round, this vegetable is particularly popular in winter when the more tender spinach is not available

---

PREPARING AND COOKING SPINACH AND SWISS CHARD

Spinach and spinach beet:
Carefully pick over the spinach, discarding any withered or damaged leaves and tough stalks. Wash thoroughly in several changes of water until no signs of earth or grit remain. Spinach should be cooked with only the water which clings to the leaves after washing. Sauté it in butter with a clove of chopped garlic for about 5 minutes; overcooked spinach will be unpleasantly watery. To stew spinach, put it in a large pan, cover and cook gently until wilted, turning it over halfway through cooking. Drain and gently squeeze out the excess moisture with your hands. Toss in butter or olive oil, season with freshly grated nutmeg or chop finely and use for gnocchi and pasta fillings.
Swiss chard leaves can be cooked in exactly the same way as spinach. The prepared stalks should be blanched until tender in salted water or vegetable stock, then baked in a sauce or tart, sautéed in butter or used as a stuffing. A popular bietola *dish is a* sformato, *a savoury, moulded, baked custard.*

Vegetables

Zucca *(squash)* **and** zucchini *(courgettes (zucchini))*

Squashes and courgettes are widely used in northern Italian cooking. Both have large, open, deep-yellow flowers, which are considered a great delicacy. Squashes come in a variety of shapes and sizes, from huge orange pumpkins to small, pale butternut squashes and green acorn squashes. They all have dense, sweet-tasting flesh. Courgettes are like small marrows, with shiny green skin and a sweet, delicate flavour. In Italy, tiny specimens are often sold with their flowers attached.

CULINARY USES

The pumpkin is the symbol of Mantua and recipes *alla mantovana* use the flesh a multitude of ways, from *tortelli alla zucca* (pumpkin-filled tortelli) to risotti, soups and sweet dessert tarts. Pumpkin flowers can be coated in batter and deep-fried, stuffed with a filling of ricotta, or chopped and added to risotti for extra colour and flavour.

Courgettes combine well with other Mediterranean vegetables, such as tomatoes and aubergines (eggplants). They can be dipped in batter and deep-fried, made into fritters or served with a white sauce seasoned with Parmesan cheese or nutmeg. Served cold with a mint-flavoured vinaigrette (*zucchini a scapece*) or tomato sauce, they can be part of an *antipasto*. They can be halved and stuffed with a meat or vegetable filling. Young courgettes can also be thinly sliced or grated and eaten raw in a salad.

BUYING AND STORING

Courgettes are available almost all year round, but are at their best in spring and summer. The smaller and skinnier courgettes are, the better they taste. They should have very glossy green skins and feel very firm. Do not buy flabby courgettes or those with blemished skins. Larger specimens are useful for stuffing. If you can find them in markets, go for tiny courgettes

Courgettes (zucchini)
These familiar vegetables combine well with other Mediterranean vegetables

Pumpkins
Italians use the flesh of these large vegetables in a multitude of ways

Small pumpkins
Like their larger cousins, these small pumpkins have dense, sweet-tasting flesh

with their flowers attached. Allow 250g/9oz courgettes per serving. They will keep in the vegetable drawer of the refrigerator for up to a week.

Squashes should feel firm and heavy for their size. It is not worth buying enormous pumpkins (other than for decorative purposes), as their flesh tends to be stringy and flavourless. All whole squashes keep well, but once they are opened, they should be wrapped in clear film (plastic wrap) and kept in the refrigerator for no more than three days.

If you are lucky enough to find squash or courgette flowers (the best way is to grow your own), they must be cooked straight away, as they are extremely perishable.

PREPARING COURGETTES (ZUCCHINI), SQUASHES AND PUMPKINS

Courgettes should be topped and tailed, then sliced, diced, cut into batons or grated as appropriate. They do not need peeling.

Flowers may contain small insects, so wash them quickly under cold running water and gently pat dry with kitchen paper. Cut off all but 2.5cm/1in of the stems. Courgettes are best sautéed in butter or olive oil flavoured with plenty of chopped garlic and parsley. Courgettes deep-fried in a light batter are a

favourite accompaniment in Italy. The flowers can be prepared in the same way. To make zucchini a scapece, slice 1kg/2¼lb courgettes thickly and brown in hot olive oil. Place in a dish and scatter over about 20 torn mint leaves and 1 finely chopped garlic clove. Season and dress with one part red wine vinegar and two parts olive oil. Mix well and leave the flavours to develop for 2 hours before serving.

Squashes and pumpkins should be peeled and the seeds and fibrous parts removed. Cut the flesh into chunks or slices. The skin of large pumpkins may be too hard to peel; if so, break open the pumpkin with a hammer or drop it on the floor, and scoop out the flesh, discarding the seeds.

Pumpkin and squash should be blanched in boiling salted water, then sweated in butter until soft and made into soup or stuffing, cooked au gratin or grated raw and added to a risotto. Pumpkin can also be sweetened and used as a pie filling.

Butternut squash
The brightly coloured flesh of butternut squashes is widely used in northern Italian cooking

Acorn squash
Once halved, these small squashes need to be seeded and peeled before cooking

Salad Leaves

Italians grow salad leaves in profusion and gather them from the wild to create inventive and interesting combinations, such as *misticanza*, a pot-pourri of wild greens and cultivated leaves. In high season, you will find at least a dozen different salad leaves in an Italian market, ranging from fresh green round (butterhead) garden lettuces to bitter dark green grass-like leaves and purplish-red radicchio. Such salads are served after the main course, dressed with olive oil and vinegar to cleanse the palate.

Cicoria di campo or dente di leone (dandelion)

Dandelion leaves are rich in iron and vitamins, and are also reputed to be a powerful diuretic. They have a pungent, peppery taste and long, fresh green indented leaves (hence the name 'lion's tooth'). They can be picked from the wild before the plant has flowered, but only the young leaves should be eaten. Cultivated dandelion leaves are available. They are more tender than wild leaves, but have a less intense flavour.

CULINARY USES
Young dandelion leaves are usually served raw in salads together with other leaves; they are particularly good with crisply cooked bacon and hard-boiled eggs. They can also be cooked like spinach.

Radicchio

This variety of red-leafed chicory comes originally from Treviso. *Radicchio di Treviso* has elongated purplish-red leaves with pronounced cream-coloured veins. The more familiar round variety is known as *radicchio di Verona*. Both types of red-leafed chicory have a bitter taste, and for salads are best used in small quantities together with other leaves. They look particularly attractive when combined with frilly-leafed frisée, pale whitish-green chicory (Belgian endive) leaves, or the darker cornsalad and rocket (arugula).

Dandelion leaves
Pick these peppery-tasting leaves from the wild before the plant has flowered

Radicchio di Verona
The more familiar round red-leafed chicory (Belgian endive)

Radicchio di Treviso
This elongated variety is delicious grilled (broiled) with olive oil

CULINARY USES
Radicchio can also be eaten as a hot vegetable, either quartered and grilled (broiled) with olive oil, or stuffed with a mixture of breadcrumbs, anchovies, capers and olives and baked – but it loses its beautiful colour when cooked. A little radicchio added to a risotto made with red wine will add to the pretty pink colour.

BUYING AND STORING
Radicchio leaves should be fresh-looking with no trace of brown at the edges. *Radicchio di Verona* should be firm with tightly packed leaves. Both types will keep in the refrigerator for up to a week.

Rucola *(rocket (arugula))*

Rocket has dark green elongated, indented leaves and a hot, pungent flavour and aroma. Like dandelions, it grows wild in the Italian countryside, but it is also cultivated commercially. Home-grown rocket has a much better flavour than the immature leaves usually found in supermarkets, but it bolts easily and should be picked as soon as the leaves are large enough.

CULINARY USES

Rocket adds zest to any green salad and can be eaten on its own with a dressing of olive oil and lemon juice or balsamic vinegar. Combined with radicchio, cornsalad and fresh herbs, rocket makes a good substitute for *misticanza*. It can be added to pasta sauces and risotti, or cooked like spinach, but cooking does diminish the pungent flavour.

BUYING AND STORING

In Italy, rocket is always sold in small bunches. The leaves should look very fresh with no sign of wilting. Rocket does not keep well unless it has been pre-packaged. To keep it for a day or two, wrap it in damp newspaper or damp kitchen paper and store in the refrigerator.

Rocket (arugula)
This hot, pungent salad leaf grows wild in the Italian countryside, but it is also cultivated commercially

Cornsalad
The delicate but distinctive flavour of this salad plant adds interest to winter salads

Valeriana *(cornsalad)*

This delicate salad plant, also called lamb's lettuce, has tender green rounded leaves bunched together in a rosette shape. It grows wild in fields in Italy, but is also cultivated and is an essential ingredient of *misticanza*. It has a delicate but distinctive flavour, which adds interest to winter salads.

CULINARY USES

Cornsalad is usually served by itself or in a mixed green salad, but it can also be cooked like spinach. The tender leaves will blacken if damaged, so take care when tossing a salad not to bruise them.

BUYING AND STORING

Cornsalad should look fresh and green, with no withered or drooping leaves. The smaller and rounder the leaves, the better the flavour. It will keep in the salad drawer of the refrigerator for several days, but take care not to squash it.

PREPARING CORNSALAD

Cornsalad is sold with the root attached, so it must be washed thoroughly before use. Dunk it in several changes of cold water to remove all the grit, then dab the leaves dry with kitchen paper, handling them very gently.

Mushrooms

Italian country-dwellers have always been passionate collectors of edible wild mushrooms; in spring and autumn, the woods and fields are alive with furtive fungi hunters in search of these flavourful delicacies. Cultivated button (white) mushrooms are rarely eaten in Italy, even when fresh wild varieties are out of season; Italians prefer to use dried or preserved wild fungi with their robust, earthy taste.

The most highly prized mushroom for use in Italian cooking is the *porcino* (cep). Since these are hugely expensive, they are most often dried and used in small quantities to add flavour to field or other wild mushrooms. Drying actually intensifies the flavour of *porcini*, so they are not regarded as inferior to the fresh mushrooms – quite the reverse. Other popular wild fungi include *gallinacci* (chanterelles), *prataioli* (field (portobello) mushroooms) and *ovoli* (Caesar's mushrooms).

HISTORY

From earliest times, primitive man gathered and ate wild mushrooms. The Greeks and Romans enjoyed many fungi, including *amanita caesarea* (Caesar's mushroom), which was popular with the Emperor Claudius and ultimately his downfall; his wife Agrippina poisoned him by adding deadly *amanita phalloides* (the aptly named deathcap) to a dish of his favourite fungi. The Romans succeeded in cultivating several types of mushrooms, but cultivation on a large scale really began in the 17th century, when a French botanist discovered how to grow mushrooms in compost all year round.

STORING

Never store mushrooms in a plastic bag, as they will sweat and turn mushy. Put them into a paper bag and keep in the vegetable drawer of the refrigerator for no more than two days.

PREPARING AND COOKING MUSHROOMS

Mushrooms should never be washed or they will become waterlogged and mushy. To clean them, cut off the earthy base of the stalk and lightly brush the caps with a soft brush or wipe them clean with a slightly damp cloth.

With very few exceptions (including ceps and Caesar's mushrooms, which can be eaten raw), wild mushrooms should be cooked to destroy any mild toxins they may contain. All mushrooms can be sliced and sauteéd in hot olive oil or a mixture of butter and olive oil with finely chopped garlic or shallots, a little red chilli and herbs (parsley, marjoram, thyme or mint are particularly good).

Chanterelles
These orangey-yellow mushrooms have a delicious, delicate flavour and a distinct apricot aroma

COOKING CHANTERELLES

Chanterelles have a delicious, delicate flavour and a slightly chewy texture; they should be cooked slowly or they may become hard. Fry them gently in butter with chopped garlic or shallots for about 10 minutes, adding some finely chopped parsley, marjoram or thyme towards the end of the cooking time. Serve them on hot buttered toast, or add to omelettes or scrambled eggs. They are particularly good with poultry, rabbit or veal and can also be dressed with a herb-flavoured vinaigrette and served warm in a salad.

CULINARY USES

Ovoli can be thinly sliced and eaten raw in a salad. They combine very well with hazelnuts.

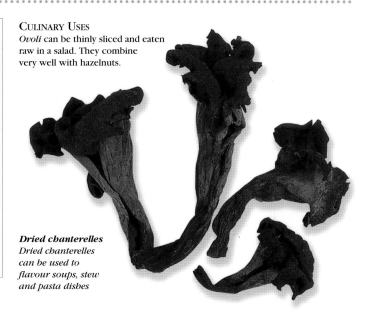

Dried chanterelles
Dried chanterelles can be used to flavour soups, stew and pasta dishes

Ovoli *(Caesar's mushrooms; Latin name amanita caesarea)*

These large mushrooms with an orangey-yellow cap have an excellent flavour and were a favourite of the Roman emperors. They are still found in Italy, but are very rare elsewhere.

Mushroom powder

Well-flavoured dried mushrooms can be crushed to a powder and used to flavour sauces, soups and stews. Some Italian delicatessens stock mushroom powder. If you make your own, store it in an airtight container.

RECONSTITUTING DRIED MUSHROOMS

Soak 25g/1oz dried mushrooms in 250ml/8fl oz/1 cup hot water for about 20 minutes until soft, then drain and use like fresh mushrooms. Keep the soaking water to use in sauces, stocks or soups; it will have an intense mushroom flavour.

DRYING CHANTERELLES

Leave the chanterelles whole, or halve them if they are large.

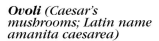

Lay them on a double thickness of newspaper and leave in a very warm, airy place (above the boiler is ideal), turning them over every few hours until they have become completely dry and brittle. Alternatively, string them like necklaces and hang them up to dry, or place in a very cool fan oven (maximum 130°C/250°F/ gas ¹/₂), leaving the door ajar. When the chanterelles are completely dry, store them in jars or paper bags. All mushrooms can be dried in this way; slice them thinly before drying. It is only worth drying perfect specimens.

Mushrooms

Porcini (ceps)

These are the king of mushrooms in Italian cooking. Their Italian name means 'little piglets', which aptly describes their bulbous stalks and rounded brown caps. In autumn, they are found in woodlands, where they can grow to an enormous size, weighing more than 500g/1¼lb each (although mushroom-hunters rarely leave them for long enough to grow to these proportions). There are many different varieties of *porcini*, all of which have a fine flavour and meaty texture.

CULINARY USES

All ceps can be cooked in the same way as other mushrooms. Young ones can be thinly sliced and eaten raw, dressed with extra virgin olive oil. Larger caps are delicious brushed with olive oil, grilled (broiled) and served with a grinding of salt and pepper. Don't discard the stalks, which have an excellent flavour; chop them and cook with the caps, or use them for sauces, stocks and soups; just trim off the earthy bits from the base.

DRYING

Ceps can be thinly sliced and dried in the same way as *gallinacci*. Dried *porcini* are commercially available. They are very expensive, but a little goes a long way. Just 25g/1oz dried porcini, soaked and drained, will enhance the flavour of 500g/1¼lb cultivated mushrooms beyond recognition. Don't be tempted to buy cheap packets of dried *porcini*, which may contain a high proportion of inferior dried mushrooms and bits of twig from the forest floor.

STORING

Fresh *porcini* can be kept in the vegetable drawer of the refrigerator for up to two days. Dried mushrooms will keep in an airtight container for at least a year.

Porcini *(ceps)*
Italian cooks consider these to be the king of mushrooms

FREEZING

Small *porcini* in perfect condition can be frozen whole. Large or blemished specimens should be sliced and lightly sautéed in butter, then drained and frozen. Do not defrost before use, or they will become mushy. Simply cook the mushrooms from frozen in hot olive oil or butter. Frozen mushrooms will only keep for about one month.

PICKLING *PORCINI*

Unblemished fresh porcini can be preserved by pickling. Choose unblemished funghi (if you haven't enough porcini, use a mixture of mushrooms), leaving small ones whole and slicing or quartering large ones.

1kg/2¼lb mushrooms
500ml/17fl oz/ generous
  2 cups white wine vinegar
500ml/17fl oz/ generous
  2 cups water
10ml/2 tsp salt
5ml/1 tsp peppercorns,
  lightly crushed
2 bay leaves
10 ml/2 tsp coriander seeds
2 garlic cloves, peeled
  and halved
4 small dried red chillies
olive oil

1 Put the mushrooms in a large pan with all the ingredients except the olive oil. Bring to the boil and simmer for 5–10 minutes until the mushrooms are tender but still firm. Drain them, reserving the pickling aromatics, and leave them to cool completely.

2 Spoon the mushrooms and aromatics into a sterilized preserving jar and fill up the jar with olive oil. Seal and leave for at least a month. Pickled mushrooms will keep for at least six months.

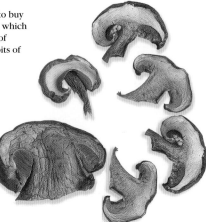

Dried *porcini (ceps)*
These dried porcini are expensive to buy, but since drying actually accentuates their flavour, a little goes a long way

Black truffles
No one has succeeded in cultivating truffles so they remain rare and expensive – the black variety are more highly prized than the white

White truffles
Found in Piedmont, northern Italy, these delicately flavoured truffles are usually served raw

Chiodini (honey fungus; Latin name armarilla mellea)

No gardener welcomes the sight of honey fungus (the Italian name means 'little nails'), as it is a parasitic fungus that destroys the trees on whose roots it grows. However, the caps of these small golden mushrooms are good to eat (the fibrous stalks should be discarded). In their raw state they are mildly toxic, but once they have been blanched in very hot oil or boiling water, then stewed in butter with a little garlic, seasoning and parsley, they make good eating.

CULINARY USES
Honey fungus makes a good filling for a *frittata* (Italian omelette). Allow 150g/ 5oz *chiodini* caps and 4 large (US extra large) eggs for two people. Season the eggs and beat them lightly with 25g/1oz grated Parmesan cheese. Heat 30ml/ 2 tbsp olive oil in a frying pan and sauté the blanched mushroom caps with 1 minced garlic clove and 15ml/1 tbsp chopped parsley for about 3 minutes. Season with salt and pepper, pour in the eggs and stir well. Cook the *frittata* until set on the bottom, then sprinkle with a little more Parmesan and place under a hot grill (broiler) until golden brown. Cut into wedges and serve.

Tartufi *(truffles)*

Truffles grow about 20cm/8in underground, usually near oak trees. They are in season from October to late December. Their irregular, knobbly, round shape conceals a pungent, earthy and delicious aroma and flavour. There are two main varieties, black and white. The more highly prized black truffles (*tuber melanosporum*) grow mostly in the Périgord region of France, but they are also found in northern Italy, in Tuscany and Piedmont. The more common Piedmont truffle is the white variety (*tuber magnatum*), which has a rather more delicate flavour.

No one has yet succeeded in cultivating truffles commercially, so they remain rare and expensive. They are sniffed out by trained pigs or dogs, who can detect their subterranean scent. In order to develop their full aroma and flavour, the truffles must be left to mature, so truffle-hunters often cover up those which the animals have unearthed (praying that nobody else will find their buried treasure) until they reach full maturity.

HISTORY
Truffles have been eaten since ancient times. They were a favourite dish of the ancient Egyptians. The Greeks and Romans believed them to have aphrodisiac properties, but in the Middle Ages they were thought to be manifestations of the devil. Louis XIV of France, however, subscribed to the earlier theory, and from his reign onwards truffles were enthusiastically consumed by all those rich enough to afford this luxury food.

CULINARY USES
Truffles can be eaten raw or cooked. White Piedmont truffles are usually served raw, shaved very thinly over fresh pasta, a *fonduta* or eggs. They can be heated briefly in butter and seasoned with salt, white pepper and nutmeg. Black or white truffles are delicious with all poultry and white meat. A few slivers of truffle will add a touch of luxury to almost any savoury sauce. A classic rich Italian dish using truffles is *vincigrassi*, sheets of fresh pasta layered with butter, cream, slivers of truffle, ham and chicken livers. It is a speciality of the Marches and the Abruzzi.

BUYING AND STORING
If you are lucky enough to find a fresh truffle, use it as soon as possible, as the flavour is volatile. Brush off the earth from the skin and peel the truffle (keep the peelings to use in a sauce). To give whole fresh eggs the most wonderful flavour, put them in a bowl with the truffle, cover and leave overnight; they will absorb the superb musty aroma.

You are more likely to buy canned or bottled truffles than fresh ones. Whole ones are extremely expensive, but cheaper pieces and even peelings are available. The most economical way to enjoy the flavour of truffles is to buy Italian oil scented with white truffles. A drop or two of this added to a dish will transform it into something really special.

Truffle oil
The most economical way to enjoy the flavour of truffles – a drop or two of this scented oil will enhance sauces, pastas and salads

Fruit & Nuts

Italians prefer to buy only those fruits and nuts that are in season, and who can blame
them? Italy produces an abundance of soft, stone and citrus fruits, all bursting with flavour
and often available fresh from the tree. There are apples and pears from the orchards of the
northern regions; nuts, peaches, plums and figs from the central plains; while the south and
Sicily produce almost every kind of fruit – grapes, cherries, oranges and lemons – as well as
pistachio nuts and almonds. Many of these fruits are indigenous to Italy and have been
grown there since time immemorial.

After a full meal of *antipasto*, pasta and a *secondo* (main course), it is hardly surprising that Italian desserts very often consist of nothing but a bowl of seasonal fresh fruit served on its own or made into a refreshing *macedonia* (fruit salad). Soft fruits form the basis of ice creams, sorbets, *granite* and *frullati* (fresh fruit milkshakes), while nuts and winter fruits (often dried or candied) are baked into tarts and pastries.

Amarena *(Morello cherry)*

Although Italy does produce sweet dessert cherries, it is best known for the bitter Morello variety, which are preserved in syrup or brandy, or made into ice cream and Maraschino liqueur. These cherries are small, with dark red skins and firm flesh. They are in season from late June to early July, and can be eaten raw, although they have quite a sharp flavour.

CULINARY USES

Morello cherries can be poached in sugar syrup and served whole, or puréed and made into a rich, dark, cherry syrup. Stone (pit) the cherries and purée them. Strain the cherries through a fine sieve (strainer) and leave the juice at room temperature for about 24 hours. Strain through muslin (cheesecloth) and add 750g/ 1lb 10 oz caster (superfine) sugar per 500ml/17fl oz/generous 2 cups cherry juice. Heat gently. When the sugar has dissolved, bring the syrup to the boil, strain again and pour into airtight bottles or containers. These cherries

also make excellent jam. A popular Venetian dish is Morello cherries poached in a red wine syrup flavoured with cinnamon. Bottled cherries in vinegar can be used in sauces for meat, duck and game.

BUYING AND STORING

Choose fresh cherries with unwrinkled and unblemished skins, which look shiny and feel firm. Stored in a plastic bag, they will keep in the refrigerator for up to a week.

Morello cherries
These dark red cherries are usually
preserved in syrup and used for
desserts. Those bottled in vinegar
can be used for savoury recipes

Arancia *(orange)*

Many varieties of oranges are grown in Sicily and southern Italy. The best-known Sicilian oranges are the small blood oranges with their bright ruby-red flesh. Other types of sweet oranges include seedless navels, which take their name from the umbilical-like end which contains an embryonic orange, and seeded late oranges, which have paler flesh and are available throughout the winter. Bitter oranges (*arance amare*) are also grown; these rough-skinned varieties are made into preserves (although rarely marmalade in Italy), candied peel and *liquore all'arancia* (orange liqueur).

HISTORY

Oranges originated in China, but bitter oranges may possibly have been known in Ancient Greece; the mythical 'golden apples of the Hesperides' are said to have been Seville oranges, although this seems historically far-fetched. They were certainly brought to Italy by Arab traders during the Roman Empire and over the centuries became a symbol of wealth and opulence – so much so that the Medici family incorporated them into their coat of arms as five golden balls. Sweet oranges did not arrive in Italy until the 17th century.

Oranges
Sweet varieties are used for both sweet and savoury recipes – they are a favourite addition to salads

Bitter oranges
This rough-skinned variety can be used to add zest to savoury dishes – it combines well with white fish, liver, duck and game – and is used for preserves

CULINARY USES

A favourite Sicilian recipe is *insalata di arance alla siciliana*, a salad of thinly sliced oranges and red onion rings dressed with black olives and their oil. Oranges also combine well with raw fennel and chicory (Belgian endive). They can be sliced and served *alla veneziana*, coated with caramel, or simply macerated in a little lemon juice with a sliver of lemon peel for a refreshing dessert. They can be squeezed for juice, or made into sorbet and *granita*. Bitter oranges combine well with white fish, calf's liver, duck or game, and add zest to a tomato sauce.

BUYING AND STORING

Oranges are available all year round, but are at their best in winter. They should have unblemished shiny skins and feel heavy for their size (this indicates that they contain plenty of juice and that the flesh is not dry). If you intend to candy the peel or incorporate it into a recipe, choose unwaxed oranges. Oranges will keep at room temperature for a week and for at least two weeks in the refrigerator. Bring them back to room temperature or warm them slightly before eating them.

Preparing Fresh Oranges

1 When peeling an orange it is important to remove all the bitter white pith and membrane. Hold the orange over a bowl to catch the juice and use a very sharp knife to cut off the peel, pith and the membrane enclosing the flesh.

2 To segment the orange, cut down between the membranes of the segments and ease out the flesh. Squeeze the membranes into the bowl to extract the juice.

3 To remove strips of orange rind, run a cannelle knife down the orange, or use a zester for finer shreds. If you cannot find unwaxed fruit, wash the oranges in warm water, rinse and dry well before removing strips of rind.

Fruit

Fico (fig)

Figs are grown all over Italy, but thanks
to the hot climate Sicilian figs are
perhaps the most luscious of all.
During the summer months you will
often find Italian farmers at the
roadside selling punnets of ripe
figs from their own trees. There
are two types of Italian figs, green
and purple. Both have thin,
tender skins and very sweet,
succulent, red flesh, and are rich
in vitamins A, B and C. They are in
season from July to October and are
best eaten straight off the tree when
they are perfectly ripe.

Purple figs
*The sweet succulent
flesh of this variety
makes a perfect partner
to nuts of all kinds*

HISTORY

Figs were said to grow in the Garden
of Eden, where Adam and Eve used
the leaves to cover their nakedness.
In fact they probably originated in
Asia Minor, although the oldest fig
tree in the world is reputed to be
growing in a garden in Palermo in
Sicily. The Greeks and Romans
certainly enjoyed figs, which are still
as highly prized today.

Green figs
*Delicious served raw with prosciutto
or salami as an* antipasto

CULINARY USES

Fresh figs are delicious served on their
own, but they have an affinity with nuts
such as walnuts, pistachios and
almonds. They can be served raw with
Parma ham or salami as an *antipasto*,
or stuffed with raspberry coulis or
mascarpone as a dessert. Poached in a
little water or wine flavoured with
cinnamon or nutmeg, they make an
excellent accompaniment to duck,
game or lamb.

BUYING AND STORING

Ripe figs are extremely delicate and
do not travel well, so it is hard to find
imported fruit at a perfect stage of
maturity. In season in Italy, however,
you can find local figs that
are just ripe for eating; they
should be soft and yielding,
but not squashy. Sometimes the skin
may have split, revealing the luscious
red or pink flesh. As long as you are
going to eat the fig immediately, this
does not matter. Take great care not to
squash the figs on your way home, or
you will end up with a squishy,
inedible mess.

Under-ripe figs can be kept at room
temperature for a day or two until the
skin softens, but they will never
develop the fine flavour of tree-
ripened figs. Ripe figs should be eaten
on the day they are bought as they do
not store well.

PREPARING
AND COOKING FIGS

*Wash the figs briefly and gently
pat dry. Discard the stalk and
peel the figs, if you wish.*

To serve as an antipasto *or
dessert, cut them downwards
from the stalk end into quarters,
leaving them attached at the
base. Open out the quarters
like flowers.*

*Perfectly ripe figs are best
eaten raw, but less perfect
specimens can be improved by
cooking. They can be gently
poached in syrup or red wine
flavoured with a cinnamon
stick or vanilla pod, or rolled
in caster (superfine) sugar and
baked in the oven until
caramelized. Barely ripe figs
also make excellent jam.*

Limone *(lemon)*

Lemons are grown all over Italy, even in the northern regions. Lake Garda even boasts a town called Limone, named for its abundance of lemon trees. But the most famous Italian lemons come from the Amalfi coast, where they grow to an extraordinary size and have such a sweet flavour that they can almost be eaten as a dessert fruit. Their aromatic flavour enhances almost any dish, and they have the added advantage of being rich in vitamin C.

HISTORY

Lemons originated in India or Malaysia and were brought by the Assyrians to Greece, which in turn took them to Italy. The Greeks and Romans greatly appreciated their culinary and medicinal qualities. Later seafarers ate them in large quantities to protect against scurvy, and society ladies used them as a beauty treatment to whiten their skin, bleach their hair and redden their lips.

CULINARY USES

Lemons are extraordinarily versatile. The juice can be squeezed to make a refreshing *spremuta di limone*, or it can be added to other cold drinks or tea. It is an anti-oxidant, which prevents discoloration when applied to other fruits and vegetables. The juice is used for dressings and for flavouring all sorts of drinks and sauces. A squeeze of lemon juice adds a different dimension to intrinsically bland foods, such as fish, poultry, veal or certain vegetables. Its acidity also helps to bring out the flavour of other fruits. The zest makes a wonderfully aromatic flavouring for cakes and pastries, and is an essential ingredient of *gremolata*, a topping of grated zest, garlic and parsley for *osso buco*. Quartered lemons are always served with *fritto misto di mare* (mixed fried fish) and other foods fried in batter.

PREPARING LEMONS

Before squeezing a lemon, warm it gently: either put it in a bowl, pour boiling water over the top and leave it to stand for about 5 minutes or, if you prefer, microwave the lemon on full power for about 30 seconds; this will significantly increase the quantity of juice you will obtain.

For sweet dishes, when you want to add the flavour of lemons, but not the grated rind, rub a sugar lump over the skin of the lemon to absorb the oil, then use the sugar as part of the recipe.

To prepare grated lemon rind, thoroughly wash and dry unwaxed lemons. Grate the rind or peel it off with a zester, taking care not to include any white pith.

BUYING AND STORING

Depending on the variety, lemons may have thick indented skin, or be perfectly smooth. Their appearance does not affect the flavour, but they should feel heavy for their size. If you intend to use the zest, buy unwaxed lemons. Lemons will keep in the refrigerator for up to two weeks.

Lemons
Lemons are grown all over Italy - their aromatic flavour enhances almost any dish

Fruit

Melone *(melon)*

Many different varieties of sweet, aromatic melons are grown in Italy, and each has its own regional name. *Napoletana* melons have a smooth pale green rind and delicately scented orange flesh. *Cantalupo* (cantaloupe) melons have a warty skin, which is conveniently marked into segments, and highly scented deep yellow flesh. A similar Tuscan melon with grey-green rind and orange flesh is called *popone*. These melons are all perfect for eating with prosciutto or salami as an *antipasto*.

Watermelons (*anguria* or *cocomero*) are grown in Tuscany. These huge green melons with their refreshing bright pink or red flesh and edible brown seeds can be round or sausage-shaped. In Florence, the feast of San Lorenzo, the patron saint of cooks, is celebrated with an orgy of watermelons on August 10th. During this season, roadside stalls groan under the weight of hundreds of these gigantic fruit.

CULINARY USES

Italians eat melon as an appetizer, usually accompanied by wafer-thin *prosciutto crudo* or cured meats. Melons and watermelons are occasionally served as a dessert fruit on their own, but more often appear in a *macedonia* (fruit salad).

BUYING AND STORING

The best way to tell whether a melon is ripe is to smell it; it should have a mild, sweet scent. If it smells highly perfumed and musky, it will be over-ripe. The fruit should feel heavy for its size and the skin should not be bruised or damaged. Gently press the rind with your thumbs at the stalk end; it should give a little. Melons will ripen quickly at room temperature and should be eaten within two or three days. Wrap cut melon tightly in clear film (plastic wrap) before storing in the refrigerator, or its scent may permeate other foods.

> ### PREPARING MELON
>
> *For serving as an* antipasto, *cut the melon into wedges, scoop out the seeds and run a flexible knife between the rind and flesh. Remove the rind before serving.*

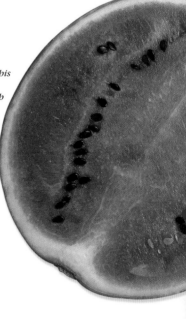

Napoletana melon
The sweet scented flesh of this and the similar cantaloupe melon is perfect for eating with prosciutto as an antipasto

Pesche (peaches) and pesche noci (nectarines)

Peaches, with their velvety skin and sweet, juicy flesh, are a summer fruit grown in central and southern Italy. The most common variety is the *pesca gialla* (yellow peach), which has succulent, yellow flesh. More highly prized are the *pesche bianche* (white peaches), whose pink-tinted flesh is full of juice and flavour.

Nectarines have smooth plum-like skins and taste very similar to peaches. They also come in yellow and white varieties and, like peaches, the white nectarines have a finer flavour. Some people prefer nectarines as a dessert fruit because they do not require peeling. Peaches and nectarines are interchangeable in cooked dishes.

CULINARY USES

Peaches and nectarines are delicious served as a dessert fruit, but can also be macerated in fortified wine or spirits or poached in white wine and syrup. They have a particular affinity with almonds; a favourite Italian dessert is *pesche ripiene alla piemontese*, halved peaches stuffed with crumbled almond-flavoured amaretti and baked in white wine. They are also delicious served with raspberries, or made into fruit drinks (the famous Bellini cocktail is made with fresh peach juice) and ice creams and sorbets.

BUYING AND STORING

Peaches are in season from June to September. Make sure they are ripe, but not too soft, with unwrinkled and unblemished skins. They should have a sweet, intense scent. Peaches and nectarines bruise very easily, so try to buy those that have been kept in compartmented trays rather than piled into punnets.

Do not keep peaches and nectarines for more than a day or two. If they are very ripe, store them in the refrigerator; under-ripe fruit will ripen in a couple of days if kept in a brown paper bag at room temperature.

PREPARING PEACHES

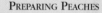

To peel peaches, place them in a heatproof bowl and pour boiling water over them. Leave for 15–30 seconds (depending on how ripe they are), then refresh in very cold water; the skins will slip off easily.

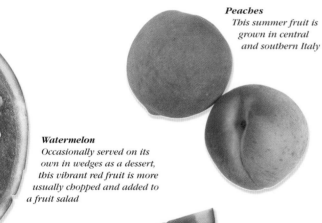

Peaches
This summer fruit is grown in central and southern Italy

Watermelon
Occasionally served on its own in wedges as a dessert, this vibrant red fruit is more usually chopped and added to a fruit salad

Nectarines
These smooth-skinned fruits are delicious served as a dessert fruit

Fruit

Uva (grapes)

Italy is the world's largest producer of grapes of all kinds. Almost every rural property boasts an expanse of vineyards, some producing wine-making grapes intended only for home consumption. Others (particularly in Chianti and the south) are destined for the enormous Italian wine-making industry. But Apulia, Abruzzo and Sicily produce sweet dessert grapes on a vast commercial scale, from large luscious Italia, with their fine muscat flavour, to Cardinal, named for its deep red colour, purple Alphonse Lavallé, and various small seedless varieties.

Despite their high calorific value, grapes are extremely good for you, since they are rich in potassium, iron and vitamins.

HISTORY
Wild grapes grew in the Caucasus as early as the Stone Age, and early man soon discovered the secret of cultivating vineyards and making wine. The Greeks and Romans discovered that drying grapes transformed them into sweet raisins and sultanas (golden raisins). The Gauls invented the wooden wine cask, and from that time wine production became a major industry.

CULINARY USES
Dessert grapes are best eaten on their own or as an accompaniment to cheese, but they can be used in pastries or as a garnish for cooked quails, guinea fowl or other poultry. The seeds are pressed into grapeseed oil, which has a neutral taste and is high in polyunsaturated fatty acids.

BUYING AND STORING
Choosing white, black or red grapes is a matter of preference; beneath the skin, the flesh is always pale green and juicy. Buy bunches of grapes with fruit which is of equal size and not too densely packed on the stalk. Check that none is withered or bad. The skin should have a delicate bloom and be firm to the touch. Try to eat one grape from a bunch to see how they taste. The flesh should be firm and very juicy and refreshing.

Grapes should be washed immediately after purchase, then placed in a bowl and kept in the refrigerator for up to three days. Keeping them in a plastic bag causes them to become over-ripe very quickly.

PREPARING GRAPES

Grapes used for cooking should be peeled and deseeded. Put them in a bowl, pour over boiling water and leave for 10-20 seconds, depending on the ripeness of the grapes. Peel off the skin. To remove the seeds, halve the grapes and scoop out the pips with the tip of a pointed knife.

Italia grapes
These luscious red and white grapes have a wonderful Muscat flavour

Nuts

Many different kinds of nuts are grown in Italy – chestnuts and hazelnuts in the north, pine nuts in the coastal regions, and almonds, pistachios and walnuts in the south. They are used in a wide variety of savoury dishes, cakes and pastries, or served as a dessert with a glass of *vin santo* (sweet white wine).

Castagne (chestnuts)

These are a mainstay of Tuscan and Sardinian cooking, dating back to the days when the peasants could not afford wheat to make flour, so they ground up the chestnuts that grow in abundance throughout the region instead. Most varieties of sweet chestnut contain two or three

Chestnuts
A mainstay of Tuscan and Sardinian cooking

separate nuts inside the spiky green husk, but commercially grown varieties contain a single, large nut, which is easier to peel and better for serving whole.

Chestnuts have shiny, rich reddish-brown shells with a wrinkled, thin skin beneath, which can be very hard to remove. They cannot be eaten raw, but once cooked, the starchy nuts are highly nutritious and very sustaining.

CULINARY USES

Chestnuts roasted over an open fire conjure up the spirit of autumn. Peeled chestnuts can be boiled, poached in red wine or milk or fried in butter as a garnish. They make hearty soups, or can be puréed into

sauces for game. In Piedmont, they are candied to make marrons glacés, and a favourite Italian dessert is *monte bianco*, a rich concoction of puréed chestnuts and cream.

Chestnut flour is still widely used in Tuscany and Liguria, where it is baked into cakes and pastries, such as *castagnaccio*, a confection with pine nuts and herbs.

BUYING AND STORING

The nicest chestnuts are those you gather yourself, but if you are buying them, look for large, shiny specimens, with no tiny maggot holes in the shells. The chestnuts should feel heavy for their size and not rattle when you shake them. They will keep in a cool place for at least two weeks. If any holes appear in the shells, discard the nut immediately, or you will very soon have an infestation of maggots.

Mandorle (almonds)

Two varieties of almonds are grown in central and southern Italy. *Mandorle dolci* (sweet almonds) are eaten as a dessert or used in cooking and baking, while *mandorle amare* (bitter almonds) are used to flavour liqueurs like amaretto or bittersweet confections such as amaretti. These almonds are not edible in their raw state; in fact, they are poisonous if consumed in large quantities. Both types of almonds have a velvety pale green outer casing; the hard light brown shell within encloses one or two oval nuts.

CULINARY USES

Early in the season (late May), sweet almonds can be eaten raw as a dessert. They have a delicious fresh flavour and the brown skin is still soft enough to be palatable. Later, dried sweet almonds are blanched, slivered or ground to be used for cakes, pastries and all sorts of confectionery, including *marzapane* (marzipan) and *croccante* (almond brittle). They can be devilled or salted as an appetizing snack with an *aperitivo*.

Toasted almonds are the classic garnish for trout, and go well with chicken or rabbit. Dried bitter almonds are used in small quantities to add a more intense flavour to cookies and cakes.

Almonds
In Italy in early spring, fresh almonds are eaten raw as a dessert

Nuts

Buying and Storing

Fresh almonds in the shell are available from late May to late June. They are difficult to crack, so you may prefer to buy ready-shelled nuts. They should look plump, and the skins should not feel too dry. Pre-blanched almonds can often be a disappointment; buy the nuts with their skins on and blanch them yourself. Store shelled almonds in an airtight container for no longer than a month.

Nocciole (hazelnuts)

Fresh hazelnuts are harvested in August and September and during these months are always sold in their frilled green husks. The small round nuts have a very sweet flavour and a milky texture when fresh. In Italy, they are generally dried and used in confectionery and cakes.

Culinary Uses

Hazelnuts are used in all sorts of confectionery, including *torrone* (a sort of nougat) and *gianduiotti*, a delicious fondant chocolate from Piedmont. The famous chocolate *baci* ('kisses') from Perugia contain a whole hazelnut in the centre. Hazelnuts are finely ground to make cakes and cookies, and are excellent in stuffings for poultry and game.

Buying and Storing

If hazelnuts are sold in their fresh green husks, you can be sure they are fresh and juicy. Otherwise, look for shiny shells that are not too thick and unblemished; cracked shells will cause the nut to shrivel and dry out. Shelled hazelnuts should be kept in an airtight container for no longer than one month.

Shelled almonds
These dried almonds are used for cakes, pastries and confectionery

Shelled hazelnuts
These dried nuts are used for confectionery and cakes

Hazelnuts
When fresh, these small nuts have a very sweet flavour

Noci (walnuts)

Walnuts grow in abundance throughout central and southern Italy. The kernels, shaped like the two halves of a brain, grow inside a pale brown, heavily indented shell enclosed by a smooth green fleshy husk or 'shuck'. Fresh walnuts have a delicious milky sweetness and a soft texture, which hardens as the nuts mature. Walnuts do not need to be skinned before eating.

Walnuts
In Italy, fresh walnuts are very often eaten straight from the shell as a dessert

---

Preparing Almonds

To blanch almonds, place them in a strainer and plunge into boiling water for a few seconds. As soon as the skin begins to loosen, transfer the almonds to a bowl of cold water and slip off the skins. Dry thoroughly before storing.

CULINARY USES

Fresh walnuts are usually eaten straight from the shell as a dessert. They can be ground or chopped and used in cakes and desserts, or halved and used for decoration. They are used to make savoury sauces for pasta, such as *salsa di noce*, a rich combination of ground walnuts, butter and cream. Walnut oil has a distinctive flavour and, used sparingly, makes an excellent salad dressing. Unripe walnuts can be pickled, and they are used to make sweet, sticky liqueurs.

BUYING AND STORING

Fresh 'wet' walnuts are available from late September to late October. They should be kept in a wicker basket and eaten within a week. Dried walnuts should not have cracked or broken shells. They will keep for at least two months. Never store walnuts in the refrigerator, as the oil they contain will harden and ruin the flavour. Dried walnut kernels will have the flavour and texture of fresh nuts if they are soaked in milk for at least 4 hours.

Pinoli *(pine nuts)*

Pine nuts (more accurately known as pine kernels) are actually the seeds from the stone pine trees that grow n profusion along the Adriatic and Mediterranean coasts of Italy. The small, oblong, cream-coloured seeds grow inside a hard husk and are extracted from between the scales of the pine cones. The soft-textured kernels, which have an oily, slightly resinous flavour, are always sold dehusked. They can be eaten raw, but are usually toasted before use to bring out the flavour.

CULINARY USES

Pine nuts are used in many Italian dishes, both sweet and savoury, but they are best known as an essential ingredient of pesto. They go well with meat and game, and make exceptionally delicious cookies and tarts.

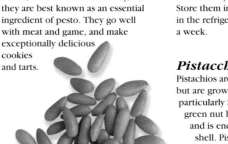

Pine nuts
The oily, slightly resinous flavour is accentuated by light toasting

Pistachio nuts
Grown in southern Italy, these sweet, delicately flavoured nuts are used in mortadella

BUYING AND STORING

Pine nuts are always sold out of the husk. Because they are very oily, they go rancid quite quickly, so buy only as much as you need at any one time. Store them in an airtight container in the refrigerator for not more than a week.

Pistacchi *(pistachios)*

Pistachios are native to the Near East, but are grown in southern Italy, particularly Sicily. The small, bright green nut has a yellowish-red skin and is enclosed in a smooth, pale shell. Pistachios have a sweet, delicate flavour, which makes them ideal for desserts, but they are also commonly used to stud mortadella and other pale cooked meat products.

CULINARY USES

Pistachios can be eaten raw or roasted and salted as a snack with an *aperitivo*. Their colour enhances most white meats and poultry. They make deliciously rich ice cream and are used in *cassata gelata*, the famous Sicilian dessert.

BUYING AND STORING

If possible, buy pistachios still in their shells. These will be easier to open if they are already slightly ajar; once open, the nut is very easy to remove. Shelled, blanched pistachios are also available. They are useful for cooking, but lack the fine flavour of whole nuts. Store blanched pistachios in an airtight container for up to two weeks. Whole nuts will keep for well over a month.

Herbs & Seasonings

Herbs are vital to Italian cooking. Their aromatic flavour adds depth and interest to what is essentially plain cooking, based on fine, fresh ingredients. It is impossible to imagine roast chicken or veal without rosemary or sage, or tomatoes or pesto without basil. Many wild herbs grow in the Italian countryside, and these are often incorporated into Italian recipes. One of the most popular is mentuccia, *a wild mint with tiny leaves and the delicate flavour of marjoram. If a recipe specifies* mentuccia *or its close relative* nepitella, *substitute a smaller quantity of mint.*

Always use fresh herbs whenever you can; the dried varieties have a stronger and often quite different taste, and lack the subtlety of fresh herbs. If you must use dried herbs, try to buy them freeze-dried; these taste much closer to the real thing. As a general rule, you will need only about one-third as much dried herb as fresh – in other words, allow about 5ml/1 tsp dried herbs for every 15ml/1 tbsp fresh.

Basilico (basil)
Basil, with its intense aroma and fresh, pungently sweet flavour, is associated with Italian cooking more than any other herb. It is an essential ingredient of pesto, but it also finds its way into soups, salads and almost all dishes based on tomatoes, with which it has an extraordinary affinity. There are over 50 varieties of this annual herb, but the one most commonly used in Italy is sweet basil, with its fresh broad green leaves and wonderfully spicy aroma.

CULINARY USES
Basil has a volatile flavour, so it is best added to dishes at the end of cooking. It can be used in any dish that contains tomatoes and is delicious sprinkled on to a pizza. It adds a pungent, sweet note to almost all salads and is particularly good with white fish and shellfish. It makes an excellent flavouring for omelettes and is often added to

minestrone. The most famous of all basil dishes is pesto, the fragrant Genoese sauce made by pounding together fresh basil, garlic, Parmesan cheese, pine nuts and olive oil.

BUYING AND STORING
In sunny climates, such as southern Italy, basil grows outdoors all through the summer. In other places it is available cut or growing in pots all year round, so there really is no reason to use dried basil. Look for sweet basil with bright green leaves – the larger the better. If you have grown your own and have a glut, you can freeze basil leaves to preserve the flavour, but they lose their fresh texture and darken in colour. Alternatively, put a bunch of basil in a jar and top up with olive oil for a fragrant flavoured oil for dressings. To store fresh cut basil, wrap it in damp kitchen paper and keep in the vegetable drawer of the refrigerator for up to two days.

Basil
More than any other, this pungent, intensely flavoured herb is associated with Italian cooking – it is an essential ingredient in many dishes, including pesto

---

PREPARING BASIL

Basil leaves are tender and bruise easily, so never chop them with a knife, but tear them lightly with your fingers immediately before using.

Pesto

To make enough pesto for 4–6 servings of pasta, put 115g/4oz basil leaves in a mortar with 25g/1oz pine nuts, 2 fat peeled garlic cloves and a large pinch of coarse salt, and crush to a paste with a pestle. Work in 50g/2oz freshly grated Parmesan

cheese. Gradually add about 120ml/4fl oz extra virgin olive oil, working it in thoroughly with a wooden spoon to make a thick, creamy sauce. Put the pesto in a screwtop jar; it will keep for several weeks in the refrigerator.

Maggiorana *(sweet marjoram)* **and origano** *(oregano)*

These two highly aromatic herbs are closely related (oregano is the wild variety), but marjoram has a much milder flavour. Marjoram is more commonly used in northern Italy, while oregano is widely used in the south to flavour tomato dishes, vegetables and pizzas. Drying greatly intensifies the flavour of both herbs, so they should be used very sparingly.

CULINARY USES

In northern Italy, sweet marjoram is used to flavour meat, poultry, vegetables and soups; the flavour goes particularly well with carrots and cucumber. Despite its rather pungent aroma, marjoram has a delicate flavour, so it should be added to long-cooked foods towards the end of cooking.

Oregano is used exclusively in southern Italian cooking, especially in tomato-based dishes. It is a classic flavouring for pizza, but should always be used in moderation.

BUYING AND STORING

Marjoram and oregano are in season throughout the summer, but cut fresh herbs are available all year round in supermarkets. The leaves dry out quickly, so store them in plastic bags in the refrigerator; they will keep for up to a week. Dried oregano should be stored in small airtight jars away from the light. It loses its pungent flavour after a few months, so only buy a little at a time.

Oregano
Widely used in the south of Italy to flavour tomato dishes

Prezzemolo *(parsley)*

Italian parsley is the flat leaf variety, which has a more robust flavour than curly parsley. It has attractive dark green leaves, which resemble fresh coriander (cilantro). It is used as a flavouring in innumerable cooked dishes, but rarely as a garnish. If flat leaf parsley is not available, curly parsley makes a perfectly adequate substitute. Parsley is an extremely nutritious herb, rich in iron and potassium and vitamin C.

Marjoram
The aromatic flavour of this herb is very similar to that of oregano, but much milder

Parsley
Italian parsley is the flat leafed variety. It has a strong, robust flavour

Herbs & Seasonings

CULINARY USES

Parsley can be used to flavour innumerable savoury dishes. It adds colour and flavour to sauces, soups and risotti. The stalks can be used to flavour stocks and stews. Chopped parsley can be sprinkled over cooked savoury dishes; whole leaves are rarely used as a garnish in Italy.

BUYING AND STORING

Parsley is available all year round, so it should never be necessary to use the dried variety. A large bunch of parsley will keep for up to a week in the refrigerator if washed and wrapped in damp kitchen paper. Chopped parsley freezes very well and can be added to cooked dishes straight from the freezer.

Rosmarino (rosemary)

Spiky evergreen rosemary bushes, with their attractive blue flowers, grow wild all over Italy. The herb has a delicious, highly aromatic flavour, which is intensifed when it is dried. The texture of rosemary leaves is quite hard and the flavour very pungent, so it is never used raw, but only in cooking. It can easily overpower a dish, so only a few leaves should be used in a dish.

CULINARY USES

Rosemary combines extremely well with roast or grilled (broiled) lamb, veal and chicken. A few needles will enhance the flavour of baked fish or any tomato dish, and it adds a wonderful flavour to roast potatoes and onions. Some rosemary branches added to the charcoal on a barbecue impart a superb flavour to whatever is being cooked. Dried rosemary can always be substituted for fresh; it is extremely pungent, so should be used very sparingly.

Salvia (sage)

Wild sage grows in profusion in the Italian countryside. There are several varieties, including the common garden sage, with furry silvery-grey leaves and spiky purple flowers, and clary sage, with hairy curly leaves, which is used to make dry vermouth. All sages have a slightly bitter aromatic flavour, which contrasts well with fatty meats such as pork. In northern Italy, particularly Tuscany, it is used to flavour veal and chicken. It is an excellent medicinal herb (the Latin name means 'good health'); an infusion of sage leaves makes a good gargle for a sore throat.

CULINARY USES

Used sparingly, sage combines well with almost all meat and vegetable dishes and is often used in minestrone. It has a particular affinity with veal (such as *osso buco*, *piccata* and, of course, calf's liver) and is an

Sage
Several varieties of this herb grow in profusion in the Italian countryside

essential ingredient of *saltimbocca alla romana*, veal escalopes (US scallops) and *prosciutto crudo* topped with sage leaves and sautéed in butter and white wine. In Tuscany, white haricot (navy) beans (*fagioli*) are often flavoured with sage.

BUYING AND STORING

Fresh sage is very easy to grow on a sunny windowsill. It is available in both fresh and dried forms from supermarkets all year round. Dried sage is very strongly flavoured, so should be used in tiny quantities. It starts to taste musty after a few weeks, so replace it fairly frequently. Fresh sage should be stored in a plastic bag in the refrigerator; it will keep for up to a week.

Rosemary
The highly aromatic flavour of this herb is intensified when it is dried

Aceto (vinegar)

Like all wine-making countries, Italy produces excellent red and white wine vinegar as a by-product. The best vinegar is made from good wines, which are fermented in oak casks to give a depth of flavour. Good vinegar should be clean-tasting and aromatic, with no trace of bitterness and it should be transparent, not cloudy. White wine vinegar is pale golden with a pinkish tinge; red wine vinegar ranges from deep pink to dark red.

Aceto balsamico (balsamic vinegar)

Balsamic vinegar is the king of vinegars. Its name means 'balm-like', reflecting its digestive qualities. Indeed, the best has a flavour so mellow and sweet that it can be drunk on its own as a *digestivo*. Balsamic vinegar is made in the area around Modena; the boiled and concentrated juice of local *trebbiano* grapes is aged in a series of barrels of decreasing size and different woods over a very long period – sometimes as long as 50 years – which gives it a

slightly syrupy texture and a rich, deep mahogany colour. Like Parmigiano Reggiano and Parma ham (prosciutto), genuine balsamic vinegar (*aceto balsamico tradizionale di Modena*) is strictly controlled by law; it must have been aged in the wood for at least 12 years. Vinegar aged 20 years or more is called *stravecchio*.

Culinary Uses

Red and white wine vinegars are principally used to make salad dressings and marinades, or to preserve vegetables *sott'aceto* for *antipasti*. They also add the requisite sharpness to sauces like *agrodolce* (sweet and sour). Good balsamic vinegar is also used as a dressing, sometimes on its own. It can be used to finish a delicate sauce for white fish, poultry or calf's liver. A few

Balsamic vinegar
This is the king of vinegars and has a wonderfully sweet and mellow flavour

drops sprinkled over ripe strawberries will enhance their flavour.

Buying and Storing

Price is usually an indication of quality where vinegar is concerned, so always buy the best you can afford. Genuine balsamic vinegar must be labelled *aceto balsamico tradizionale di Modena*; products that purport to be the real thing but are not labelled as such have either not been aged for long enough or, worse, are just red wine vinegar coloured and flavoured with caramel. Proper balsamic vinegar is expensive, but the flavour is so concentrated that a little goes a long way, and it is worth paying more for the genuine article. Vinegar will keep in a cool dark place for many months.

Red and white wine vinegars
These vinegars have a sharp flavour and are used principally for salad dressings

Herbs & Seasonings

Aglio (garlic)

Garlic is not, as you might suppose, a type of onion, but is a member of the lily family. The bulb or 'head' is a collection of cloves held together by a papery white or purplish skin. When crushed or chopped it releases a pungent, slightly acrid oil with a very distinctive flavour and smell. Freshly picked garlic is milder than older, dried garlic, and the large, mauve-tinged variety has a more delicate flavour than the smaller white variety.

Garlic finds its way into many Italian dishes, but it is generally used with discretion so as not to flavour the food too aggressively. It is indispensable to certain dishes like *bagna cauda* (hot anchovy and garlic dip), *spaghetti all'aglio e olio* (garlic and olive oil) and pesto. In the south, garlic is used to flavour tomato sauces and fish soups.

CULINARY USES

Used in small quantities, garlic enlivens almost any sauce, soup or stew. It can be roasted with lamb and potatoes, or baked in its skin for a mellower flavour. Blanched, crushed garlic will aromatize olive oil to make an excellent dressing for salads or to use in cooking where only a hint of garlic flavour is required. Raw skinned garlic cloves can be rubbed over toasted croutons to make flavourful *bruschetta* bases.

BUYING AND STORING

Garlic sold loose by the head or kilo is usually fresher and better than pre-packaged varieties. The heads should feel firm and the skin should not be too papery. Do not buy garlic that is sprouting green shoots; the cloves will be soft and of no culinary value.

Stored in a cool dry place, garlic will keep for many months. If possible, hang the heads in bunches to keep them aerated. Once garlic has become soft or wizened, throw it away.

Garlic
Italian cooks prefer to use garlic with discretion, but it is indispensable to many dishes. The purple-skinned variety has a more delicate flavour than the white variety

---

PREPARING AND COOKING GARLIC

To peel garlic, cut off the root end with a small sharp knife and peel the skin upwards.

Alternatively, lay a garlic clove on the work surface, place the flat side of a heavy knife blade on top and bring the side of your fist sharply down on to the blade. This will flatten the garlic and split the skin.

To chop garlic, halve the clove and remove the bitter-tasting green shoot. Chop the garlic as finely as possible.

For very fine garlic, crush it in a garlic press.

Garlic should be softened gently in oil or butter; it will become very bitter if allowed to brown. For a subtle flavour, heat a whole clove of garlic in the oil, then remove it before adding the other ingredients. The flavour of garlic dissipates quite quickly during cooking, so for long-cooked dishes add it towards the end of the cooking time.

Olive *(olives)*

A wide variety of olives is cultivated all over Italy. Most are destined to be pressed into oil (nearly 20 per cent of their weight is oil), but some are kept as table olives to be salted, pickled or marinated, and served as part of an *antipasto* or used in cooking. There are two main types of olive, green (immature) and black (mature); both are bitter and inedible in their natural state. All olives have a high calorific content and are rich in iron, potassium and vitamins.

Green olives are the unripe fruit, which are picked in October or November. They have a sharper flavour and crunchier texture than black olives, which continue to ripen on the tree and are not harvested until December. Among the best Italian table olives are the small, shiny black Gaeta olives from Liguria. Wrinkled black olives from Lazio have a strong, salty flavour, while Sardinian olives are semi-ripened and are brown or purplish in colour. The largest olives come from Apulia and Sicily, where giant, green specimens are grown. These are sometimes pitted and stuffed with pimento, anchovy or almonds. Cured olives can be flavoured with all sorts of aromatics, such as garlic, local herbs, orange or lemon zest and dried chillies.

HISTORY

Olive trees have been grown in the Mediterranean since biblical times, when they were brought there from the East by the Romans. Ancient civilizations venerated the olive tree; the Egyptians believed that the goddess Isis discovered the secret of extracting oil from the fruit.

CULINARY USES

Olives can be served on their own or as a garnish or topping for pizza. They are used as an ingredient in many Italian recipes, such as *caponata*. Sicilian *caponata* is a dome-shaped salad of fried aubergines (eggplants) with celery, onions, tomatoes, capers and green olives, while the Ligurian dish of the same name consists of stale cookies or bread soaked in olive oil and topped with a mixture of chopped olives, garlic, anchovies and oregano. Olives combine well with Mediterranean ingredients like tomatoes, aubergines, anchovies and capers and are used in sauces for rabbit, chicken and firm-fleshed fish. Made into a paste with red wine vinegar, garlic and olive oil, they make an excellent topping for *crostini*.

BUYING AND STORING

Cured olives vary enormously in flavour, so ask to taste one before making your selection. Loose olives can be kept in an airtight container in the refrigerator for up to a week.

Green olives
These unripe olives have a sharper flavour than black olives

Capperi *(capers)*

Capers are the immature flower buds of a wild Mediterranean shrub. They are pickled in white wine vinegar or preserved in brine which gives them a piquant, peppery flavour. Sicilian capers are packed in whole salt, which should be rinsed off before using the capers. Bottled nasturtium flower buds are sometimes sold as a cheaper alternative to true capers. Caper berries look like large, fat capers on a long stalk, but they are actually the fruit of the caper shrub. They can be served as a cocktail snack or in a salad.

Black olives
Olives are among the oldest fruits known to man. They are grown all over Italy

Caper berries
The pickled fruit of the caper shrub can be served as a cocktail snack

Herbs & Seasonings

CULINARY USES

Capers are mainly used as a condiment or garnish, but they also add zest to shellfish and fish dishes, salads, pizzas and pasta sauces such as the famous Sicilian *pasta colle sarde*, a mixture of sardines, parsley, tomatoes, pine nuts and raisins.

BUYING AND STORING

Choosing pickled or brined capers is a matter of taste, as is whether or not you should rinse them before use. Large capers are usually cheaper than small ones; there is no difference in flavour, but small capers make a more attractive garnish. Salt-packed capers are always sold loose by the *etto* (100g/3½oz); they should be used as soon as possible. Once opened, jars of capers should be kept in the refrigerator. Make sure any capers left in the jar are covered with the preserving liquid.

Salted capers
These are used to add zest to fish dishes, salads and pasta sauces

Pickled capers
Rinsing these capers before use softens their sharp, piquant flavour

Olio di oliva (olive oil)

Unlike other oils, which are extracted from the seeds or dried fruits of plants, olive oil is pressed from the pulp of ripe olives, which gives it an inimitable richness and flavour. Different regions of Italy produce distinctively different olive oils; Tuscan oil (considered the best) is pungent and peppery, Ligurian oil is lighter and sweeter, while the oils from the south and Sicily are powerful and nutty.

The best olive oil is *extra vergine*, which is strictly controlled and regulated like wine. This is made simply by pressing the olives to extract the oil, with no further processing. Extra virgin olive oil must have an acidity level of less than 1 per cent. The distinctive fruity flavour of this oil makes it ideal for dressings and using raw. Virgin olive oil is pressed in the same way, but has a higher acidity level and a less refined flavour. It, too, can be used as a condiment, but is also suitable for cooking. Unclassified olive oil is refined, then blended with virgin oil to add flavour. It has an undistinguished taste, but is ideal for cooking; it should not be used as a condiment.

BUYING AND STORING

The best olive oil comes from Lucca in Tuscany and is very expensive. It is made with slightly under-ripe olives, which give it a luminous green colour. If your budget does not stretch to this, buy the best extra virgin oil you can afford to use 'neat' or in dressings. Experiment with small bottles of different extra virgin oils to see which you prefer. For cooking, pure olive oil is fine. Once opened, olive oil should be kept in a cool place away from the light. The best oil will soon lose its savour, so use it within six months.

Extra virgin olive oil
The distinctive fruity flavour makes this oil ideal for salad dressings

COOKING WITH OLIVE OIL

Olive oil can be heated to very high temperatures without burning or smoking, which makes it ideal for frying, sauce-making and other cooking. Extra virgin olive oil should be saved for dressing fish, vegetables and salads.

Peperoncini (dried red chillies)

Hot flakes of dried chillies are added to many southern Italian dishes, such as *arrabiata* sauce and the famous *pasta all'aglio, olio e peperoncino* (dressed with garlic, oil and chillies). Chillies are unusual in that their 'hotness' is usually in inverse proportion to their size, so larger dried varieties are generally milder than the smaller ones. In summer, bunches of tiny fresh red chillies can be bought in Italian markets. These can be used fresh, preserved in olive oil to make a spicy dressing or to drizzle over a pizza, or hung up to dry and crumbled to add 'oomph' to a dish. Crushed chilli flakes are available in jars.

CULINARY USES

A small pinch of dried chilli flakes spices up stews and sauces, particularly those made with tomatoes. For a really hot pizza, crumble a few flakes over the top. Dried chillies are extremely fiery and should be used very sparingly.

BUYING AND STORING

Dried chillies will last for years, but they do lose their savour over a period of time, so buy only small quantities. Whole *peperoncini* should be hung up in bunches and crumbled directly into the dish you are cooking.

Dried red chilli flakes
Just a small pinch of these fiery flakes spices up stews and sauces

Zafferano (saffron)

Saffron consists of the dried stigmas of the saffron crocus. It takes about 80,000 crocuses to produce about 500g/1¼lb of spice and these have to be hand-picked, so it is hardly surprising that saffron is the world's most expensive spice. Saffron stigmas or threads are a vivid orangey-red colour with a pungent aroma. They are also sold ground into powder. Saffron has a highly aromatic flavour and will impart a wonderful, rich golden colour to risotti and sauces.

Dried chillies
These are often used in fiery southern Italian dishes, such as arrabbiata sauce

Saffron threads
Used to flavour and colour the classic risotto alla milanese

HISTORY

Saffron originated in Asia Minor, where it was used by ancient civilizations as a flavouring, as a dye, in perfumery and for medicinal purposes. Arab traders brought the spice to the Mediterranean in the 10th century; for centuries it was so highly prized that stealing or adulterating it was punishable by death. The best saffron is nowadays cultivated in Spain, but it is also grown in Italy.

CULINARY USES

In Italy, saffron is mainly used to flavour and colour risotti, like the classic *risotto alla milanese*. It is excellent in sauces for fish and poultry and can be used to flavour cookies and cakes.

BUYING AND STORING

Saffron threads are sold in small boxes or jars containing only a few grams. The wiry threads should be a deep orangey-red in colour; paler yellowish-orange threads are probably the much cheaper and less desirable safflower, which will add colour but not flavour to a dish. Powdered saffron is convenient to use, but less reliable, as it may have been adulterated with safflower. Stored in small, airtight containers, saffron will keep for months.

COOKING WITH SAFFRON

Do not add saffron directly to a dish. Infuse threads in a little hot water for at least 5 minutes before blending into a dish to bring out the flavour and ensure even colouring. Add the soaking water together with the threads. Never fry saffron in hot oil or butter; this will ruin the flavour.

Cakes, Cookies & Breads

In Italy it is perfectly normal and acceptable for a hostess to buy a dolce *(cake or dessert) to serve at the end of a meal, rather than make it herself. Pastry shops and bakeries sell a wide variety of traditional tarts, spiced yeast cakes and cookies to be enjoyed with coffee or a glass of vin santo, sweet dessert wine or a liqueur. Some of these, such as* panettone *and* pastiera napoletana, *are reserved for special occasions like Christmas and Easter, and almost every town has its own speciality for its local saint's day.*

Amaretti (macaroons)

Amaretti are made from ground almonds, egg whites and sugar. They have a distinctive flavour, which comes from the addition of bitter almonds. They originated in Venice during the Renaissance and their English name of macaroons comes from the Venetian macerone, meaning 'fine paste'. They come in dozens of different forms, from the famous crunchy sugar-encrusted cookies wrapped in pairs in twists of crisp white paper to soft-centred macaroons wrapped in brightly-coloured foil. Amaretti are delicious dipped into hot coffee. They can also be crumbled to make a stuffing for baked peaches or apricots.

Panettone
This light-textured yeast cake is a speciality of Milan

Cantucci

These hard, high-baked lozenge-shaped cookies from Tuscany are designed to be dipped into *espresso* coffee or *vin santo*. When moistened, they become deliciously soft and crumbly. They are usually studded with almonds or other nuts and flavoured with aniseed or vanilla.

Cantucci

Amaretti
These crunchy sugar-encrusted cookies are delicious dipped into hot coffee

Panettone

Literally meaning 'big bread', *panettone* is a light-textured spiced yeast bread containing sultanas (golden raisins) and candied fruit. Originally a speciality of Milan, it is now sold all over Italy as a Christmas delicacy and is traditionally given as a gift. *Panettoni* can vary in size from small to enormous. They are sometimes sold in pastel-coloured dome-shaped boxes, which are often hung from the ceiling of bakeries and delicatessens, and look very festive. At Easter, they are baked into the shape of a lamb (*agnello*) or a dove (*colomba*). *Panettone* is sliced into wedges and eaten like cake.

Crumiri

These sweet elbow-shaped cookies are a speciality of Piedmont. The rich golden brown dough is made with polenta and honey and piped through a fluted nozzle to give the cookies their characteristic ridged texture. Although the cookies seem hard on the outside, the polenta flour gives the *crumiri* a pleasantly crunchy texture. *Crumiri* are good tea-time cookies, but they are also excellent dipped in hot coffee.

Panforte

Somewhat resembling a Christmas pudding in flavour, but shaped like a flat disc, *panforte* is a rich, dark spiced cake crammed with dried fruit and toasted nuts. It is a speciality of Siena and is sold in a colourful glossy wrapping, often depicting Sienese scenes. It is extremely rich, so can only be eaten in small quantities, which is just as well, since it is also quite expensive.

Panettone
The characteristic box often hangs from the ceiling in Italian delicatessens

Panforte
This Italian spice cake is packed full of fruit and nuts

Savoiardi
These soft-textured, Italian sponge finger cookies are used as a base for tiramisu

Savoiardi (sponge cookies)

As their name suggests, *savoiardi* come from the Savoy region of Piedmont. They are plumper and wider than sponge fingers and have a softer texture. They are excellent dunked into tea or coffee, and are traditionally served with zabaglione; but they are best of all used as a base for tiramisu, the wickedly rich Italian coffee and mascarpone dessert.

Pane (Bread)

No Italian meal is ever served without bread to accompany the food. Indeed, it often constitutes one of the dishes in a meal in the form of *crostini* and *bruschetta* (toasted canapés), soups such as *pancotto*, *panzanella* (bread salad) or pizza. In Tuscany, bread plays a more important part in the food of the region than pasta. A favourite antipasto is *fettunta*, toasted bread rubbed with garlic, anointed with plenty of olive oil and sprinkled with coarse salt. When a topping is added, it becomes *bruschetta*.

Italians buy or make fresh bread every day, but stale or leftover loaves are never wasted. Instead they are made into breadcrumbs and used for thickening sauces and stews, or for stuffings, salads or wonderfully sustaining soups.

There are hundreds of different types of Italian bread with many regional variations to suit the local food. Traditional Tuscan country bread is made without salt, since it is designed to be served with salty cured meats such as salami and *prosciutto crudo*. (If you prefer salted bread, ask for *pane salato*.) Southern Italian breads often contain olive oil, which goes well with tomatoes. *Pane integrale* (wholemeal (whole-wheat) bread) is traditionally baked in a wood oven. The texture and flavour of the bread depends on the type of flour used and the amount of seasoning, but nearly all Italian breads are firm-textured with substantial crusts. You will never find flabby damp white sandwich loaves in an Italian bakery, although the inside of traditional white *panini* (bread rolls) can sometimes resemble cotton wool.

Ciabatta

These flattish, slipper-shaped loaves with squared or rounded ends are made with olive oil and are often flavoured with fresh or dried herbs, olives or sun-dried tomatoes. They have an airy texture inside and a pale, crisp crust. *Ciabatta* is delicious served warm, and is excellent for sandwiches.

Ciabatta
These popular loaves are available plain or flavoured with olives or sun-dried tomatoes

Wholemeal
(whole-wheat) bread
In Italy this bread is traditionally baked in a wooden oven

Focaccia

A dimpled flat bread similar to pizza dough, *focaccia* is traditionally oiled and baked in a wood oven. A whole *focaccia* from a bakery weighs several kilos and is sold by weight, cut into manageable pieces. A variety of ingredients can be worked into the dough or served as a topping – onions, *pancetta*, rosemary or oregano, ham, cheese or olives. *Focaccine* are small versions, which are split and served with fillings like a sandwich. In Apulia, *focaccia del Venerdi Santo*, with its topping of fennel, chicory (Belgian endive), anchovies, olives and capers, is traditionally served on Good Friday.

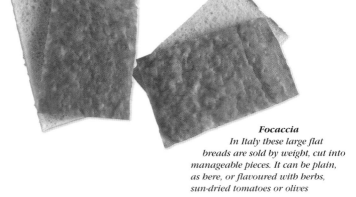

Focaccia
In Italy these large flat breads are sold by weight, cut into manageable pieces. It can be plain, as here, or flavoured with herbs, sun-dried tomatoes or olives

White bread
Like nearly all Italian breads, this one is firm-textured, with a substantial crust

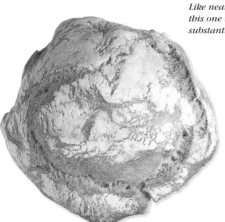

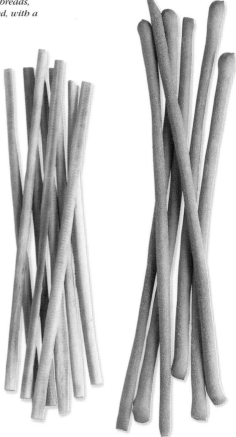

Grissini
The cover charge in every Italian restaurant invariably includes packets of bread sticks

Grissini

These crisp golden bread sticks originated in Turin, but are now found in almost every Italian restaurant, packed in long envelopes. They range in size from matchstick-thin to hefty, knobbly, home-baked batons. Italian bakers often use up any leftover dough to make *grissini*, which are sold loose by weight. They can be rolled in sesame or poppy seeds for extra flavour.

Store Cupboard

One of the great joys of Italian food is that you can create a delicious meal almost instantly using ingredients from your store cupboard (pantry). Rice and pasta can be combined with any number of bottled or tinned vegetables, shellfish or sauces to make a speedy and nutritious meal. Unopened jars and cans last for months, if not years, so it is worth keeping a selection in your store cupboard for an impromptu meal that you can rustle up in moments.

Pesto

Although nothing is as good as home-made pesto, there are some excellent bottled varieties of this fragrant green basil sauce. Traditional pesto is made with basil, pine nuts, Parmesan or Pecorino cheese and olive oil, but you may also find a red version based on sweet red (bell) peppers.

CULINARY USES

Pesto can be used as an instant dressing for any type of pasta or potato gnocchi. It gives a lift to risotti and tomato sauces, and is delicious stirred into minestrone or tomato-based soups. A spoonful of pesto will add a new dimension to bottled mayonnaise, creating a rich, pungent *maionese verde*. For a quick, attractive cocktail snack, halve some cherry tomatoes, scoop out the seeds and fill the tomatoes with pesto.

Pesto
Both the traditional green version shown here and a red type based on sweet red (bell) peppers are used to flavour sauces and pasta

Pomodori secchi (sun-dried tomatoes)

Sun-drying tomatoes intensifies their flavour to an astonishing sweetness and pungency and allows you to enjoy the full savour of tomatoes even in winter. If you are extremely lucky, you may still find in markets in southern Italy locally grown tomatoes that have been spread out to dry in the sun, but the commercially produced 'sun-dried' varieties are actually air-dried by machine. Wrinkled red dried tomatoes are available dry in packets or preserved in olive oil. Dry tomatoes are brick-red in colour and have a chewy texture. They can be eaten on their own as a snack, but for cooking they should be soaked in hot water until soft (the tomato-flavoured soaking water can be used for a soup or sauce). Bottled sun-dried tomatoes are sold in chunky pieces or as a paste.

Dried tomatoes
Dried tomatoes should always be softened in water before use

Sun-dried tomatoes
These strong-flavoured tomatoes add extra piquancy to dishes

CULINARY USES

Sun-dried tomatoes add piquancy to vegetable dishes, soups or sauces. They can be chopped and added to a simple *sugo di pomodori* or a meaty *ragù* for extra flavour. They make an excellent *antipasto* combined with sliced tomatoes, mozzarella cheese and basil or with other preserved or pickled vegetables. They go well with fresh Mediterranean vegetables such as fennel, aubergines (eggplants) and courgettes (zucchini), and add a special something to egg dishes, such as *frittata*. Use the oil in which the tomatoes are preserved for salad dressings or for sweating vegetables for a soup or sauce.

The paste can be used in small quantities for sauces and soups, or used on its own or with a little butter as a dressing for pasta.

Black olive paste

Legumi sott'olio (vegetables preserved in oil)

Italians produce a wide variety of vegetables preserved in olive or sunflower oil, or a mixture of both. The choicest are often cooked *alla brace* (grilled (broiled)) before being packed in the best olive oil – tiny *carciofini* (artichokes), *funghi* and *porcini* (button (white) and wild mushrooms), *peperoni* (red and yellow peppers) and *melanzane* (aubergines) – which look as beautiful as they taste. You will sometimes find large bulbous jars containing colourful layers of different vegetables in oil; these are packed by hand and are very expensive.

CULINARY USES

A mixture of oil-preserved vegetables combined with a selection of cured meats makes a wonderful *antipasto*. They can also be chopped or sliced and used to dress hot or cold pasta, or stirred into rice for a substantial cold salad. They make a delicious topping for *crostini* or pizza.

Passata (bottled strained tomatoes)
This rich tomato pureé varies in fineness from the ultra-smooth to the chunkier sugocasa

Green olive paste

Passata (bottled strained tomatoes)

Rich red passata is simply sieved ripe tomatoes, a wonderfully convenient short-cut wherever tomato pulp is required. Depending on the degree of sieving, it can be perfectly smooth or slightly chunky (*polpa di pomodoro* or *passata rustica*: 'rustic passata'). The chunky variety is sold in tall jars, while the smoothest type is available in cartons or jars. More highly concentrated tomato paste or purée (*concentrato di pomodoro*) is packed in small cans or tubes. Tomato purée (paste) is extremely strong and should only be used in small quantities.

CULINARY USES

Passata can be used as a basis for soups and sauces, and as a substitute for fresh tomatoes in all recipes where they require long cooking. For a very quick pasta sauce, sweat some finely chopped onion and garlic in olive oil, add a jar of passata and bubble the sauce while the pasta is cooking. Flavour with fresh basil, oregano, parsley or some chopped olives, capers and/or anchovies. For more body and depth and a richer colour, stir in a spoonful or two of tomato concentrate.

Pasta di olive (olive paste)

Green or, more usually, black olives are pounded to a paste with salt and olive oil and packed in small jars. Olive paste tends to be very salty and rich, so a little goes a long way.

CULINARY USES

Olive paste can be spread very thinly over pizza bases, or scraped on to toasted croûtons and topped with tomatoes or mushrooms to make *crostini*. Mixed with olive oil and a little lemon juice, it can be a dip for raw vegetables. For an interesting *antipasto*, mash a little olive paste into the yolks of halved hard-boiled eggs, spoon the mixture back into the cavity and top with a few capers.

A little olive paste adds a rich flavour to a tomato sauce, while a spoonful stirred into a vinaigrette makes a good dressing for a robust salad. If you are a real olive lover, stir a small amount into hot pasta for the simplest of dressings.

Artichoke hearts
These olive oil-packed vegetables are often combined with sliced cured meats to make an antipasto

Store Cupboard

Giardiniera (pickled vegetables)

Mixed pickled vegetables are sold packed *in agrodolce* (vinegar and oil). Single varieties like peeled or unpeeled aubergines (eggplants) and courgettes (zucchini) are available, but a mixture of these vegetables along with artichokes, baby (pearl) onions, carrots, celery and (bell) peppers is more colourful. These vegetables are sometimes described as *alla contadina* (peasant-style).

CULINARY USES
Pickled vegetables can be served with salami and ham as an *antipasto*, or drained and mixed with raw vegetables and mayonnaise for a piquant version of *insalata russa* (Russian salad). Their vinegary taste makes an excellent counterpoint to plain cold roast meats or poultry.

Filetti di acciughe (anchovy fillets)

Anchovy fillets are available preserved in salt or oil. The salted fillets have a superior flavour, but they are are only available in catering tins to be sold by the *etto* (100g/3¹/₂oz) in delicatessens. You can buy these and soak them for 30 minutes, then dry them thoroughly and pack them in olive oil, but it is more practical to buy ready canned or bottled anchovies.

CULINARY USES
Anchovies can be chopped and added to tomato sauces and salad dressings. They can be stirred into a fish risotto, or mixed with tomatoes and capers for a topping for pizzas or *crostini*. They are best of all made into *bagna cauda*, a delicious and quick hot dip for raw vegetables. For six people, heat 150ml/5fl oz/²/₃ cup olive oil with 50g/2oz/4 tbsp unsalted butter. As soon as it begins to foam, add 3 finely chopped garlic cloves and soften but do not brown. Drain and roughly chop a 50g/2oz can of anchovy fillets, add to the pan and stir over low heat until they have disintegrated to a paste. Keep the sauce hot and dip in the vegetables.

Bottarga (salted roe)

The pressed, salted and dried roe of the grey mullet or tuna, also known as *buttariga, butarega and ovotarica*, is a speciality of Sardinia, Sicily and the Veneto, where it is regarded as a great delicacy. It is usually packed in a sausage shape inside a skin that should be removed before preparing. Wrapped in clear film (plastic wrap), it will keep for several months.

CULINARY USES
Bottarga can be served as an *antipasto* thinly sliced and dressed with a little extra virgin olive oil and lemon juice. In Sicily, it is served with *caponata*, a dome-shaped salad of fried aubergines (eggplants) and celery. It is delicious simply grated over hot pasta with a knob (pat) of unsalted butter and a little chopped fresh parsley or dried chilli flakes.

Anchovy fillets
Usually chopped and added to sauces or salads for extra flavour. These are available packed in oil or salt – the salted variety have a better flavour

Peppers
The vinegary flavour of these pickled vegetables goes well with cold roast meats

Baccalà
(salted dried cod)
Air-drying is the oldest known method of preserving fish. Before the days of deep-freezing, dried fish was invaluable for people who wished to observe meatless days, but who lived far from the sea, because the salting and drying process ensures that it remains edible for many months. The most popular dried fish in Italy is salt cod, which is traditionally eaten on Good Friday. It is sometimes known confusingly as *stoccafisso* (although true stockfish is unsalted). It looks rather unappealing, like a flat, greyish board, but once it has been soaked and reconstituted it is absolutely delicious. Unlike other store-cupboard (pantry) ingredients, *baccalà* must be prepared a day in advance, but it is worth the effort.

Clams in brine

Salt cod
This is the favourite Italian dried fish – it looks unappealing, but once it is soaked and cooked, it is delicious

Vongole *(clams)*
Tiny clams are sold packed in brine in glass jars. These miniature golden nuggets need no further cooking and can be simply heated through and tossed into hot pasta or risotto, or combined with tomato sauce. If you have time, drain the clams and reduce the juice in which they are packed with finely chopped garlic and a few dried chilli flakes to make a more intense sauce.

Mostarda di Cremona
(mustard fruit chutney)
This sweet crystallized fruit chutney with its piquant undertone of the mustard was first produced over a hundred years ago in Cremona and Venice. Its vibrant multi-colour comes from the assortment of candied fruits from which it is made – cherries, pears, melons, figs, apricots and clementines, infused in mustard seed oil. Also known as *mostarda di frutta*, the chutney is traditionally served with sausages such as zampone and cotechino, or roast and boiled beef, veal and pork. For an unusual and delicious dessert, serve the chutney as a topping for creamy mascarpone.

CULINARY USES
Before using *baccalà*, it must be soaked under cold running water for at least 8 hours to rehydrate it and remove the excess salt. Once this has been done, it can be creamed with olive oil, garlic, cream and parsley to make *baccalà mantecato*, a famous Venetian dish, which is served on fried polenta. In the Florentine version, the salt cod is cut into chunks, coated with flour and fried with tomatoes and onions. *Baccalà* combines well with all Mediterranean flavours and can be stewed or baked with red peppers, potatoes, fennel or celery, capers, olives and anchovies. Many recipes also include pine nuts and raisins or sultanas (golden raisins). For a simple pasta sauce, mix some flaked salt cod with cream and chopped herbs and stir it into the hot pasta.

Mustard fruit chutney

Aperitifs & Liqueurs

Behind every bar in Italy is displayed row upon row of bottles containing dozens of different aperitivi *and* digestivi, *many of them never found outside Italy. They are consumed at any hour of the day; a favourite Italian morning drink is* caffè corretto, *espresso coffee laced with grappa or Stock (Italian brandy). Many of the vermouths and spirits are made from local ingredients, such as herbs, nuts, lemons, artichokes or regional wines. The Italians have an unshakeable belief in the digestive properties of such drinks, many of which are so bitter that most non-Italians find them completely unpalatable. At the end of a restaurant meal, you will always find the men clustered around the bar aiding their digestion with a small glass of spirit or liqueur.*

Amaro

Fernet-Branca

Campari soda

Amaro

A very bitter *aperitivo* much beloved of the Italians, *amaro* is flavoured with gentian, herbs and orange peel and contains quinine and iron. Marginally less bitter than straight *amaro* are the wine-based *amari* such as Campari, which is usually mixed with soda water and drunk before a meal to stimulate the appetite and cleanse the palate. Others, such as Fernet-Branca, are served as a pick-me-up and cure for stomach upsets. *Amaro* is reputed to have excellent digestive and tonic properties, to cure hangovers and to have aphrodisiac qualities, which probably explains its popularity in Italy.

Campari

A bright crimson *aperitivo* from the *amaro* family, wine-based Campari has a bitter, astringent flavour. It was first produced in the 19th century by the Campari brothers from Milan, and has been produced by the same family ever since. Campari is sold in triangular single-portion bottles ready-mixed with soda (Campari soda). The neat bitters are an essential ingredient of cocktails such as *Negroni* and *Americano*.

Cynar

This dark brown, intensely bitter, aperitif with an alcoholic content of 17 per cent is made from artichokes. Too bitter to swallow on its own, it is usually served as a long drink with ice and soda water.

Punt e Mes

The name of this intensely bitter red *aperitivo* means 'point and a half'. It is said to have been created by the Carpano distillery when customers ordered their drinks to be mixed according to their own specification. Punt e Mes is usually drunk on its own, but can be served with ice and soda.

Cynar

Vermouth

All vermouths, both white and red, are made from white wine flavoured with aromatic herbal extracts and spices. The first vermouth was made in Turin in the 18th century, and vermouth is still produced there. Red vermouths, like Cinzano and sweet Martini, are sweetened with sugar and tinted with caramel to give them a deep red colour. These sweet red varieties are generically called 'Italian' vermouth – the 'it' in a Gin and It cocktail. Dry vermouth is white and contains less sugar. It is known as 'French', but is also produced in Italy by companies such as Martini and Rossi. Other well-known brands include Riccadonna and Gancia.

Punt e Mes

CULINARY USES

Although the Italians tend to use white wine rather than vermouth in their cooking, dry white vermouth can be substituted in sauces and veal, rabbit or poultry dishes. It adds a touch of dryness and intensity.

Extra-dry white Vermouth

Fortified Wines

Marsala

This rich brown fortified wine has a sweet, musky flavour and an alcoholic content of about 18 per cent. It is made in the west of Sicily, near the town from which it takes its name. The best Marsala (*vergine*) has been matured for at least five years to give an intensity of flavour and colour. Although sweet Marsala is better known, dry varieties (*ambra secco*) are also produced; their flavour is reminiscent of medium sherry. The sweetest version is *Marsala all'uovo*, an intensely rich and sticky dessert wine enriched with egg yolks, which can only be drunk in tiny quantities. Dry Marsala is generally served as an *aperitivo*, while the sweet version is served after a meal, usually with little cookies to dip into the wine. Unlike sherry, sweet Marsala does not deteriorate once the bottle is opened, so it makes a very useful standby in the kitchen.

Vin santo

This 'holy wine' from Tuscany is made from semi-dried grapes with a long slow fermentation, followed by many years ageing to produce a syrupy golden wine. Although not a fortified wine, its intense flavour has some similarity to sherry and it is drunk in much the same way. Vin santo can be dry or sweet, but the sweet version is more common. It is generally served with a plate of *cantucci* or *biscotti di Prato*, hard slipper-shaped cookies studded with nuts. These are dunked into the wine to make a delicious dessert.

Vin santo

Culinary Uses

Sweet Marsala is probably best known as an essential ingredient of *zabaglione*, a light frothy dessert made from whisked egg yolks, sugar and Marsala. It is used in *zuppa inglese* (trifle) and many other desserts. Dry Marsala is widely used in Italian cooking, particularly in veal dishes such as *scaloppine* and *piccata alla Marsala* and sautéed chicken livers. A few spoonfuls of Marsala added to the pan in which veal or poultry has been sautéed will mingle with the pan juices to make a delicious syrupy sauce. It adds extra flavour to wild mushrooms or a mushroom risotto.

Marsala
The sweet variety is used to flavour zabaglione

Dry Marsala
Widely used by Italian cooks for flavouring veal and poultry dishes

Amaretto

This sweet liqueur is made from apricot kernels and flavoured with almonds and aromatic extracts. There are several brands produced, but the best is Disaronno Amaretto, which comes in a distinctive squarish rippled glass bottle with a square cap.

CULINARY USES

The distinctive almond flavour of Amaretto enhances many desserts, such as *macedonia* (fruit salad), *zuppa inglese* (trifle) and *panna* (whipped cream).

Galliano

A bright yellow liqueur from Lombardy, Galliano is flavoured with herbs and spices and tastes a little like a bittersweet Chartreuse. It is occasionally drunk on its own as a *digestivo*, but is best known as an ingredient for cocktails such as Harvey Wallbanger or Golden Cadillac.

Galliano

Amaretto

Liqueurs & Digestivi

Grappa

A pungent colourless brandy with an alcoholic content of about 40 per cent, distilled from the pressed skins and pips of the grapes left after wine-making. At its crudest, grappa tastes of raw spirit, but after maturing the taste becomes refined and the best grappa can be as good as a fine French *marc*. Grappa is made in many regions, usually from local grapes, which lend each variety its characteristic flavour. On the whole, you get what you pay for; cheap grappa is fiery and pungent, while expensive, well-matured varieties can be very smooth. The very best grappa often comes in exquisite hand-blown bottles. The spirit can be flavoured with various aromatics, including rose petals and lemon peel.

CULINARY USES

Grappa is not widely used in Italian cooking, except in *capretto alla piemontese* (braised kid). It can be used for flambéeing and for preserving soft fruits. The spirit takes on the flavour of the fruits and can be drunk as a *digestivo* after the fruits have been eaten.

Liquore al limone or Cedro

This sticky sweet liqueur is made from the peel of the lemons that grow in profusion around the Amalfi coast. Almost every delicatessen in the region sells a home-made version of this opaque yellow drink, whose sweetness is tempered by the tangy citrus fruit. It should be served ice-cold straight from the refrigerator or freezer and makes a refreshing *aperitivo* or *digestivo*.

Liquore al limone

Maraschino

This sweet, colourless cherry liqueur is made from fermented bitter Maraschino cherries. It can be drunk on its own as a *digestivo*, but is more commonly used for flavouring cocktails or sweet dishes.

Maraschino

Grappa

Nocino

This sticky, dark brown liqueur from Emilia-Romagna is made from unripe green walnuts steeped in spirit. It has an aromatic but bittersweet flavour.

Sambuca

A colourless liqueur with a strong taste of aniseed, although it is actually distilled from witch elder. Traditionally it is served in a schooner-shaped glass, flambéed and with a coffee bean floating on top. The coffee bean is crunched as the Sambuca is drunk, so that its bitterness counteracts the intense sweetness of the liqueur. This method of serving Sambuca is known as *colla mosca* ('with the fly'), the 'fly' being the coffee bean.

Strega

A bright yellow liqueur made from herbs and flowers, strega (meaning 'witch'), has a bittersweet flavour and is definitely an acquired taste!

Sambuca

Strega

Nocino

The Recipes

*The recipes in this collection cover a range of styles,
from regional specialities to popular modern
classics. More unusual, innovative offerings are here
too, destined to become future favourites.
All of the recipes use ingredients that can be found
easily outside Italy, and all are as delicious
to eat as they are easy to make.
Buon Appetito.*

Antipasti

Antipasto means 'before the meal', and no respectable
Italian meal would start without it. The recipes in
this chapter are typical of Italian antipasti -
appetizing and easy on the eye, light and tasty.
Vegetables, fish and salads are the mainstay, not only
for their lightness and freshness, but also
for their colour.

Roast Pepper Terrine

Torta di peperoni al forno

This terrine is perfect for a dinner party because it tastes better if made ahead. Prepare the salsa on the day of serving. Serve with hot Italian bread.

Ingredients

8 (bell) peppers (red, yellow and orange)
675g/1½lb/3 cups mascarpone
3 eggs, separated
30ml/2 tbsp each roughly chopped flat
 leaf parsley and shredded basil
2 large garlic cloves, roughly chopped
2 red, yellow or orange peppers, seeded
 and roughly chopped
30ml/2 tbsp extra virgin olive oil
10ml/2 tsp balsamic vinegar
a few basil sprigs
a pinch of sugar
salt and freshly ground black pepper
serves 8

1 Place the peppers under a hot grill (broiler) for 8 – 10 minutes, turning them frequently until the skins are charred and blistered on all sides. Put the hot peppers in plastic bags, seal and leave until cold.

2 ▲ Rub off the pepper skins under cold running water. Break open the flesh and rub out the cores and seeds. Drain the peppers, dry them on kitchen paper, then cut seven of them lengthways into thin, even strips. Reserve the remaining pepper for the salsa.

Variation

For a lower-fat version of this terrine, use ricotta cheese instead of the mascarpone.

3 Put the mascarpone in a bowl with the egg yolks, herbs and half the garlic. Add salt and pepper to taste. Beat well. In a separate bowl, whisk the egg whites to a soft peak, then fold into the cheese mixture until evenly incorporated.

4 ▲ Preheat the oven to 180°C/350°F/ Gas 4. Line the base of a lightly oiled 900g/2lb loaf tin (pan). Put one-third of the cheese mixture in the tin and spread level. Arrange half the pepper strips on top in an even layer. Repeat until all the cheese and peppers are used.

5 Cover the tin with foil and place in a roasting pan. Pour in boiling water to come halfway up the sides of the tin. Bake for 1 hour. Leave to cool in the water bath, then lift out and chill overnight.

6 A few hours before serving, make the salsa. Place the remaining roast pepper and fresh peppers in a food processor. Add the remaining garlic, oil and vinegar.

7 Set aside a few basil leaves for garnishing and add the rest to the processor. Process until finely chopped. Tip the mixture into a bowl, add salt and pepper to taste and mix well. Cover with clear film (plastic wrap) and chill until ready to serve.

8 Turn out the terrine, peel off the paper and slice thickly. Garnish with the basil leaves and serve cold, with the sweet pepper salsa.

Pan-fried Chicken Liver Salad

Insalata di fegatini

This Florentine salad uses vin santo, a sweet dessert wine from Tuscany, but this is not essential – any dessert wine will do, or a sweet or cream sherry.

Ingredients

75g/3oz fresh baby spinach leaves
75g/3oz lollo rosso leaves
75ml/5 tbsp olive oil
15ml/1 tbsp butter
225g/8oz chicken livers, trimmed and
    thinly sliced
45ml/3 tbsp vin santo
50–75g/2–3oz fresh Parmesan cheese,
    shaved into curls
salt and freshly ground black pepper
serves 4

1 ▲ Wash and dry the spinach and lollo rosso. Tear the leaves into a large bowl, season with salt and pepper to taste and toss gently to mix.

2 ▲ Heat 30ml/2 tbsp of the oil with the butter in a large, heavy frying pan. When foaming, add the chicken livers and toss over a medium to high heat for 5 minutes or until the livers are browned on the outside but still pink in the centre. Remove from the heat.

3 ▲ Remove the livers from the pan with a slotted spoon, drain them on kitchen paper, then place on top of the spinach.

4 ▲ Return the pan to a medium heat, add the remaining oil and the vin santo and stir until sizzling.

5 Pour the hot dressing over the spinach and livers and toss to coat. Put the salad in a serving bowl and sprinkle over the Parmesan shavings. Serve immediately.

Salad Leaves with Gorgonzola

Insalata verde con gorgonzola

Crispy fried pancetta makes tasty croûtons, which contrast well in texture and flavour with the softness of mixed salad leaves and the sharp taste of Gorgonzola.

Ingredients
225g/8oz pancetta rashers (strips), any
 rinds removed, coarsely chopped
2 large garlic cloves, roughly chopped
75g/3oz rocket (arugula) leaves
75g/3oz radicchio leaves
50g/2oz/¹/₂ cup walnuts,
 roughly chopped
115g/4oz Gorgonzola cheese
60ml/4 tbsp olive oil
15ml/1 tbsp balsamic vinegar
salt and freshly ground black pepper
serves 4

Variation
Use walnut oil instead of olive oil, or
hazelnuts and hazelnut oil instead of
walnuts and olive oil.

1 ▲ Put the chopped pancetta and
garlic in a non-stick or heavy frying
pan and heat gently, stirring constantly,
until the pancetta fat runs. Increase
the heat and fry until the pancetta and
garlic are crisp.

2 Remove the pancetta with a slotted
spoon and drain on kitchen paper.
Leave the pancetta fat in the pan, off
the heat.

3 ▲ Tear the rocket and radicchio
leaves into a salad bowl. Sprinkle over
the walnuts, pancetta and garlic. Add
salt and pepper and toss to mix.
Crumble the Gorgonzola on top.

4 Return the frying pan to a medium
heat and add the oil and balsamic
vinegar to the pancetta fat. Stir until
sizzling, then pour over the salad.
Serve at once, to be tossed at the table.

Tomato and Mozzarella Toasts

Bruschetta casalinga

These resemble mini pizzas and are good with drinks before a dinner party. Prepare them several hours in advance and pop them in the oven just as your guests arrive.

Ingredients
3 *sfilatini* (thin ciabatta)
about 250ml/8fl oz/1 cup sun-dried
 tomato paste
3 x 150g/5oz packets mozzarella
 cheese, drained
about 10ml/2 tsp dried oregano or
 mixed herbs
30–45ml/2–3 tbsp olive oil
freshly ground black pepper
serves 6–8

Variations
Use red or green pesto instead of
the sun-dried tomato paste – a
combination of colours is especially
effective if the toasts are served on a
large platter. Halved olives can be
pressed into the cheese, or criss-cross
strips of anchovy.

1 ▲ Cut each *sfilatino* on the diagonal
into 12-15 slices, discarding the ends.
Toast lightly on both sides.

2 Preheat the oven to 220°C/425°F/
Gas 7. Spread sun-dried tomato paste
on one side of each slice of toast. Cut
the mozzarella into small pieces and
arrange over the tomato paste.

3 ▲ Put the toasts on baking trays,
sprinkle with herbs and pepper to
taste and drizzle with oil. Bake for
5 minutes or until the mozzarella has
melted and is bubbling. Leave the
toasts to settle for a few minutes
before serving.

Genoese Squid Salad

Calamari in insalata alla genovese

This is a good salad for summer, when French beans and new potatoes are at their best.

Serve it for a first course or light lunch.

Ingredients

450g/1lb prepared squid, cut into rings
4 garlic cloves, roughly chopped
300ml/¹/₂ pint/1¹/₄ cups Italian red wine
450g/1lb waxy new potatoes,
    scrubbed clean
225g/8oz French (green) beans, trimmed
    and cut into short lengths
2–3 drained sun-dried tomatoes in oil,
    thinly sliced lengthways
60ml/4 tbsp extra virgin olive oil
15ml/1 tbsp red wine vinegar
salt and freshly ground black pepper
serves 4–6

Cook's Tips

The French potato called Charlotte is perfect for this type of salad because it retains its shape and does not break up when boiled. Prepared squid can be bought from supermarkets with fresh fish counters, and from fishmongers.

1 ▲ Preheat the oven to 180°C/350°F/ Gas 4. Put the squid rings in an earthenware dish with half the garlic, the wine and pepper to taste. Cover and cook for 45 minutes or until the squid is tender.

2 Put the potatoes in a pan, cover with cold water and add a good pinch of salt. Bring to the boil, cover and simmer for 15–20 minutes or until tender. Using a slotted spoon, lift out the potatoes and set aside. Add the beans to the boiling water and cook for 3 minutes. Drain.

3 ▲ When the potatoes are cool enough to handle, slice them thickly on the diagonal and place them in a bowl with the warm beans and sundried tomatoes. Whisk the oil, wine vinegar and the remaining garlic in a jug (pitcher) and add salt and pepper to taste. Pour over the potato mixture.

4 Drain the squid and discard the wine and garlic. Add the squid to the potato mixture and fold very gently to mix. Arrange the salad on individual plates and grind pepper liberally all over. Serve warm.

Tuna Carpaccio

Carpaccio di tonno

Fillet (tenderloin) of beef is most often used for carpaccio, but meaty fish such as tuna make an unusual change. The secret is to freeze the fish before slicing it wafer thin.

Ingredients

2 fresh tuna steaks, about 450g/1lb
    total weight
60ml/4 tbsp extra virgin olive oil
15ml/1 tbsp balsamic vinegar
5ml/1 tsp caster (superfine) sugar
30ml/2 tbsp drained bottled green
    peppercorns or capers
salt and freshly ground black pepper
lemon wedges and green salad,
    to serve

serves 4

Cook's Tip

Raw fish is safe to eat as long as it is very fresh, so check with your fishmonger before purchase, and make and serve carpaccio on the same day. Do not buy fish that has been frozen and thawed.

1 ▲ Remove the skin from each tuna steak and place each steak between two sheets of clear film (plastic wrap) or non-stick baking parchment. Pound with a rolling pin until flattened slightly.

2 Roll up the tuna as tightly as possible, then wrap tightly in clear film and place in the freezer for 4 hours or until firm.

3 ▲ Unwrap the tuna and cut crossways into the thinnest possible slices. Arrange on individual plates.

4 Whisk together the remaining ingredients, season and pour over the tuna. Cover and allow to come to room temperature for 30 minutes before serving with lemon wedges and green salad.

Marinated Vegetable Antipasto

Verdura marinata per antipasto

Antipasto means 'before the meal' and traditionally consists of a selection of marinated vegetable dishes served with cured meats. Serve in attractive bowls, with plenty of crusty bread.

2 Thickly slice the mushrooms and place in a large bowl. Heat the oil in a small pan and add the garlic and rosemary. Pour in the wine.

3 Bring the mixture to the boil, then lower the heat and simmer gently for 3 minutes. Add salt and pepper to taste.

4 ▲ Pour the mixture over the mushrooms. Mix well and leave until cool, stirring occasionally. Cover and marinate overnight. Serve at room temperature, garnished with rosemary sprigs.

Ingredients

For the peppers
3 red (bell) peppers
3 yellow peppers
4 garlic cloves, sliced
a handful fresh basil, plus extra to garnish
extra virgin olive oil
salt and freshly ground black pepper

For the mushrooms
450g/1lb open cap mushrooms
60ml/4 tbsp extra virgin olive oil
1 large garlic clove, crushed
15ml/1 tbsp chopped fresh rosemary
250ml/8fl oz/1 cup dry white wine
fresh rosemary sprigs, to garnish

For the olives
1 dried red chilli, crushed
grated rind of 1 lemon
120ml/4fl oz/¹/₂ cup extra virgin olive oil
225g/8oz/1¹/₃ cups Italian black olives
30ml/2 tbsp chopped fresh flat leaf parsley
1 lemon wedge, to serve
serves 4

1 ▲ Place the peppers under a hot grill (broiler). Turn occasionally until blackened and blistered all over. Remove from the heat and place in a large plastic bag. When cool, remove the skin, halve the peppers and remove the seeds. Cut the flesh into strips lengthways and place them in a bowl with the sliced garlic and basil leaves. Add salt, to taste, cover with oil and marinate for 3–4 hours before serving, tossing occasionally. When serving, garnish with more basil leaves.

5 ▲ Prepare the olives. Place the chilli and lemon rind in a small pan with the oil. Heat gently for about 3 minutes. Add the olives and heat for 1 minute more. Tip into a bowl and leave to cool. Marinate overnight. Sprinkle the parsley over just before serving with the lemon wedge.

Cook's Tip
The (bell) pepper antipasto can be stored in the refrigerator for up to 2 weeks covered in oil in a screw-top jar.

Stuffed Roast Peppers with Pesto

Peperoni arrostiti con pesto

Serve these scallop- and pesto-filled sweet red peppers with Italian bread, such as ciabatta or focaccia, to mop up the garlicky juices.

Ingredients

4 squat red (bell) peppers
2 large garlic cloves, cut into thin slivers
60ml/4 tbsp olive oil
4 shelled scallops
45ml/3 tbsp pesto
salt and freshly ground black pepper
freshly grated Parmesan cheese,
    to serve
salad leaves and fresh basil sprigs,
    to garnish
serves 4

Cook's Tip

Scallops are available from most fishmongers and supermarkets with fresh fish counters. Never cook scallops for longer than the time stated in the recipe or they will be tough and rubbery.

1 Preheat the oven to 180°C/350°F/ Gas 4. Cut the peppers in half lengthways, through their stalks. Scrape out and discard the cores and seeds. Wash the pepper shells to remove any seeds and pat dry.

2 ▲ Put the peppers, cut-side up, in an oiled roasting pan. Divide the slivers of garlic equally among them and sprinkle with salt and pepper to taste. Spoon the oil into the peppers, then roast for 40 minutes.

3 ▲ Cut each of the shelled scallops in half to make two flat discs. Remove the peppers from the oven and place a scallop half in each pepper half. Top with pesto.

4 Return the pan to the oven and roast for 10 minutes more. Transfer the peppers to individual serving plates, sprinkle with grated Parmesan and garnish each plate with a few salad leaves and fresh basil sprigs. Serve warm.

Mozzarella Skewers

Spiedini alla romana

Stacks of flavour – layers of oven-baked mozzarella, tomatoes, basil and bread.

Ingredients

12 slices white country bread, each about
  1cm/¹/₂ in thick
45ml/3 tbsp olive oil
225g/8oz mozzarella cheese, cut into
  5mm/¹/₄in slices
3 plum tomatoes, cut into
  5mm/¹/₄in slices
15g/¹/₂oz/¹/₂ cup fresh basil leaves,
  plus extra to garnish
salt and freshly ground black pepper
30ml/2 tbsp chopped fresh flat
  leaf parsley, to garnish
serves 4

Cook's Tip

If you use wooden skewers, soak them
in water first, to prevent scorching.

1 ▲ Preheat the oven to 220°C/425°F/
Gas 7. Trim the crusts from the bread
and cut each slice into four equal
squares. Arrange on a baking sheet
and brush on one side (or both sides)
with half the olive oil. Bake for
3–5 minutes until the squares are
pale golden.

2 Remove from the oven and place
the bread squares on a board with the
other ingredients.

3 ▲ Make 16 stacks, each starting
with a square of bread, then a slice
of mozzarella topped with a slice of
tomato and a basil leaf. Sprinkle with
salt and pepper, then repeat, ending
with the bread. Push a skewer through
each stack and place on the baking
sheet. Drizzle with the remaining oil
and bake for 10–15 minutes until the
cheese begins to melt. Garnish with
fresh basil leaves and serve scattered
with chopped fresh flat leaf parsley.

Aubergine Fritters

Frittelle di melanzane

These simply delicious fritters make a superb starter or vegetarian supper dish.

Ingredients

1 large aubergine (eggplant), about
  675g/1¹/₂lb, cut into 1cm/¹/₂in
  thick slices
30ml/2 tbsp olive oil
1 egg, lightly beaten
2 garlic cloves, crushed
60ml/4 tbsp chopped fresh parsley
130g/4¹/₂oz/2¹/₄ cups fresh
  white breadcrumbs
90g/3¹/₂oz/generous 1 cup grated
  Parmesan cheese
90g/3¹/₂oz/generous 1 cup feta
  cheese, crumbled
45ml/3 tbsp plain (all-purpose) flour
sunflower oil, for shallow frying
salt and freshly ground black pepper

To serve

natural (plain) yogurt, flavoured with fried
  red chillies and cumin seeds
lime wedges
serves 4

1 ▲ Preheat the oven to 190°C/375°F/
Gas 5. Brush the aubergine slices with
the olive oil, then place them on a
baking sheet and bake for about
20 minutes until golden and tender.
Chop the slices finely and place them
in a bowl with the egg, garlic, parsley,
breadcrumbs, Parmesan and feta. Add
salt and pepper to taste, and mix well.
Leave the mixture to rest for about
20 minutes. If the mixture looks
very sloppy, add more breadcrumbs.

2 ▲ Divide the mixture into eight
balls and flatten them slightly. Place
the flour on a plate and season with
a little salt and pepper. Coat the
fritters in the seasoned flour, shaking
off any excess.

3 Shallow fry the fritters in batches for
1 minute on each side, until golden
brown. Drain on kitchen paper and
serve with the flavoured yogurt and
lime wedges.

Soups

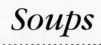

The Italians are great soup eaters, and some of the best
soups in the world come from Italy. Clear broth, brodo,
and delicate puréed soups are served as a first course
before a main meal. More substantial chunky soups,
minestre, are often main meals in themselves, usually
served in the evening if the main meal of the day has
been at lunchtime.

Onion Soup

La cipollata

This warming winter soup comes from Umbria, where it is sometimes thickened with beaten eggs and grated Parmesan cheese. It is then served on top of hot toasted croûtes.

Ingredients

115g/4oz pancetta rashers
    (strips), any rinds removed,
    roughly chopped
30ml/2 tbsp olive oil
15g/¹/₂oz/1 tbsp butter
675g/1¹/₂lb onions, thinly sliced
10ml/2 tsp sugar
about 1.2 litres/2 pints/5 cups
    chicken stock
350g/12oz ripe Italian plum tomatoes,
    peeled and roughly chopped
a few basil leaves, shredded
salt and freshly ground
    black pepper
freshly grated Parmesan cheese,
    to serve

serves 4

3 ▲ Add the stock, tomatoes and salt and pepper and bring to the boil, stirring. Lower the heat, half cover the pan and simmer, stirring occasionally, for about 30 minutes.

4 Check the consistency of the soup and add a little more stock or water if it is too thick.

5 Just before serving, stir in most of the basil and taste for seasoning, adjusting as necessary. Serve hot, garnished with the remaining shredded basil. Hand round the freshly grated Parmesan separately.

Cook's Tip
Look for Vidalia onions to make this soup. They are available at large supermarkets, and have a very sweet flavour and attractive yellowish flesh.

1 ▲ Put the chopped pancetta in a large pan and heat gently, stirring constantly, until the fat runs. Increase the heat to medium, add the oil, butter, onions and sugar and stir well to mix.

2 ▲ Half cover the pan and cook the onions gently for about 20 minutes until golden. Stir frequently and lower the heat if necessary.

Cream of Courgette Soup

Vellutata di zucchini

The beauty of this soup is its delicate colour, rich and creamy texture and subtle taste. If you prefer a more pronounced cheese flavour, use Gorgonzola instead of Dolcelatte cheese.

Ingredients

30ml/2 tbsp olive oil
15g/¹/₂oz/1 tbsp butter
1 medium onion, roughly chopped
900g/2lb courgettes (zucchini), trimmed
    and sliced
5ml/1 tsp dried oregano
about 600ml/1 pint/2¹/₂ cups vegetable or
    chicken stock
115g/4oz Dolcelatte cheese, rind
    removed, diced
300ml/¹/₂ pint/1¹/₄ cups single (light) cream
salt and freshly ground black pepper
fresh oregano and extra Dolcelatte,
    to garnish
serves 4–6

1 ▲ Heat the oil and butter in a large pan until foaming. Add the onion and cook gently for about 5 minutes, stirring frequently, until softened but not brown.

2 ▲ Add the courgettes and oregano, with salt and pepper to taste. Cook over a medium heat for 10 minutes, stirring frequently.

3 ▲ Pour in the stock and bring to the boil, stirring. Lower the heat, half cover the pan and simmer gently, stirring occasionally, for about 30 minutes. Stir in the diced Dolcelatte until melted.

Cook's Tip

To save time, trim off and discard the ends of the courgettes (zucchini), cut them into thirds, then chop in a food processor fitted with the metal blade.

4 ▲ Process in a blender or food processor until smooth. Press through a sieve (strainer) into a clean pan.

5 Add two-thirds of the cream and stir over a low heat until hot, but not boiling. Check the consistency and add more stock if the soup is too thick. Taste for seasoning, then pour into heated bowls. Swirl in the remaining cream. Garnish with oregano and extra cheese and serve.

Wild Mushroom Soup

Zuppa di porcini

Wild mushrooms are expensive. Dried porcini have an intense flavour, so only a small quantity is needed. The beef stock helps to strengthen the earthy flavour of the mushrooms.

Ingredients

25g/1oz/2 cups dried porcini mushrooms
30ml/2 tbsp olive oil
15g/¹/₂oz/1 tbsp butter
2 leeks, thinly sliced
2 shallots, roughly chopped
1 garlic clove, roughly chopped
225g/8oz/3 cups fresh wild mushrooms
about 1.2 litres/2 pints/5 cups beef stock
2.5ml/¹/₂ tsp dried thyme
150ml/¹/₄ pint/²/₃ cup double
    (heavy) cream
salt and freshly ground
    black pepper
fresh thyme sprigs,
    to garnish
serves 4

Cook's Tip

Porcini are ceps. Italian cooks would make this soup with a combination of fresh and dried ceps, but if fresh ceps are difficult to obtain, you can use other wild mushrooms, such as chanterelles.

1 ▲ Put the dried porcini in a bowl, add 250ml/8fl oz/1 cup warm water and leave to soak for 20–30 minutes. Lift out of the liquid and squeeze over the bowl to remove as much of the soaking liquid as possible. Strain all the liquid and reserve to use later. Finely chop the porcini.

2 Heat the oil and butter in a large pan until foaming. Add the sliced leeks, chopped shallots and garlic and cook gently for about 5 minutes, stirring frequently, until softened but not coloured.

3 ▲ Chop or slice the fresh mushrooms and add to the pan. Stir over a medium heat for a few minutes until they begin to soften. Pour in the stock and bring to the boil. Add the porcini, soaking liquid, dried thyme and salt and pepper. Lower the heat, half cover the pan and simmer gently for 30 minutes, stirring occasionally.

4 ▲ Pour about three-quarters of the soup into a blender or food processor and process until smooth. Return to the soup remaining in the pan, stir in the cream and heat through. Check the consistency and add more stock if the soup is too thick. Taste for seasoning. Serve hot, garnished with thyme sprigs.

Tomato and Fresh Basil Soup

Crema di pomodori al basilico

This intensely flavoured and vivid soup is best made in late summer when fresh tomatoes are at their most delicious and are often available cheaply at markets.

Ingredients
15ml/1 tbsp olive oil
25g/1oz/2 tbsp butter
1 medium onion, finely chopped
900g/2lb ripe plum tomatoes, chopped
1 garlic clove, roughly chopped
about 750ml/1¼ pints/3 cups chicken
    or vegetable stock
120ml/4fl oz/½ cup dry white wine
30ml/2 tbsp sun-dried tomato paste
30ml/2 tbsp shredded fresh basil,
    plus a few whole leaves, to garnish
150ml/¼ pint/ ⅔ cup double
    (heavy) cream
salt and freshly ground black pepper
serves 4–6

1 ▲ Heat the oil and butter in a large pan until foaming. Add the onion and cook gently for about 5 minutes, stirring frequently, until softened but not brown.

2 ▲ Stir in the tomatoes and garlic, then add the stock, white wine and sun-dried tomato paste, with salt and pepper to taste. Bring to the boil, then lower the heat, half cover the pan and simmer for 20 minutes, stirring occasionally to stop the tomatoes sticking to the base of the pan.

3 ▲ Process the soup with the shredded basil in a blender or food processor, then press through a sieve (strainer) into a clean pan.

4 ▲ Add the double cream and heat through, stirring. Do not allow the soup to approach boiling point. Check the consistency and add more stock if necessary and then taste for seasoning. Pour into heated bowls and garnish with basil. Serve at once.

Variation
The soup can also be served chilled. Pour it into a container after sieving and chill for at least 4 hours. Serve in chilled bowls.

Minestrone with Pasta and Beans

Minestrone alla milanese

This classic minestrone from Lombardy includes pancetta for a pleasant touch of saltiness.

Milanese cooks vary the recipe according to what is on hand, and you can do the same.

Ingredients
45ml/3 tbsp olive oil
115g/4oz pancetta, any rinds removed,
   roughly chopped
2–3 celery sticks, finely chopped
3 medium carrots, finely chopped
1 medium onion, finely chopped
1–2 garlic cloves, crushed
2 x 400g/14oz cans chopped tomatoes
about 1 litre/1¾ pints/4 cups
   chicken stock
400g/14oz can cannellini beans,
   drained and rinsed
50g/2oz/½ cup short–cut macaroni
30–60ml/2–4 tbsp chopped flat leaf
   parsley, to taste
salt and freshly ground black pepper
shaved Parmesan cheese, to serve
serves 4

Variation
Use long grain rice instead of the
pasta, and borlotti beans instead
of cannellini beans.

1 ▲ Heat the oil in a large pan. Add the pancetta, celery, carrots and onion and cook over a low heat for 5 minutes, stirring constantly, until the vegetables are softened.

2 Add the garlic and tomatoes, breaking them up well with a wooden spoon. Pour in the stock. Add salt and pepper to taste and bring to the boil. Half cover the pan, lower the heat and simmer gently for about 20 minutes, until the vegetables are soft.

3 ▲ Drain the beans and add them to the pan with the macaroni. Bring to the boil again. Cover, lower the heat and continue to simmer for about 20 minutes more. Check the consistency and add more stock if necessary. Stir in the parsley and taste for seasoning.

4 Serve hot, sprinkled with plenty of Parmesan cheese. This makes a meal in itself if served with chunks of crusty Italian bread.

Summer Minestrone

Minestrone estivo

This brightly coloured, fresh-tasting soup makes the most of summer vegetables.

Ingredients
45ml/3 tbsp olive oil
1 large onion, finely chopped
15ml/1 tbsp sun-dried tomato paste
450g/1lb ripe Italian plum tomatoes,
   peeled and finely chopped
225g/8oz green courgettes (zucchini),
   trimmed and roughly chopped
225g/8oz yellow courgettes, trimmed
   and roughly chopped
3 waxy new potatoes, diced
2 garlic cloves, crushed
about 1.2 litres/2 pints/5 cups chicken
   stock or water
60ml/4 tbsp shredded fresh basil
50g/2oz/⅔ cup grated Parmesan cheese
salt and freshly ground black pepper
serves 4

1 ▲ Heat the oil in a large pan, add the onion and cook gently for about 5 minutes, stirring constantly, until softened. Stir in the sun-dried tomato paste, chopped tomatoes, courgettes, diced potatoes and garlic. Mix well and cook gently for 10 minutes, uncovered, shaking the pan frequently to stop the vegetables sticking to the base.

2 ▲ Pour in the stock. Bring to the boil, lower the heat, half cover the pan and simmer gently for 15 minutes or until the vegetables are just tender. Add more stock if necessary.

3 Remove the pan from the heat and stir in the basil and half the cheese. Taste for seasoning. Serve hot, sprinkled with the remaining cheese.

Clam and Pasta Soup

Zuppa alle vongole

This soup is a play on the pasta dish - spaghetti alle vongole - *using store-cupboard (pantry)*

ingredients. Serve it with hot focaccia or ciabatta for an informal supper with friends.

Ingredients
30ml/2 tbsp olive oil
1 large onion, finely chopped
2 garlic cloves, crushed
400g/14oz can chopped tomatoes
15ml/1 tbsp sun-dried tomato paste
5ml/1 tsp sugar
5ml/1 tsp dried mixed herbs
about 750ml/1¼ pints/3 cups fish or
    vegetable stock
150ml/¼ pint/ ²/₃ cup red wine
50g/2oz/½ cup small pasta shapes
150g/5oz jar or can clams in
    natural juice
30ml/2 tbsp finely chopped flat leaf
    parsley, plus a few whole leaves,
    to garnish
salt and freshly ground black pepper
serves 4

1 ▲ Heat the oil in a large pan. Cook the onion gently for 5 minutes, stirring frequently, until softened.

2 ▲ Add the garlic, tomatoes, tomato paste, sugar, herbs, stock and wine, with salt and pepper to taste. Bring to the boil. Lower the heat, half cover the pan and simmer for 10 minutes, stirring occasionally.

3 ▲ Add the pasta and continue simmering, uncovered, for about 10 minutes or until al dente. Stir occasionally, to prevent the pasta shapes from sticking together.

Cook's Tip
This soup has a fuller flavour if it is made the day before and reheated.

4 ▲ Add the clams and their juice to the soup and heat through for 3 – 4 minutes, adding more stock if required. Do not let it boil or the clams will be tough. Remove from the heat, stir in the parsley and taste the soup for seasoning. Serve hot, sprinkled with coarsely ground black pepper and parsley leaves.

Tuscan Bean Soup

Zuppa di fagioli alla toscana

There are lots of versions of this wonderful soup. This one uses cannellini beans, leeks,

cabbage and good olive oil - and tastes even better reheated.

Ingredients

45ml/3 tbsp extra virgin olive oil
1 onion, roughly chopped
2 leeks, roughly chopped
1 large potato, peeled and diced
2 garlic cloves, finely chopped
1.2 litres/2 pints/5 cups vegetable stock
400g/14oz can cannellini beans, drained,
     liquid reserved
175g/6oz Savoy cabbage, shredded
45ml/3 tbsp chopped fresh flat
     leaf parsley
30ml/2 tbsp chopped fresh oregano
75g/3oz/1 cup Parmesan cheese, shaved
salt and freshly ground black pepper

For the garlic toasts

30–45ml/2–3 tbsp extra virgin olive oil
6 thick slices country bread
1 garlic clove, peeled and bruised
serves 4

1 ▲ Heat the oil in a large pan and gently cook the onion, leeks, potato and garlic for 4–5 minutes.

2 ▲ Pour the stock into the pan along with the reserved liquid from the cannellini beans. Cover and simmer for 15 minutes.

3 ▲ Stir in the cabbage and beans, with half the herbs, season and cook for 10 minutes more. Spoon about one-third of the soup into a food processor or blender and process until fairly smooth. Return to the soup to the pan, taste for seasoning and adjust as necessary, then heat the soup through for 5 minutes.

4 ▲ Meanwhile make the garlic toasts. Drizzle a little oil over the slices of bread, then rub both sides of each slice with the garlic. Toast until browned on both sides. Ladle the soup into bowls. Sprinkle with the remaining herbs and the Parmesan shavings. Add a drizzle of olive oil and serve with the toasts.

Lentil Soup with Tomatoes

Minestra di lenticchie

A classic rustic Italian soup flavoured with rosemary, delicious served with garlic bread.

Ingredients
225g/8oz/1 cup dried green or
    brown lentils
45ml/3 tbsp extra virgin olive oil
3 rindless streaky (fatty) bacon rashers
    (strips), cut into small dice
1 onion, finely chopped
2 celery sticks, finely chopped
2 carrots, finely diced
2 rosemary sprigs, finely chopped
2 bay leaves
400g/14oz can plum tomatoes
1.75 litres/3 pints/7½ cups
    vegetable stock
salt and freshly ground black pepper
bay leaves and rosemary sprigs,
    to garnish
serves 4

Cook's Tip
Look out for the small green lentils in
Italian groceries or delicatessens.

1 Place the lentils in a bowl and cover
with cold water. Leave to soak for
2 hours. Rinse and drain well.

2 ▲ Heat the oil in a large pan. Add
the bacon and cook for about
3 minutes, then stir in the onion and
cook for 5 minutes until softened.
Stir in the celery, carrots, rosemary,
bay leaves and lentils. Toss over the
heat for 1 minute until thoroughly
coated in the oil.

3 ▲ Tip in the canned plum tomatoes
and stock and bring to the boil. Break
up the tomatoes using a wooden
spoon. Lower the heat, half cover the
pan, and simmer for about 1 hour, or
until the lentils are perfectly tender
without being mushy.

4 Remove the bay leaves, add salt
and pepper to taste and serve with
a garnish of fresh bay leaves and
rosemary sprigs.

Spinach and Rice Soup

Minestra di riso e spinaci

Use very fresh, young spinach leaves to prepare this light and fresh-tasting soup.

Ingredients
675g/1½lb fresh spinach, washed
45ml/3 tbsp extra virgin olive oil
1 small onion, finely chopped
2 garlic cloves, finely chopped
1 small fresh red chilli, seeded and
    finely chopped
115g/4oz/generous 1 cup risotto rice
1.2 litres/2 pints/5 cups vegetable stock
60ml/4 tbsp grated Pecorino cheese
salt and freshly ground black pepper
serves 4

1 Place the spinach in a large pan with
just the water that clings to its leaves
after washing. Add a large pinch of
salt. Heat gently until the spinach has
wilted, then remove from the heat and
drain, reserving any liquid.

2 ▲ Either chop the spinach finely
using a large knife or place in a food
processor and process to a fairly
coarse purée.

3 ▲ Heat the oil in a large pan and
gently cook the onion, garlic and chilli
for 4–5 minutes until softened. Stir in
the rice until well coated, then pour in
the stock and reserved spinach liquid.
Bring to the boil, lower the heat and
simmer for 10 minutes.

4 Add the spinach and season. Cook
for 5–7 minutes more, until the rice is
tender. Check the seasoning and serve
with the Pecorino cheese.

Pasta & Gnocchi

·······························

In Italy, pasta and gnocchi are traditionally served as first courses after the antipasti *and before the second course of fish or meat. Everyday dishes are often simple, served with nothing more than olive oil or butter, grated Parmesan and basil. Outside of Italy there are no hard-and-fast rules, and nowadays people eat pasta and gnocchi whenever they like.*

Cannelloni with Tuna

Cannelloni sorpresa

Children love this pasta dish. Fontina cheese has a sweet, nutty flavour and very good melting qualities. Look for it in large supermarkets and Italian delicatessens.

Ingredients

50g/2oz/¼ cup butter
50g/2oz/½ cup plain (all-purpose) flour
about 900ml/1½ pints/3 ¾ cups hot milk
2 x 200g/7oz cans tuna, drained
115g/4oz/1 cup Fontina cheese, grated
1.5ml/¼ tsp grated nutmeg
12 no-precook cannelloni tubes
50g/2oz/⅔ cup freshly grated
   Parmesan cheese
salt and freshly ground black pepper
fresh herbs, to garnish

serves 4–6

1 ▲ Melt the butter in a heavy pan, add the flour and stir over a low heat for 1–2 minutes. Remove the pan from the heat and gradually add 350ml/12fl oz/1½ cups of the milk, beating vigorously after each addition. Return the pan to the heat and whisk for 1–2 minutes until the sauce is very thick and smooth. Remove from the heat.

2 ▲ Mix the drained tuna with about 120ml/4fl oz/½ cup of the warm white sauce in a bowl. Add salt and black pepper to taste. Preheat the oven to 180°C/350°F/Gas 4.

3 ▲ Gradually whisk the remaining milk into the rest of the sauce, then return to the heat and simmer, whisking constantly, until thickened. Add the grated Fontina and nutmeg, with salt and pepper to taste. Simmer for a few more minutes, stirring frequently. Pour about one-third of the sauce into a baking dish and spread to the corners.

4 ▲ Fill the cannelloni tubes with the tuna mixture, pushing it in with the handle of a teaspoon. Place the cannelloni in a single layer in the dish. Thin the remaining sauce with a little more milk if necessary, then pour it over the cannelloni. Sprinkle with Parmesan cheese and bake for 30 minutes or until golden. Serve hot, garnished with herbs.

Shellfish Lasagne

Lasagne alla marinara

Rich and creamy, this flavoursome lasagne makes a good supper-party dish. You can make the filling in advance and assemble the lasagne on the day.

Ingredients

65g/2 ¹/₂oz/5 tbsp butter
450g/1lb monkfish fillets, skinned and
    diced small
225g/8oz fresh prawns (shrimp), shelled,
    deveined and roughly chopped
225g/8oz/3 cups button (white)
    mushrooms, chopped
40g/1¹/₂oz/3 tbsp plain (all-purpose) flour
600ml/1 pint/2 ¹/₂ cups hot milk
300ml/¹/₂ pint/1¹/₄ cups double
    (heavy) cream
400g/14oz can chopped tomatoes
30ml/2 tbsp shredded fresh basil
8 sheets no-precook lasagne
75g/3oz/1 cup grated Parmesan cheese
salt and freshly ground black pepper
fresh herbs, to garnish

serves 6

1 ▲ Melt 15g/¹/₂oz/1 tbsp of the butter in a large pan, add the monkfish and prawns and sauté over a medium to high heat for 2–3 minutes. As soon as the prawns turn pink, transfer them to a bowl with a slotted spoon.

2 Add the mushrooms to the pan and sauté for 5 minutes, until the juices run and the mushrooms are soft. Remove with a slotted spoon and add to the fish.

3 Melt the remaining butter in a pan, add the flour and stir over a low heat for 1–2 minutes. Remove from the heat and gradually whisk in the milk. Return to the heat and bring to the boil, whisking. Lower the heat and simmer for 2–3 minutes, whisking occasionally, until thick. Whisk in the cream and cook over a low heat for 2 minutes more.

4 ▲ Remove the sauce from the heat and stir in the fish and mushroom mixture with all the juices that have collected in the bowl. Add salt to taste, and plenty of pepper. Preheat the oven to 190°C/375°F/Gas 5.

5 Spread half the chopped tomatoes over the bottom of a baking dish. Sprinkle with half the basil and season to taste. Ladle one-third of the sauce over the tomatoes.

6 ▲ Cover the sauce with four lasagne sheets. Spread the remaining tomatoes over the lasagne and sprinkle with the remaining basil and salt and pepper to taste. Ladle half the remaining sauce over. Arrange the remaining lasagne sheets on top, top with the remaining sauce and cover with the cheese.

7 Bake for 30–40 minutes until golden and bubbling. Serve hot, garnished with fresh herbs.

Spaghetti with Clams and White Wine

Spaghetti alle vongole

Raid the pantry to make this quick and easy pasta dish with an intense flavour.

Ingredients

30ml/2 tbsp olive oil
1 onion, very finely chopped
2 garlic cloves, crushed
400g/14oz can chopped tomatoes
150ml/¹/₄ pint/ ²/₃ cup dry white wine
150g/5oz jar or can clams in natural juice,
    drained with juice reserved
350g/12oz dried spaghetti
30ml/2 tbsp finely chopped fresh
    flat leaf parsley, plus extra
    to garnish
salt and freshly ground black pepper
serves 4

Cook's Tip

The tomato sauce can be made several
days ahead of time and kept in the
refrigerator. Add the clams and heat
them through at the last minute
– but don't let them boil or they
will toughen.

1 Heat the oil in a pan, add the onion
and cook gently, stirring frequently, for
about 5 minutes until softened, but
not brown.

2 ▲ Stir in the garlic, tomatoes, wine
and reserved clam juice, with salt to
taste. Add a generous grinding of black
pepper. Bring to the boil, stirring, then
lower the heat. Cover the pan and
simmer the sauce gently for about
20 minutes, stirring from time to time.

3 ▲ Meanwhile, coil the spaghetti into
a large pan of rapidly boiling salted
water and cook for 12 minutes or until
it is al dente.

4 Drain the spaghetti. Add the clams
and parsley to the tomato sauce and
heat through, then taste for seasoning.
Tip the spaghetti into a warmed serving
bowl, pour over the tomato sauce and
toss to mix. Serve immediately,
sprinkled with more parsley.

Pasta with Cream and Parmesan

Pasta Alfredo

*This popular classic originated in Rome. It is incredibly quick and simple to make – perfect
for a midweek supper when time is short.*

Ingredients

350g/12oz dried fettuccine
25g/1oz/2 tbsp butter
300ml/¹/₂ pint/1¹/₄ cups double
    (heavy) cream
50g/2oz/ ²/₃ cup grated Parmesan cheese,
    plus extra to serve
30ml/2 tbsp finely chopped fresh flat leaf
    parsley, plus extra to garnish
salt and freshly ground black pepper
serves 3–4

Variation

In Rome, fettuccine would
traditionally be served with this sauce,
but tagliatelle can be used if you
prefer. Pasta shapes, such as penne,
rigatoni or farfalle, are also suitable.

1 Cook the fettuccine in a large pan
of rapidly boiling salted water for
8–10 minutes or until al dente.

2 ▲ Meanwhile, melt the butter in a
large flameproof casserole and add the
cream and Parmesan, with salt and
pepper to taste. Stir over a medium
heat until the cheese has melted and
the sauce has thickened.

3 ▲ Drain the fettuccine thoroughly
and add it to the sauce with the
chopped parsley. Fold the pasta
and sauce together over a medium
heat until the strands of pasta are
generously coated. Grind more
black pepper over and garnish with
the extra chopped parsley. Serve
immediately, with a bowl of grated
Parmesan handed round separately.

Tagliatelle with Bolognese Sauce

Tagliatelle alla bolognese

Most people think of bolognese sauce, the famous ragù from Bologna, as being served with spaghetti. To be absolutely correct, it should be served with tagliatelle.

Ingredients

30ml/2 tbsp olive oil
1 onion, finely chopped
1 carrot, finely chopped
1 celery stick, finely chopped
1 garlic clove, crushed
350g/12oz minced (ground) beef
150ml/¼ pint/⅔ cup red wine
250ml/8fl oz/1 cup milk
400g/14oz can chopped tomatoes
15ml/1 tbsp sun-dried tomato paste
350g/12oz dried tagliatelle
salt and freshly ground black pepper
shredded fresh basil, to garnish
grated Parmesan cheese, to serve
serves 4

1 ▲ Heat the oil in a large pan. Add the onion, carrot, celery and garlic and cook gently, stirring frequently, for about 10 minutes until softened. Do not allow the vegetables to colour.

2 ▲ Add the minced beef to the pan with the vegetables and cook over a medium heat until the meat changes colour, stirring constantly and breaking up any lumps with a wooden spoon.

3 ▲ Pour in the wine. Stir frequently until it has evaporated, then add the milk and continue cooking and stirring until this has evaporated, too.

Cook's Tip

Don't skimp on the cooking time – it is essential for a full-flavoured bolognese sauce. Some Italian cooks insist on cooking it for 3–4 hours, so the longer the better.

4 ▲ Stir in the tomatoes and tomato paste, with salt and pepper to taste. Simmer the sauce uncovered, over the lowest possible heat for at least 45 minutes.

5 Cook the tagliatelle in a large pan of rapidly boiling salted water for 8–10 minutes or until al dente. Drain thoroughly and tip into a warmed large bowl. Pour over the sauce and toss to combine. Garnish with basil and serve immediately, with Parmesan cheese handed separately.

Penne with Pancetta and Cream

Penne alla carbonara

This simple yet delicious recipe makes a gloriously rich supper dish. Follow it with a simple salad dressed with lemon juice and extra virgin olive oil.

Ingredients

300g/11oz dried penne
30ml/2 tbsp olive oil
1 small onion, finely chopped
175g/6oz pancetta rashers (strips), any
    rinds removed, cut into bitesize strips
1–2 garlic cloves, crushed
5 egg yolks
175ml/6fl oz/¾ cup double (heavy) cream
115g/4oz/1⅓ cups grated Parmesan
    cheese, plus extra to serve
salt and freshly ground black pepper

serves 3–4

1 ▲ Cook the penne in a large pan of rapidly boiling salted water for about 10 minutes or until al dente.

2 Meanwhile, heat the oil in a large flameproof casserole. Add the onion and cook gently for about 5 minutes, stirring frequently, until softened. Add the pancetta and garlic. Cook until the pancetta is cooked but not crisp. Remove from the heat and set aside.

3 ▲ Put the egg yolks in a jug (cup) and add the cream and Parmesan cheese. Grind in plenty of black pepper. Beat well to mix.

4 ▲ Drain the penne thoroughly, tip into the casserole and toss over a medium to high heat until the pancetta mixture is evenly mixed with the pasta.

5 Remove from the heat, pour in the egg yolk mixture and toss well to combine. Spoon into a large, shallow serving dish, grind a little black pepper over and sprinkle with some of the extra Parmesan. Serve the rest of the Parmesan separately.

Cook's Tip

Serve this dish the moment it is ready or it will not be hot enough. Having added the egg yolks, don't return the pan to the heat or attempt to reheat the pasta and sauce together or the egg yolks will scramble and give the pasta a curdled appearance.

Farfalle with Mushrooms and Cheese

Farfalle boscaiole

Fresh wild mushrooms are very good in this sauce, but they are expensive. To cut the cost,

use half wild and half cultivated, or as many wild as you can afford.

Ingredients

15g/¹/₂oz/1 cup dried porcini mushrooms
25g/1oz/2 tbsp butter
1 small onion, finely chopped
1 garlic clove, crushed
225g/8oz/3 cups fresh mushrooms,
    thinly sliced
a few fresh sage leaves, very
    finely chopped, plus a few whole
    leaves, to garnish
150ml/¹/₄ pint/ ²/₃ cup dry white wine
225g/8oz/2 cups dried farfalle
115g/4oz/¹/₂ cup mascarpone
115g/4oz/1 cup Gorgonzola or torta di
    Gorgonzola cheese, crumbled
salt and freshly ground black pepper
serves 4

5 ▲ Cook the farfalle in a large pan of rapidly boiling salted water for about 10 minutes or according to the packet instructions, until al dente.

Variation

For a lighter sauce, use crème fraîche instead of mascarpone.

6 ▲ Meanwhile, stir the mascarpone and Gorgonzola into the mushroom sauce. Heat through, stirring, until melted. Taste for seasoning. Drain the pasta thoroughly, add to the sauce and toss to mix. Serve immediately, with black pepper ground liberally on top. Garnish with sage leaves.

1 ▲ Put the dried porcini in a small bowl with 250ml/8fl oz/1 cup warm water and leave to soak for about 20–30 minutes. Remove the mushrooms from the liquid and squeeze the porcini over the bowl to extract as much liquid as possible.

2 Strain the liquid and set it aside. Finely chop the porcini.

3 Melt the butter in a large pan, add the onion and chopped porcini and cook gently, stirring for about 3 minutes until the onion is soft.

4 Add the garlic and fresh mushrooms, chopped sage, salt and plenty of black pepper. Cook over a medium heat, stirring frequently, for about 5 minutes or until the mushrooms are soft and juicy. Stir in the soaking liquid and the wine and simmer.

Pasta with Tomato and Chilli Sauce

Pasta all'arrabbiata

This is a speciality of Lazio – the word arrabbiata means rabid or angry, and describes the heat that comes from the chilli. This quick version is made with bottled sugocasa.

Ingredients

500g/1lb sugocasa (see Cook's Tip)
2 garlic cloves, crushed
150ml/¼ pint/⅔ cup dry white wine
15ml/1 tbsp sun-dried tomato purée (paste)
1 fresh red chilli
300g/11oz penne or tortiglioni
60ml/4 tbsp finely chopped fresh
    flat leaf parsley
salt and freshly ground black pepper
freshly grated Pecorino cheese, to serve
serves 4

1 ▲ Put the sugocasa, garlic, wine, tomato paste and whole chilli in a pan and bring to the boil. Cover and simmer gently.

2 ▲ Drop the pasta into a large pan of rapidly boiling salted water and simmer for 10–12 minutes or until al dente.

Cook's Tip

Sugocasa is sold in bottles sometimes labelled 'crushed Italian tomatoes'. It is finer than canned chopped tomatoes and coarser than passata (bottled strained tomatoes), and so is ideal for pasta sauces, soups and stews.

3 ▲ Remove the chilli from the sauce and add half the parsley. Taste for seasoning. If you prefer a hotter taste, chop some or all of the chilli and return it to the sauce.

4 ▲ Drain the pasta and tip into a warmed large bowl. Pour the sauce over the pasta and toss to mix. Serve immediately, sprinkled with grated Pecorino and the remaining parsley.

Three-cheese Lasagne
Lasagne ai tre formaggi

The cheese makes this lasagne quite expensive, so reserve it for a special occasion.

Ingredients
30ml/2 tbsp olive oil
1 onion, finely chopped
1 carrot, finely chopped
1 celery stick, finely chopped
1 garlic clove, crushed
675g/1½lb minced (ground) beef
400g/14oz can chopped tomatoes
300ml/½ pint/1¼ cups beef stock
300ml/½ pint/1¼ cups red wine
30ml/2 tbsp sun-dried tomato paste
10ml/2 tsp dried oregano
9 sheets no-precook lasagne
3 x 150g/5oz packets mozzarella cheese,
    thinly sliced
450g/1lb/2 cups ricotta cheese
115g/4oz Parmesan cheese, grated
salt and freshly ground black pepper
serves 6–8

1 Heat the oil and gently cook the onion, carrot, celery and garlic, stirring for 10 minutes, until softened.

2 Add the beef and cook until it changes colour, stirring constantly and breaking up the meat.

3 ▲ Add the tomatoes, stock, wine, tomato paste, oregano and salt and pepper and bring to the boil, stirring. Cover, lower the heat and simmer gently for 1 hour, stirring occasionally.

4 ▲ Preheat the oven to 190°C/375°F/ Gas 5. Check for seasoning, then ladle one-third of the meat sauce into a 23 x 33cm/9 x 13in baking dish and cover with three sheets of lasagne. Arrange one-third of the mozzarella slices over the top, dot with one-third of the ricotta, then sprinkle with one-third of the Parmesan.

5 Repeat these layers twice, then bake for 40 minutes. Leave to cool for 10 minutes before serving.

Tortiglioni with Spicy Sausage Sauce
Tortiglioni alla siciliana

This heady pasta dish is not for the faint-hearted. Serve it with a robust Sicilian red wine.

Ingredients
30ml/2 tbsp olive oil
1 onion, finely chopped
1 celery stick, finely chopped
2 large garlic cloves, crushed
1 fresh red chilli, seeded and chopped
450g/1lb ripe Italian plum tomatoes,
    peeled and finely chopped
30ml/2 tbsp tomato purée (paste)
150ml/¼ pint/⅔ cup red wine
5ml/1 tsp sugar
300g/11oz dried tortiglioni
175g/6oz spicy salami, rind removed
salt and freshly ground black pepper
30ml/2 tbsp chopped fresh parsley,
    to garnish
grated Parmesan cheese, to serve
serves 4

Cook's Tip
Buy the salami for this dish in one piece so that you can chop it into large chunks.

1 ▲ Heat the oil, then add the onion, celery, garlic and chilli and cook gently, stirring frequently, for about 10 minutes until softened.

2 Add the tomatoes, tomato purée, wine, sugar and salt and pepper to taste and bring to the boil, stirring. Lower the heat, cover and simmer gently, stirring occasionally, for about 20 minutes. Add a few spoonfuls of water from time to time if the sauce becomes too thick.

3 ▲ Meanwhile, drop the pasta into a large pan of rapidly boiling salted water and simmer, uncovered, for 10 - 12 minutes.

4 Chop the salami into bitesize chunks and add to the sauce. Heat through, then taste for seasoning.

5 Drain the pasta, tip it into a large bowl, then pour the sauce over and toss to mix. Scatter over the parsley and serve with grated Parmesan.

Pasta and Bolognese Bake

Pasticcio

Pasticcio is Italian for pie, and in some regions this is made with a pastry topping. This simple version makes a great family supper because it's such a favourite with children.

Ingredients
225g/8oz dried conchiglie
1 quantity hot Bolognese Sauce (see
     Tagliatelle with Bolognese Sauce
     page 158)
salt and freshly ground black pepper

For the white sauce
50g/2oz/¼ cup butter
50g/2oz/½ cup plain (all-purpose) flour
750ml/1¼ pints/3 cups milk
75g/3oz/1 cup grated Parmesan cheese
1 egg, beaten
a good pinch of grated nutmeg
mixed salad leaves, to serve
serves 4

1 Cook the conchiglie in a large pan of rapidly boiling salted water for 10–12 minutes or until al dente.

2 Meanwhile, make the white sauce. Melt the butter in a pan until foaming, add the flour and stir over a low heat for 1–2 minutes. Remove the pan from the heat and gradually whisk in the milk. Return the pan to the heat and bring to the boil, whisking constantly. Lower the heat and simmer for 2–3 minutes, whisking occasionally, until the sauce thickens. Remove the pan from the heat.

3 ▲ Preheat the oven to 190°C/375°F/ Gas 5. Drain the pasta thoroughly, transfer it to a 20 x 30cm/8 x 12in baking dish and mix in the hot bolognese sauce. Level the surface.

4 ▲ Stir about two-thirds of the Parmesan into the white sauce, then stir in the beaten egg and nutmeg, with salt and pepper to taste.

5 Pour over the pasta and sauce and sprinkle with the remaining Parmesan. Bake for 20 minutes or until golden and bubbling. Serve hot, straight from the dish. Add a salad garnish to each plate.

Cook's Tip
This recipe is a good way of using up leftover bolognese sauce and cooked pasta – the quantities do not need to be exact.

Pasta with Aubergines

Pasta alla Norma

This Sicilian recipe is traditionally made from fried aubergines. This version is lighter as the aubergines are roasted. It is a great make-ahead family dish.

Ingredients

2 medium aubergines (eggplants), about
    225g/8oz each, diced small
45ml/3 tbsp olive oil
275g/10oz dried macaroni or fusilli
50g/2oz/²/₃ cup grated Pecorino cheese
salt and freshly ground black pepper
shredded fresh basil leaves, to garnish
crusty bread, to serve

For the tomato sauce

30ml/2 tbsp olive oil
1 onion, finely chopped
400g/14oz can chopped tomatoes
    or 400g/14oz passata (bottled
    strained tomatoes)
serves 4

Cook's Tip

In Sicily, a cheese called ricotta salata is used for this recipe. This is a matured salted ricotta that is grated. It is unlikely that you will find ricotta salata outside Sicily; Pecorino is the best substitute.

1 Soak the diced aubergine in a bowl of cold salted water for 30 minutes.

2 Meanwhile, preheat the oven to 220°C/425°F/Gas 7. Make the sauce. Heat the oil in a large pan, add the onion and cook gently for about 3 minutes until softened. Add the tomatoes, and season. Bring to the boil, lower the heat, cover and simmer for about 20 minutes. Stir the sauce and add a few spoonfuls of water from time to time, to prevent it from becoming too thick. Remove from the heat.

3 ▲ Drain the aubergines and pat dry. Spread out in a roasting pan, add the oil and toss to coat. Bake the aubergines for 20–25 minutes, turning every 4–5 minutes so that they brown evenly.

4 Cook the pasta in a large pan of rapidly boiling salted water for 10–12 minutes or until al dente. Reheat the tomato sauce.

5 ▲ Drain the pasta and add it to the tomato sauce, with half the roasted aubergines and half the Pecorino. Toss to mix, then taste for seasoning.

6 Spoon the pasta and sauce mixture into a warmed large serving dish and top with the remaining roasted aubergines. Scatter the shredded fresh basil leaves over the top, followed by the remaining Pecorino. Serve with generous chunks of crusty bread.

Spinach and Ricotta Gnocchi

Gnocchi de spinaci e ricotta

The mixture for these tasty little herb dumplings needs to be handled very carefully to achieve light and fluffy results. Serve with a sage butter and grated Parmesan.

Ingredients
6 garlic cloves, unpeeled
25g/1oz mixed fresh herbs, such as
    parsley, basil, thyme, coriander
    (cilantro) and chives, finely chopped
225g/8oz fresh spinach leaves
250g/9oz/generous 1 cup ricotta cheese
1 egg yolk
50g/2oz/²/₃ cup grated Parmesan cheese
75g/3oz/²/₃ cup plain (all-purpose) flour
50g/2oz/¹/₄ cup butter
30ml/2 tbsp fresh sage, chopped
salt and freshly ground
    black pepper
serves 4

1 Cook the garlic cloves in boiling water for 4 minutes. Drain and pop out of the skins. Place in a food processor with the herbs and blend to a purée or mash the garlic with a fork and add the herbs to mix well.

2 ▲ Place the spinach in a large pan with just the water that clings to the leaves and cook gently until wilted. Leave to cool then squeeze out as much liquid as possible. Chop finely.

3 Place the ricotta in a bowl and beat in the egg yolk, spinach, herbs and garlic. Stir in half the Parmesan, sift in the flour and mix well.

Cook's Tip
Squeeze the spinach dry to ensure the gnocchi are not wet and to give a lighter result. The mixture should be fairly soft and will be easier to handle if chilled for an hour before preparing the dumplings.

4 ▲ Using floured hands, break off pieces of the mixture slightly smaller than a walnut and roll them into small dumplings.

5 Bring a large pan of salted water to the boil and carefully add the gnocchi. When they rise to the top of the pan they are cooked; this should take about 3 minutes.

6 ▲ The gnocchi should be light and fluffy all the way through. If not, simmer for a further 1 minute. Drain well. Meanwhile, melt the butter in a frying pan and add the sage. Simmer gently for 1 minute. Add the gnocchi to the frying pan and toss in the butter over a gentle heat for 1 minute, then serve sprinkled with the remaining Parmesan.

Gnocchi with Gorgonzola Sauce

Gnocchi alla gorgonzola

Gnocchi are prepared all over Italy with different ingredients used in different regions. These are gnocchi di patate, *potato dumplings.*

Ingredients
450g/1lb potatoes, unpeeled
1 large egg
115g/4oz/1 cup plain (all-purpose) flour
fresh thyme sprigs, to garnish
salt and freshly ground black pepper

For the sauce
115g/4oz Gorgonzola cheese
60ml/4 tbsp double (heavy) cream
15ml/1 tbsp fresh thyme, chopped
60ml/4 tbsp freshly grated
    Parmesan cheese, to serve
serves 4

1 Cook the potatoes in boiling salted water for about 20 minutes until they are tender. Drain and, when cool enough to handle, remove the skins.

2 ▲ Force the potatoes through a sieve (strainer), pressing through using the back of a spoon, into a mixing bowl. Add plenty of seasoning and then beat in the egg until completely incorporated. Add the flour a little at a time, stirring well with a wooden spoon after each addition until you have a smooth dough. (You may not need all the flour.)

3 Turn the dough out on to a floured surface and knead for about 3 minutes, adding more flour if necessary, until it is smooth and soft and not sticky to the touch.

Cook's Tips
Choose dry, floury potatoes. Avoid new or red-skinned potatoes which do not have the right dry texture.

4 ▲ Divide the dough into six equal pieces. Flour your hands and gently roll each piece between your hands into a log shape measuring 15 - 20cm/ 6 - 8in long and 2.5cm/1in around. Cut each log into 6-8 pieces, about 2.5cm/1 in long, then gently roll each piece in the flour.

5 Form into gnocchi by gently pressing each piece on to the floured surface with the tines of a fork to leave ridges in the dough.

6 ▲ To cook, drop the gnocchi into a pan of boiling water about 12 at a time. Once they rise to the surface, after about 2 minutes, cook for 4-5 minutes more. Remove and drain.

7 Place the Gorgonzola, cream and thyme in a large frying pan and heat gently until the cheese melts to form a thick, creamy consistency and heat through. Add the drained gnocchi and toss well to combine. Serve with Parmesan and garnish with thyme.

Rice, Polenta & Pizzas

In the north of Italy, rice is served as a first course, as
creamy risotto, but you can serve it as a main dish,
with a salad and Italian bread. Polenta, also from the
north of Italy, is most often served with the main
course, especially with meaty casseroles. Pizzas hail
from the south, where they are eaten at any time of
day, the ultimate convenience food.

Risotto with Spring Vegetables

Risotto primavera

This is one of the prettiest risottos, especially if you can get yellow courgettes. Green courgettes can be used instead if the yellow ones are unavailable.

Ingredients

150g/5oz/1 cup shelled fresh peas
115g/4oz/1 cup French (green) beans,
    cut into short lengths
30ml/2 tbsp olive oil
75g/3oz/6 tbsp butter
2 small yellow courgettes (zucchini),
    cut into matchsticks
1 onion, finely chopped
275g/10oz/1½ cups risotto rice
120ml/4 floz/½ cup Italian dry
    white vermouth
about 1 litre/1¾ pints/4 cups boiling
    chicken stock
75g/3oz/1 cup grated Parmesan cheese
a small handful of fresh basil leaves,
    finely shredded, plus a few whole
    leaves, to garnish
salt and freshly ground black pepper
serves 4

1 Blanch the peas and beans in
a large pan of lightly salted boiling
water for 2–3 minutes, until just
tender. Drain, refresh under cold
running water, drain again and set
aside until required.

2 ▲ Heat the oil and 25g/1oz/2 tbsp
of the butter in a medium pan until
foaming. Add the courgettes and cook
gently for 2–3 minutes or until just
softened. Remove with a slotted spoon
and set aside. Add the onion to the
pan and cook gently for about
3 minutes, stirring frequently, until
it is softened.

3 ▲ Stir in the rice until the grains
start to swell and burst, then add the
vermouth. Stir until the vermouth stops
sizzling and most of it has been
absorbed by the rice. Add a few ladlefuls
of stock and season. Stir over low heat
until the stock has been absorbed.

4 Continue cooking and stirring for
20–25 minutes, adding the remaining
stock a few ladlefuls at a time. The
rice should be al dente and the risotto
should have a creamy appearance.

5 ▲ Gently stir in the vegetables,
the remaining butter and about half the
Parmesan. Heat through, then stir in
the basil and taste for seasoning.
Garnish with a few whole basil leaves
and serve hot, with the remaining
grated Parmesan handed separately.

Variations
Shelled broad (fava) beans could be
used instead of the peas and asparagus
tips can be used instead of the French
(green) beans.

Rice with Peas, Ham and Cheese

Risi e bisi

A classic risotto from the Veneto. Although it is traditionally served as an appetizer in Italy,

risi e bisi *makes an excellent supper dish served with hot crusty bread.*

Ingredients
75g/3oz/6 tbsp butter
1 small onion, finely chopped
about 1 litre/1¾ pints/4 cups boiling
    chicken stock
275g/10oz/1½ cups risotto rice
150ml/¼ pint/⅔ cup dry white wine
225g/8oz/2 cups frozen petits pois
    (baby peas), thawed
115g/4oz cooked ham, diced
salt and freshly ground black pepper
50g/2oz/⅔ cup Parmesan cheese,
    to serve
serves 4

1 ▲ Melt 50g/2oz/4 tbsp of the butter in a pan until foaming. Add the onion and cook gently for about 3 minutes, stirring frequently, until softened. Have the hot stock ready in an adjacent pan.

2 ▲ Add the rice to the onion mixture. Stir until the grains start to burst, then pour in the wine. Stir until it stops sizzling and most of it has been absorbed, then pour in a little hot stock, with salt and pepper to taste. Stir over a low heat until the stock has been absorbed.

3 ▲ Add the remaining stock, a little at a time, allowing the rice to absorb all the liquid before adding more, and stirring constantly. Add the peas towards the end. After 20–25 minutes, the rice should be al dente and the risotto moist and creamy.

4 ▲ Gently stir in the diced cooked ham and the remaining butter. Heat through until the butter has melted, then taste for seasoning. Transfer to a warmed serving bowl. Grate or shave a little Parmesan over the top and hand round the rest separately.

Saffron Risotto

Risotto alla milanese

This classic risotto is always served with osso buco in Italy, but makes a delicious first course or light supper dish in its own right.

Ingredients
about 1.2 litres/2 pints/5 cups beef or
   chicken stock
a good pinch of saffron threads or
   1 sachet of saffron powder
75g/3oz/6 tbsp butter
1 onion, finely chopped
275g/10oz/1½ cups risotto rice
75g/3oz/1 cup grated Parmesan cheese
salt and freshly ground black pepper
serves 4

1 Bring the stock to the boil, then reduce to a low simmer. Ladle a little stock into a small bowl. Add the saffron threads or powder and leave to infuse.

2 Melt 50g/2oz/4 tbsp of the butter in a large pan until foaming. Add the finely chopped onion and cook gently for about 3 minutes, stirring frequently, until softened.

3 Add the rice. Stir until the grains start to swell and burst, then add a few ladlefuls of the stock, with the saffron liquid. Season to taste. Stir over a low heat until the stock is absorbed.

4 Add the remaining stock, a few ladlefuls at a time, allowing the rice to absorb all the liquid before adding more, and stirring constantly. After 20–25 minutes, the rice should be al dente and the risotto golden yellow, moist and creamy.

5 ▲ Gently stir in about two-thirds of the grated Parmesan and the remaining butter. Heat through until the butter has melted, then taste for seasoning. Transfer the risotto to a warmed serving bowl or platter and serve hot, with the remaining grated Parmesan sprinkled on top.

Polenta Elisa

Polenta Elisa

This dish comes from the valley around Lake Como. Serve it solo as a starter, or with a mixed salad and some sliced salami or prosciutto for a midweek supper.

Ingredients
250ml/8 floz/1 cup milk
225g/8oz/2 cups pre-cooked polenta
115g/4oz/1 cup grated Gruyère cheese
115g/4oz/1 cup torta di Dolcelatte
   cheese, crumbled
50g/2oz/¼ cup butter
2 garlic cloves, roughly chopped
a few fresh sage leaves, chopped
salt and freshly ground black pepper
prosciutto, to serve
serves 4

1 Preheat the oven to 200°C/400°F/ Gas 6. Lightly butter a 20–25cm/ 8–10in baking dish.

Cook's Tip
Pour the polenta into the boiling liquid in a continuous stream, stirring constantly with a wooden spoon or balloon whisk. If using a whisk, change to a wooden spoon once the polenta thickens.

2 ▲ Bring the milk and 750ml/ 1¼ pints/3 cups water to the boil in a large pan, add 5ml/1 tsp salt, then pour in the polenta. Cook for about 8 minutes or according to the instructions on the packet.

3 Spoon half the polenta into the baking dish and level. Cover with half the grated Gruyère and crumbled Dolcelatte. Spoon the remaining polenta evenly over the top and sprinkle with the remaining cheeses.

4 Melt the butter in a small pan until foaming, add the garlic and sage and fry, stirring, until the butter turns golden brown.

5 ▲ Drizzle the butter mixture over the polenta and cheese and grind black pepper liberally over the top. Bake for 5 minutes. Serve hot, with slices of prosciutto.

Risotto with Four Cheeses

Risotto ai quattro formaggi

This is a very rich dish. Serve it for a dinner-party first course with sparkling white wine, or as a substantial lunch for four people with a simple green salad.

Ingredients

40g/1½oz/3 tbsp butter
1 small onion, finely chopped
1 litre/1¾ pints/4 cups boiling
   chicken stock
350g/12oz/1¾ cups risotto rice
200ml/7 floz/scant 1 cup sparkling dry
   white wine
50g/2oz/½ cup grated Gruyère cheese
50g/2oz/½ cup Fontina cheese,
   diced small
50g/2oz/½ cup Gorgonzola
   cheese, crumbled
50g/2oz/⅔ cup grated
   Parmesan cheese
salt and freshly ground black pepper
fresh flat leaf parsley, to garnish
serves 6

Cook's Tip
If you're feeling extravagant you
can use champagne for this risotto,
although asti spumante is more
often used.

1 Melt the butter in a pan until
foaming. Add the onion and cook
gently, stirring frequently, for about
3 minutes until softened. Have the hot
stock ready in an adjacent pan.

2 ▲ Add the rice and stir until the
grains start to swell and burst, then
add the sparkling wine. Stir until it
stops sizzling and most of it has been
absorbed by the rice, then pour in a
little of the hot stock. Season. Stir
until the stock has been absorbed.

3 Add more stock, a little at a time,
allowing the rice to absorb it before
adding more, stirring constantly for
20–25 minutes until the rice is al dente.

4 ▲ Turn off the heat under the pan,
then add the Gruyère, Fontina,
Gorgonzola and 30ml/2 tbsp of the
Parmesan. Stir gently until the cheeses
have melted, then taste for seasoning.
Tip into a serving bowl and garnish
with parsley. Serve the remaining
Parmesan separately.

Polenta with Mushroom Sauce

Polenta con salsa di funghi

Polenta is made from maize flour. Here, it is cooked until it forms a soft dough, then flavoured with Parmesan. Its subtle taste works well with the rich mushroom sauce.

Ingredients
1.2 litres/2 pints/5 cups vegetable stock
350g/12oz/3 cups polenta
50g/2oz/²/₃ cup grated Parmesan cheese
salt and freshly ground black pepper

For the sauce
15g/¹/₂oz/1 cup dried porcini
   mushrooms
15ml/1 tbsp olive oil
50g/2oz/¹/₄ cup butter
1 onion, finely chopped
1 carrot, finely chopped
1 celery stick, finely chopped
2 garlic cloves, crushed
450g/1lb/6 cups mixed chestnut
   and large flat mushrooms,
   roughly chopped
120ml/4 floz/¹/₂ cup red wine
400g/14oz can chopped tomatoes
5ml/1 tsp tomato purée (paste)
15ml/1 tbsp chopped fresh
   thyme leaves

serves 4

1 ▲ Make the sauce. Put the dried mushrooms in a bowl, add 150ml/ ¹/₄ pint/²/₃ cup of hot water and soak for 20 minutes. Drain the mushrooms, reserving the liquid, and chop roughly.

2 Heat the oil and butter in a pan and add the onion, carrot, celery and garlic. Cook over a low heat for about 5 minutes until the vegetables are beginning to soften.

3 Raise the heat and add the fresh and soaked dried mushrooms to the pan of vegetables. Cook for 8 – 10 minutes until the mushrooms are softened and golden.

4 ▲ Pour in the wine and cook rapidly for 2–3 minutes until reduced, then add the tomatoes and reserved mushroom liquid. Stir in the tomato purée with the thyme and plenty of salt and pepper. Lower the heat and simmer for 20 minutes until the sauce is rich and thick.

Cook's Tip
The polenta will spit during cooking, so use a long-handled spoon and wrap a towel around your hand to protect it while stirring.

5 ▲ Meanwhile, heat the stock in a large, heavy pan. Add a generous pinch of salt. As soon as it simmers, pour in the polenta in a fine stream, whisking until the mixture is smooth.

6 Cook for 30 minutes, stirring constantly, until the polenta comes away from the pan. Remove from the heat and stir in half the Parmesan and some pepper.

7 Divide among four heated bowls and top each with sauce. Sprinkle with the remaining Parmesan.

Butternut Squash and Sage Pizza

Pizza con zucca e salvia

The combination of the sweet butternut squash, sage and sharp goat's cheese works

wonderfully on this pizza. Pumpkin and winter squashes are popular in northern Italy.

Ingredients

15g/¹/₂oz/1 tbsp butter
30ml/2 tbsp olive oil
2 shallots, finely chopped
1 butternut squash, peeled, seeded and
    cubed, about 450g/1lb prepared weight
16 sage leaves
1 quantity risen Pizza Dough
    (see page 177)
1 quantity Tomato Sauce (see page 177)
115g/4oz/1 cup mozzarella cheese, sliced
115g/4oz/¹/₂ cup firm goat's cheese
salt and freshly ground black pepper
serves 4

1 ▲ Preheat the oven to 200°C/400°F/
Gas 6. Oil four baking sheets. Put the
butter and oil in a roasting pan and
heat in the oven for a few minutes.
Add the shallots, squash and half the
sage leaves. Toss to coat. Roast for
15–20 minutes until tender.

2 ▲ Raise the oven temperature to
220°C/425°F/Gas 7. Divide the pizza
dough into four equal pieces and roll
out each piece on a lightly floured
surface to a 25cm/10in round.

3 ▲ Transfer each pizza dough round
to a separate baking sheet and spread
with the tomato sauce, leaving a
1cm/¹/₂in border all around. Spoon the
squash and shallot mixture over the
top of the tomato sauce.

4 ▲ Arrange the slices of mozzarella
over the squash mixture and crumble
the goat's cheese over. Sprinkle the
remaining sage leaves over and season.
Bake for 15–20 minutes until the cheese
has melted and the crust is golden.

Ricotta and Fontina Pizza

Pizza con ricotta e fontina

The earthy mixed mushrooms' flavours are delicious when combined with the creamy cheeses in this hearty and sustaining pizza.

Ingredients
For the pizza dough
2.5ml/¹/₂ tsp active dried yeast
a pinch of sugar
450g/1lb/4 cups strong white bread flour
5ml/1 tsp salt
30ml/2 tbsp olive oil

For the tomato sauce
400g/14oz can chopped tomatoes
150ml/¹/₄ pint/²/₃ cup passata (bottled
    strained tomatoes)
1 large garlic clove, finely chopped
5ml/1 tsp dried oregano
1 bay leaf
10ml/2 tsp malt vinegar
salt and freshly ground black pepper

For the topping
30ml/2 tbsp olive oil
1 garlic clove, finely chopped
350g/12oz/4 cups mixed mushrooms
    (chestnut, flat or button (white)), sliced
30ml/2 tbsp chopped fresh oregano, plus
    whole leaves, to garnish
250g/9oz/generous 1 cup ricotta cheese
225g/8oz Fontina cheese, sliced
makes 4 x 25cm/10in thin crust pizzas

1 ▲ Make the dough. Put 300ml/¹/₂ pint/ 1¹/₄ cups warm water in a measuring jug (cup). Add the yeast and sugar and leave for 5–10 minutes until frothy. Sift the flour and salt into a large bowl and make a well in the centre. Gradually pour in the yeast mixture and the oil. Mix to make a smooth dough. Knead on a lightly floured surface for about 10 minutes until smooth and elastic. Place in a floured bowl, cover and leave to rise in a warm place for 1¹/₂ hours.

2 Meanwhile, make the tomato sauce. Place all the ingredients in a pan, cover and bring to the boil. Lower the heat, remove the lid and simmer for 20 minutes, stirring occasionally, until reduced.

3 ▲ Make the topping. Heat the oil in a frying pan. Add the garlic and mushrooms, with salt and pepper to taste. Cook, stirring, for about 5 minutes or until the mushrooms are tender and golden. Set aside.

4 ▲ Preheat the oven to 220°C/425°F/ Gas 7. Brush four baking sheets with oil. Knead the dough for 2 minutes, then divide into four equal pieces. Roll out each piece to a 25cm/10in round and place on a baking sheet.

5 Spoon the tomato sauce over each dough round. Brush the edge with a little olive oil. Add the mushrooms, oregano and cheese. Bake for about 15 minutes until golden brown and crisp. Sprinkle over the oregano leaves.

Fried Pizza Pasties

Panzerotti

These tasty little morsels are served all over central and southern Italy as a snack food or as part of a hot antipasti. Although similar to calzone they are fried instead of baked.

Ingredients
$^1/_2$ quantity risen Pizza Dough
   (see page 177)
$^1/_2$ quantity Tomato Sauce (see page 177)
225g/8oz mozzarella cheese, chopped
115g/4oz Italian salami, thinly sliced
a handful of fresh basil leaves, torn
sunflower oil, for deep-frying
salt and freshly ground black pepper
serves 4

Cook's Tip
To test that the oil is ready, carefully drop a piece of bread into the oil. If it sizzles instantly, the oil is ready.

1 Preheat the oven to 200°C/400°F/ Gas 6. Brush two baking sheets with oil. Divide the dough into 12 and roll out each to a 10cm/4in round.

2 ▲ Spread the centre of each pizza dough round with a little of the tomato sauce, leaving sufficient border all round for sealing the pasty, then top with a few pieces of mozzarella and a few salami slices. Sprinkle with salt and freshly ground black pepper and add a few fresh basil leaves to each round.

3 ▲ Brush the edges of the dough rounds with a little water, then fold over and press together to seal.

4 Heat oil to a depth of about 10cm/4in in a heavy pan. When hot, deep-fry the pasties, a few at a time, for 8–10 minutes until golden. Drain on kitchen paper and serve hot.

Sicilian Pizza

Pizza alla siciliana

This robust-flavoured pizza is topped with mozzarella and Pecorino cheeses.

Ingredients
1 small aubergine (eggplant), thinly sliced
30ml/2 tbsp olive oil
$^1/_2$ quantity risen Pizza Dough
   (see page 177)
$^1/_2$ quantity Tomato Sauce (see page 177)
175g/6oz mozzarella cheese, sliced
50g/2oz/$^1/_2$ cup pitted black olives
15ml/1 tbsp drained capers
60ml/4 tbsp grated Pecorino cheese
salt and freshly ground black pepper
serves 2

Cook's Tip
For best results choose olives that have been marinated in extra virgin olive oil and flavoured with herbs and garlic.

1 ▲ Preheat the oven to 200°C/400°F/ Gas 6. Brush one or two baking trays with oil. Brush the aubergine slices with olive oil and arrange them on the baking tray(s). Bake for 10–15 minutes, turning once, until browned and tender. Remove the aubergine slices from the baking tray(s) and drain on kitchen paper.

2 Raise the oven temperature to 220°C/425°F/Gas 7. Roll out the pizza dough to two 25cm/10 in rounds. Transfer to baking sheets and spread with the tomato sauce.

3 ▲ Pile the aubergine slices on top of the tomato sauce and cover with the mozzarella. Dot with the black olives and capers. Sprinkle the Pecorino cheese liberally over the top, and season with plenty of salt and pepper. Bake for 15–20 minutes, until the crust on each pizza is golden.

Fish & Shellfish

Italy has such an extensive coastline – and so many lakes, rivers and streams – that it is small wonder that fish and shellfish are so popular. Of course there are many different types that are unique to the country itself, but the most common varieties are available outside Italy. Cooking methods are very simple and quick, and any accompanying sauces light and fresh.

Monkfish with Tomato and Olive Sauce

Pesce alla calabrese

This dish comes from the coast of Calabria in southern Italy. Garlic-flavoured mashed potato is delicious with its robust sauce.

Ingredients

450g/1lb fresh mussels, scrubbed
a few fresh basil sprigs
2 garlic cloves, roughly chopped
300ml/½ pint/1¼ cups dry white wine
30ml/2 tbsp olive oil
15g/½oz/1 tbsp butter
900g/2lb monkfish fillets, skinned and
    cut into large chunks
1 onion, finely chopped
500g/1¼lb jar sugocasa or passata
    (bottled strained tomatoes)
15ml/1 tbsp sun-dried tomato paste
115g/4oz/1 cup pitted black olives
salt and freshly ground black pepper
extra fresh basil leaves, to garnish
serves 4

1 ▲ Put the mussels in a flameproof casserole with the basil, garlic and wine. Cover and bring to the boil. Lower the heat and simmer for 5 minutes, shaking the pan often. Remove the mussels, discarding any that fail to open. Strain the cooking liquid and reserve.

2 ▲ Heat the oil and butter until foaming, add the monkfish pieces and sauté over a medium heat until they just change colour. Remove.

3 ▲ Add the onion to the juices in the casserole and cook gently for about 5 minutes, stirring frequently, until softened. Add the sugocasa or passata, the reserved cooking liquid from the mussels and the tomato paste. Season with salt and pepper to taste. Bring to the boil, stirring, then lower the heat, cover and simmer for 20 minutes, stirring occasionally.

4 ▲ Pull off and discard the top shells from the mussels. Add the monkfish pieces to the tomato sauce and cook gently for 5 minutes. Gently stir in the olives and remaining basil, then taste for seasoning. Place the mussels in their half shells on top of the sauce, cover the pan and heat the mussels through for 1–2 minutes. Serve immediately, garnished with basil.

Chargrilled Squid

If you like your food hot, chop some – or all – of the chilli seeds with the flesh. If not, cut the chillies in half lengthways, scrape out the seeds and discard them before chopping the flesh.

Ingredients

2 whole prepared squid, with tentacles
75ml/5 tbsp olive oil
30ml/2 tbsp balsamic vinegar
2 fresh red chillies, finely chopped
60ml/4 tbsp dry white wine
salt and freshly ground black pepper
hot cooked risotto rice, to serve
sprigs of fresh parsley, to garnish
serves 2

3 ▲ Cut the cooked squid bodies into diagonal strips. Pile the hot risotto rice in the centre of heated soup plates and top with the strips of squid, arranging them criss-cross fashion. Keep hot.

4 ▲ Add the chopped tentacles and chillies to the pan and toss over a medium heat for 2 minutes. Stir in the wine, then drizzle over the squid and rice. Garnish with the parsley and serve immediately.

1 ▲ Make a lengthways cut down the body of each squid, then open out the body flat. Score the flesh on both sides of the bodies in a criss-cross pattern with the tip of a sharp knife. Chop the tentacles. Place all the squid in a china or glass dish. Whisk the oil and vinegar in a small bowl. Add salt and pepper to taste and pour over the squid. Cover and leave to marinate for about 1 hour.

2 ▲ Heat a ridged cast-iron pan until hot. Add the body of one of the squid. Cook over a medium heat for 2–3 minutes, pressing the squid with a fish slice to keep it flat. Repeat on the other side. Cook the other squid body in the same way.

Pan-fried Prawns in their Shells

Gamberi fritti in padella

Although expensive, this is a very quick and simple dish, ideal for an impromptu supper with friends. Serve with hot crusty Italian bread to scoop up the juices.

Ingredients
60ml/4 tbsp extra virgin olive oil
32 large fresh prawns (shrimp),
    in their shells
4 garlic cloves, finely chopped
120ml/4fl oz/¹/₂ cup Italian dry
    white vermouth
45ml/3 tbsp passata (bottled
    strained tomatoes)
salt and freshly ground black pepper
chopped fresh flat leaf parsley,
    to garnish
crusty bread, to serve
serves 4

Cook's Tip
Prawns (shrimp) in their shells are sweet and juicy, and fun to eat with your fingers. They can be quite messy though, so provide guests with finger bowls and napkins.

1 ▲ Heat the olive oil in a large, heavy frying pan until just sizzling. Add the prawns and toss over a medium to high heat until their shells just begin to turn pink. Sprinkle the garlic over the prawns in the pan and toss again, then add the vermouth and let it bubble, tossing the prawns constantly so that they cook evenly and absorb the flavours of the garlic and vermouth.

2 ▲ Keeping the pan on the heat, add the passata and season to taste. Stir until the prawns are thoroughly coated in the sauce. Serve immediately, sprinkled with the parsley and accompanied by plenty of hot crusty bread.

Grilled Red Mullet with Rosemary

Triglie al rosmarino

This recipe is very simple – the taste of the cooked red mullet is so good in itself that it needs very little to bring out the flavour.

Ingredients
4 red mullet, cleaned, about
    275g/10oz each
4 garlic cloves, cut lengthways into
    thin slivers
75ml/5 tbsp olive oil
30ml/2 tbsp balsamic vinegar
10ml/2 tsp very finely chopped fresh
    rosemary or 5ml/1 tsp dried rosemary
freshly ground black pepper
coarse sea salt, to serve
fresh rosemary sprigs and lemon
    wedges, to garnish
serves 4

Variation
Red mullet are extra delicious cooked on the barbecue. If possible, enclose them in a basket grill (broiler) so that they are easy to turn over.

1 ▲ Cut three diagonal slits in both sides of each fish. Push the garlic slivers into the slits. Place the fish in a single layer in a shallow dish. Whisk the oil, vinegar and rosemary, with ground black pepper to taste.

2 ▲ Pour over the fish, cover with clear film (plastic wrap) and leave to marinate in a cool place for 1 hour. Put the fish on the rack of a grill (broiler) pan and grill (broil) for 5 – 6 minutes on each side, turning once and brushing with the marinade. Serve hot, sprinkled with salt and garnished with rosemary sprigs and lemon wedges.

Pan-fried Sole with Lemon

Sogliole al limone

The delicate flavour and texture of sole is brought out in this simple, classic recipe. Lemon sole is used here because it is easier to obtain – and less expensive – than Dover sole.

Ingredients
30–45ml/2–3 tbsp plain (all-purpose) flour
4 lemon sole fillets
45ml/3 tbsp olive oil
50g/2oz/¼ cup butter
60ml/4 tbsp lemon juice
30ml/2 tbsp rinsed bottled capers
salt and freshly ground black pepper
fresh flat leaf parsley and lemon wedges,
    to garnish
serves 2

Cook's Tip
It is important to cook the pan juices to the right colour after removing the fish. Too pale, and they will taste insipid, too dark, and they may taste bitter. Take great care not to be distracted at this point so that you can watch the colour of the juices change to a golden brown.

1 ▲ Season the flour with salt and black pepper. Coat the sole fillets evenly on both sides. Heat the oil with half the butter in a large shallow pan until foaming. Add two sole fillets and fry over a medium heat for 2–3 minutes on each side.

2 Lift out the sole fillets with a fish slice and place on a warmed serving platter. Keep hot. Fry the remaining sole fillets.

3 ▲ Remove the pan from the heat and add the lemon juice and remaining butter. Return the pan to a high heat and stir vigorously until the pan juices are sizzling and beginning to turn golden brown. Remove from the heat and stir in the capers.

4 Pour the pan juices over the sole, sprinkle with salt and pepper to taste and garnish with the parsley. Add the lemon wedges and serve immediately.

Three-colour Fish Kebabs

Spiedini tricolore

Don't let the fish marinate for more than an hour. The lemon juice will start to break down the fibres of the fish after this time and it will be difficult not to overcook it.

Ingredients

120ml/4fl oz/½ cup olive oil
finely grated rind and juice of
   1 large lemon
5ml/1 tsp crushed chilli flakes
350g/12oz monkfish fillet, cubed
350g/12oz swordfish fillet, cubed
350g/12oz thick salmon fillet or
   steak, cubed
2 red, yellow or orange (bell) peppers,
   cored, seeded and cut into squares
30ml/2 tbsp finely chopped fresh
   flat leaf parsley
salt and freshly ground black pepper

**For the sweet tomato and
  chilli salsa**

225g/8oz ripe tomatoes, finely chopped
1 garlic clove, crushed
1 fresh red chilli, seeded and chopped
45ml/3 tbsp extra virgin olive oil
15ml/1 tbsp lemon juice
15ml/1 tbsp finely chopped fresh
   flat leaf parsley
a pinch of sugar
serves 4

1 ▲ Put the oil in a shallow glass or china bowl and add the lemon rind and juice, the chilli flakes and pepper to taste. Whisk to combine, then add the fish chunks. Turn to coat evenly.

2 Add the pepper squares, stir, then cover with clear film (plastic wrap) and marinate in a cool place for 1 hour, turning occasionally.

Variation
Use tuna instead of swordfish if you prefer. It has a similar meaty texture and combines well with the other fish.

3 ▲ Thread the fish and peppers on to eight oiled metal skewers, reserving the marinade. Barbecue or grill (broil) the skewered fish for 5 – 8 minutes, turning once.

4 Meanwhile, make the salsa by mixing all the ingredients in a bowl, and seasoning to taste with salt and pepper. Heat the reserved marinade in a small pan, remove from the heat and stir in the parsley, with salt and pepper to taste. Serve the kebabs hot, with the marinade spooned over, accompanied by the salsa.

Roast Sea Bass

Branzino al forno

Sea bass has meaty flesh. It is an expensive fish, best cooked as simply as possible. Avoid elaborate sauces, which would mask its delicate flavour.

Ingredients

1 fennel bulb with fronds, about
    275g/10oz
2 lemons
120ml/4fl oz/½ cup olive oil
1 small red onion, diced
2 sea bass, about 500g/1¼lb each,
    cleaned with heads left on
120ml/4fl oz/½ cup dry white wine
salt and freshly ground black pepper
lemon slices, to garnish

serves 4

1 ▲ Preheat the oven to 190°C/375°F/ Gas 5. Cut the fronds off the top of the fennel and reserve for the garnish. Cut the fennel bulb lengthways into thin wedges, then into dice. Cut one half lemon into four slices. Squeeze the juice from the remaining lemon half and the other lemon.

2 ▲ Heat 30ml/2 tbsp of the oil in a frying pan, add the diced fennel and onion and cook gently, stirring frequently, for about 5 minutes until softened. Remove from the heat.

3 ▲ Make three diagonal slashes on both sides of each sea bass with a sharp knife. Brush a roasting pan generously with oil, add the fish and tuck two lemon slices in each cavity. Scatter the softened fennel and onion over the fish.

Cook's Tip

Farmed or wild sea bass are available all year round from the fishmonger. They are expensive, but well worth buying for a special main course. Sizes vary from the ones used here, which are a very good size for two servings, to 1.5-1.75kg/ 3-4½lb, which take up to 50 minutes to cook.

4 ▲ Whisk the remaining oil, the lemon juice and salt and pepper to taste and pour over the fish. Cover with foil and roast for 30 minutes or until the flesh flakes, removing the foil for the last 10 minutes. Discard the lemon slices, transfer the fish to a heated serving platter and keep hot.

5 Put the roasting pan on top of the stove. Add the wine and stir over a medium heat to incorporate all the pan juices. Bring to the boil, then spoon the juices over the fish. Garnish with the reserved fennel fronds and lemon slices and serve immediately.

Stuffed Swordfish Rolls

Involtini di pesce spada

This is a very tasty dish, with strong flavours from the tomato, olive and caper sauce – and

from the salty Pecorino cheese. If you like, substitute Parmesan cheese, which is milder.

Ingredients
30ml/2 tbsp olive oil
1 small onion, finely chopped
1 celery stick, finely chopped
450g/1lb ripe Italian plum
 tomatoes, chopped
115g/4oz pitted green olives, half roughly
 chopped, half left whole
45ml/3 tbsp drained bottled capers
4 large swordfish steaks, each about
 1cm / ¹/₂in thick and 115g/4oz in weight
1 egg
50g/2oz/²/₃ cup grated Pecorino cheese
25g/1oz/¹/₂ cup fresh white breadcrumbs
salt and freshly ground black pepper
sprigs of fresh parsley, to garnish
serves 4

Cook's Tip
This dish is not for the inexperienced
cook because the pounding, stuffing
and rolling of the fish is quite tricky.
If you prefer, you can omit the stuffing
and simply cook the swordfish steaks
in the sauce.

1 ▲ Heat the oil in a large, heavy frying
pan. Add the onion and celery and
cook gently for about 3 minutes,
stirring frequently. Stir in the tomatoes,
olives and capers, with salt and
pepper to taste. Bring to the boil, then
lower the heat, cover and simmer for
about 15 minutes. Stir occasionally and
add a little water if the sauce becomes
too thick.

2 Remove the fish skin and place each
steak between two sheets of clear film
(plastic wrap). Pound lightly with a
rolling pin until each steak is reduced
to about 5mm/¹/₄in thick.

3 ▲ Beat the egg in a bowl and add
the cheese, breadcrumbs and a few
spoonfuls of the sauce. Stir well to
mix to a moist stuffing. Spread one-
quarter of the stuffing over each
swordfish steak, then roll up into a
sausage shape. Secure with wooden
cocktail sticks (toothpicks).

4 ▲ Add the rolls to the sauce in the
pan and bring to the boil. Lower
the heat, cover and simmer for about
30 minutes, turning once. Add a little
water as the sauce reduces.

5 Remove the rolls from the sauce and
discard the cocktail sticks. Place on
warmed dinner plates and spoon the
sauce over and around. Garnish with
the parsley and serve hot.

Poultry & Meat

······································

The Italians eat a wide variety of different meats, and tastes vary according to region. Veal, pork and poultry are popular all over the country, while beef is farmed and eaten more in the north, and lamb is a great Roman speciality. All meats are eaten as a second course – secondo piatto *– usually simple and served solo, with vegetables to follow.*

Beef Stew with Tomatoes, Wine and Peas

Spezzatino

It seems there are as many spezzatino *recipes as there are Italian cooks. This one traditional is perfect for a winter lunch or dinner. Serve it with boiled or mashed potatoes.*

Ingredients

30ml/2 tbsp plain (all-purpose) flour
10ml/2 tsp chopped fresh thyme or
    5ml/1 tsp dried thyme
1kg/2¼lb braising or stewing steak,
    cut into large cubes
45ml/3 tbsp olive oil
1 medium onion, roughly chopped
450g/1lb jar sugocasa or passata
    (bottled strained tomatoes)
250ml/8fl oz/1 cup beef stock
250ml/8fl oz/1 cup red wine
2 garlic cloves, crushed
30ml/2 tbsp tomato purée (paste)
275g/10oz/2 cups shelled fresh peas
5ml/1 tsp sugar
salt and freshly ground
    black pepper
fresh thyme, to garnish
serves 4

3 ▲ Add the onion to the pan, scraping the base of the pan to mix in any sediment. Cook gently for about 3 minutes, stirring frequently, until softened, then stir in the sugocasa or passata, stock, wine, garlic and tomato purée. Bring to the boil, stirring. Return the beef to the pan and stir well to coat with the sauce. Cover and cook in the oven for 1½ hours.

4 ▲ Stir in the peas and sugar. Return the casserole to the oven and cook for 30 minutes more, or until the beef is tender. Taste for seasoning. Garnish with fresh thyme before serving.

Variation
Use thawed frozen peas instead of fresh. Add them 10 minutes before the end of cooking.

1 ▲ Preheat the oven to 160°C/325°F/ Gas 3. Put the flour in a shallow dish and season with the thyme and salt and pepper. Add the beef cubes and coat evenly.

2 ▲ Heat the oil in a large flameproof casserole, add the beef and brown on all sides over a medium to high heat. Remove with a slotted spoon and drain on kitchen paper.

Meatballs with Peperonata

Polpette di manzo

These delicious light meatballs taste very good with creamed potatoes to soak up the juices.

Use a potato ricer to get them really smooth.

Ingredients

400g/14oz minced (ground) beef
115g/4oz/2 cups fresh white breadcrumbs
50g/2oz/²/₃ cup grated Parmesan cheese
2 eggs, beaten
a pinch of paprika
a pinch of grated nutmeg
5ml/1 tsp dried mixed herbs
2 thin slices of mortadella or prosciutto
    (total weight about 50g/2oz), chopped
vegetable oil, for shallow frying
salt and freshly ground black pepper
snipped fresh basil leaves, to garnish

For the peperonata

30ml/2 tbsp olive oil
1 small onion, thinly sliced
2 yellow (bell) peppers, cored, seeded
    and cut lengthways into thin strips
2 red peppers, cored, seeded and cut
    lengthways into thin strips
275g/10oz/1¹/₄ cups chopped tomatoes or
    passata (bottled strained tomateos)
15ml/1 tbsp chopped fresh parsley

serves 4

1 ▲ Put the minced beef in a bowl. Add half the breadcrumbs and all the remaining ingredients, including salt and ground black pepper to taste. Mix well with clean wet hands. Divide the mixture into 12 equal portions and roll each into a ball. Flatten the meat balls slightly so they are about 1cm/ ¹/₂in thick.

2 Put the remaining breadcrumbs on a plate and roll the meatballs in them, a few at a time, until they are evenly coated. Place on a plate, cover with clear film (plastic wrap) and chill for about 30 minutes to firm up.

3 ▲ Meanwhile, make the peperonata. Heat the oil in a medium pan, add the onion and cook gently for about 3 minutes, stirring frequently, until softened. Add the pepper strips and cook for 3 minutes, stirring constantly. Stir in the tomatoes or passata and parsley, with salt and pepper to taste. Bring to the boil, stirring.

4 Cover and cook for about 15 minutes, then remove the lid and continue to cook, stirring frequently, for 10 minutes more, or until reduced and thick. Taste for seasoning. Keep hot.

5 ▲ Pour oil into a frying pan to a depth of about 2.5cm/1in. When hot but not smoking, shallow fry the meatballs for 10–12 minutes, turning them 3–4 times and pressing them flat with a fish slice. Remove and drain on kitchen paper.

6 Serve the meatballs hot, with the peperonata alongside. Garnish with the basil.

Variation

Instead of minced (ground) beef, used half minced pork and half minced veal.

Veal Shanks with Tomatoes and White Wine   *Osso buco*

This famous Milanese dish is rich and hearty. It is traditionally served with risotto alla milanese, but plain boiled rice goes equally well. The lemony gremolata garnish helps to cut the richness of the dish, as does a crisp green salad – serve it after the osso buco and before the dessert, to refresh the palate.

Ingredients
30ml/2 tbsp plain (all-purpose) flour
4 pieces of osso buco
2 small onions
30ml/2 tbsp olive oil
1 large celery stick, finely chopped
1 medium carrot, finely chopped
2 garlic cloves, finely chopped
400g/14oz can chopped tomatoes
300ml/½ pint/1¼ cups dry white wine
300ml/½ pint/1¼ cups chicken or
    veal stock
1 strip of thinly pared lemon rind
2 bay leaves, plus extra for
    garnishing (optional)
salt and freshly ground black pepper

For the gremolata
30ml/2 tbsp finely chopped fresh
    flat leaf parsley
finely grated rind of 1 lemon
1 garlic clove, finely chopped
serves 4

1 ▲ Preheat the oven to 160°C/325°F/ Gas 3. Season the flour with salt and pepper and spread it out in a shallow bowl. Add the pieces of veal and turn them in the flour until evenly coated. Shake off any excess flour.

2 ▲ Slice one of the onions and separate it into rings. Heat the oil in a large flameproof casserole, then add the veal, with the onion rings, and brown the veal on both sides over a medium heat. Remove the veal shanks with tongs and set aside on kitchen paper to drain.

3 ▲ Chop the remaining onion and add it to the pan with the celery, carrot and garlic. Stir the bottom of the pan to incorporate the pan juices and sediment. Cook gently, stirring frequently, for about 5 minutes until the vegetables soften slightly.

4 ▲ Add the chopped tomatoes, wine, stock, lemon rind and bay leaves, then season to taste with salt and pepper. Bring to the boil, stirring. Return the veal to the pan and coat with the sauce.

5 Cover and cook in the oven for 2 hours or until the veal feels tender when pierced with a fork.

6 Meanwhile, make the gremolata. In a small bowl, mix together the chopped parsley, lemon rind and the chopped garlic.

7 Remove the casserole from the oven and lift out and discard the strip of lemon rind and the bay leaves. Taste the sauce for seasoning.

8 Serve the osso buco hot, sprinkled with the gremolata and garnished with extra bay leaves, if you like.

Cook's Tip
Osso buco is usually widely available from large supermarkets and good butchers. Choose pieces about 2cm/¾in thick.

Calf's Liver with Balsamic Vinegar

Fegato all'aceto balsamico

This quick and easy sweet and sour liver dish is a speciality of Venice. Serve it very simply, with green beans sprinkled with browned breadcrumbs.

Ingredients
15ml/1 tbsp plain (all-purpose) flour
2.5ml/¹/₂ tsp finely chopped fresh sage
4 thin slices of calf's liver, cut into
  serving pieces
45ml/3 tbsp olive oil
25g/1oz/2 tbsp butter
2 small red onions, sliced and separated
  into rings
150ml/¹/₄ pint/²/₃ cup dry white wine
45ml/3 tbsp balsamic vinegar
a pinch of sugar
salt and freshly ground black pepper
fresh sprigs of sage, to garnish
green beans sprinkled with browned
  breadcrumbs, to serve
serves 2

Cook's Tip
Never overcook calf's liver, because it
quickly turns tough. Its delicate flesh
is at its most tender when it is served
slightly underdone and pink – like a
rare steak.

1 ▲ Spread out the flour in a shallow
bowl. Season it with the sage and
plenty of salt and pepper. Turn the
liver in the flour until well coated.

2 Heat 30ml/2 tbsp of the oil with half
of the butter in a wide heavy pan or
frying pan until foaming. Add the
onion rings and cook gently, stirring
frequently, for about 5 minutes until
softened but not coloured. Remove
the onions with a fish slice or slotted
spoon and set aside.

3 ▲ Heat the remaining oil and butter
in the pan until foaming, add the liver
and cook over medium heat for
2–3 minutes on each side. Transfer to
heated dinner plates and keep hot.

4 Add the wine and vinegar to the pan,
then stir to mix with the pan juices
and any sediment. Add the onions and
sugar and heat through, stirring. Spoon
the sauce over the liver, garnish with
sage sprigs and serve immediately
with the green beans.

Veal Escalopes with Lemon

Scaloppine al limone

Popular in Italian restaurants, this dish is very easy to make at home. Rose veal is cheaper and, for many, preferable to traditional veal, so ask your butcher whether they stock it.

Ingredients

4 veal escalopes (US scallops)
30–45ml/2–3 tbsp plain (all-purpose) flour
50g/2oz/¼ cup butter
60ml/4 tbsp olive oil
60ml/4 tbsp Italian dry white vermouth or
    dry white wine
45ml/3 tbsp lemon juice
salt and freshly ground black pepper
lemon wedges and fresh parsley, to garnish
green beans and peperonata, to serve
serves 4

1 ▲ Put each escalope between two sheets of clear film (plastic wrap) and pound until very thin.

2 Cut the pounded escalopes in half or quarters, if you like, and coat them generously in the flour, seasoned with salt and pepper.

3 ▲ Melt the butter with half the oil in a large, heavy frying pan until sizzling. Add as many escalopes as the pan will hold. Fry over a medium to high heat for 1–2 minutes on each side until lightly coloured. Remove with a fish slice and keep hot.

4 Add the remaining oil to the pan and cook the remaining escalopes in the same way.

5 Remove the pan from the heat and add the vermouth or wine and the lemon juice. Stir vigorously to mix with the pan juices, then return to the heat and return all the veal to the pan. Spoon the sauce over the veal. Shake the pan over a medium heat until all of the escalopes are coated in the sauce and heated through.

6 Serve immediately, garnished with lemon wedges and parsley. Lightly cooked green beans and peperonata make a delicious accompaniment.

Variation

Use skinless chicken breast fillets instead of the veal. If they are thick, cut them in half before pounding.

Roast Lamb with Rosemary

Agnello al rosmarino

In Italy, lamb is traditionally served at Easter. This simple roast with potatoes owes its wonderful flavour to the fresh rosemary and garlic. It makes the perfect Sunday lunch at any time of year, served with one or two types of lightly cooked fresh vegetables, such as broccoli, spinach or baby carrots.

Ingredients

¹/₂ leg of lamb, about 1.4kg/3lb
2 garlic cloves, cut lengthways into
    thin slivers
leaves from 4 sprigs of fresh rosemary,
    finely chopped
105ml/7 tbsp olive oil
about 250ml/8fl oz/1 cup lamb or
    vegetable stock
675g/1¹/₂lb potatoes, cut into
    2.5cm/1 in cubes
a few fresh sage leaves, chopped
salt and freshly ground black pepper
lightly cooked baby carrots, to serve
serves 4

1 ▲ Preheat the oven to 230°C/450°F/ Gas 8. Using the point of a sharp knife, make deep incisions in the lamb, especially near the bone, and insert the slivers of garlic.

2 ▲ Put the lamb in a roasting pan and rub it all over with 45ml/3 tbsp of the oil. Sprinkle over about half of the chopped rosemary, patting it on firmly, and season with plenty of salt and pepper. Roast for 30 minutes, turning once.

3 ▲ Lower the oven temperature to 190°C/375°F/Gas 5. Turn the lamb over again and add 120ml/4fl oz/ ¹/₂ cup of the stock.

4 Roast for a further 1¹/₄ –1¹/₂ hours until the lamb is tender, turning the joint two or three times more and adding the rest of the stock in two or three batches. Baste the lamb each time it is turned.

5 ▲ Meanwhile, put the potatoes in a separate roasting pan and toss with the remaining oil and rosemary and the sage. Roast, on the same oven shelf if possible, for 45 minutes, turning the potatoes several times until they are golden and tender.

6 ▲ Transfer the lamb to a carving board, tent with foil and leave in a warm place for 10 minutes so that the flesh firms for easier carving. Serve whole or carved into thin slices, surrounded by the potatoes and accompanied by baby carrots.

Cook's Tip
If you like, the cooking juices can be strained and used to make a thin gravy with stock and red wine.

Pork in Sweet and Sour Sauce

Scaloppine di maiale in agrodolce

The combination of sweet and sour flavours is popular in Venetian cooking, especially with meat and liver. This recipe is given extra bite with the addition of crushed mixed peppercorns.

Ingredients
1 whole pork fillet (tenderloin),
    about 350g/12oz
25ml/1¹/₂ tbsp plain (all-purpose) flour
30–45ml/2–3 tbsp olive oil
250ml/8fl oz/1 cup dry white wine
30ml/2 tbsp white wine vinegar
10ml/2 tsp sugar
15ml/1 tbsp mixed peppercorns,
    coarsely ground
salt and freshly ground black pepper
broad (fava) beans tossed with grilled
    (broiled) bacon, to serve
serves 2

1 ▲ Cut the pork fillet diagonally into thin slices. Place between two sheets of clear film (plastic wrap) and pound lightly with a rolling pin to flatten them evenly.

2 ▲ Spread out the flour in a shallow bowl. Season well and coat the meat.

Cook's Tip
Grind the peppercorns in a pepper grinder, or crush them with a mortar and pestle.

3 ▲ Heat 15ml/1 tbsp of the oil in a wide, heavy pan or frying pan and add as many slices of pork as the pan will hold. Fry over a medium to high heat for 2–3 minutes on each side until crispy and tender. Remove with a fish slice and set aside. Repeat with the remaining pork, adding more oil as necessary.

4 ▲ Mix the wine, wine vinegar and sugar in a jug (cup). Pour into the pan and stir vigorously over a high heat until reduced, scraping the pan to incorporate the sediment. Stir in the peppercorns and return the pork to the pan. Spoon the sauce over the pork until it is evenly coated and heated through.

Chicken with Tomatoes and Prawns
Pollo alla marengo

This Piedmontese dish was created especially for Napoleon after the battle of Marengo.

Versions of it appear in both Italian and French recipe books.

Ingredients
120ml/4fl oz/¹/₂ cup olive oil
8 chicken thighs on the bone, skinned
1 onion, finely chopped
1 celery stick, finely chopped
1 garlic clove, crushed
350g/12oz ripe Italian plum tomatoes,
    peeled and roughly chopped
250ml/8fl oz/1 cup dry white wine
2.5ml/¹/₂ tsp finely chopped rosemary
15ml/1 tbsp butter
8 small triangles of thinly sliced white
    bread, without crusts
175g/6oz large raw prawns
    (shrimp), shelled
salt and freshly ground black pepper
finely chopped flat leaf parsley, to garnish
serves 4

1 ▲ Heat about 30ml/2 tbsp of the oil in a frying pan, add the chicken thighs and sauté over a medium heat for about 5 minutes until they have changed colour on all sides. Transfer to a flameproof casserole.

2 ▲ Add the onion and celery to the frying pan and cook gently, stirring frequently, for about 3 minutes until softened. Add the garlic, tomatoes, wine, rosemary and salt and pepper to taste. Bring to the boil, stirring.

3 Pour the tomato sauce over the chicken. Cover and cook gently for 40 minutes or until the chicken is tender when pierced.

4 ▲ About 10 minutes before serving, add the remaining oil and the butter to the frying pan and heat until hot but not smoking. Add the triangles of bread and shallow-fry until crisp and golden on each side. Drain on kitchen paper.

5 ▲ Add the prawns to the tomato sauce and heat until the prawns are cooked. Taste the sauce for seasoning. Dip one of the tips of each fried bread triangle in parsley. Serve the dish hot, garnished with the bread triangles.

Variation
To make the dish look more like its original, authentic version, garnish it with a few large crayfish or prawns (shrimp) in their shells.

Chicken with Chianti

Pollo al chianti

Together the robust, full-flavoured red wine and red pesto give this sauce a rich colour and almost spicy flavour, while the grapes add a delicious sweetness. Serve the stew with grilled (broiled) polenta or warm crusty bread, and accompany with a piquant salad, such as watercress, tossed with a tasty dressing.

Ingredients
45ml/3 tbsp olive oil
4 part-boned chicken breast
    portions, skinned
1 medium red onion
30ml/2 tbsp red pesto
300ml/¹/₂ pint/1¹/₄ cups Chianti
300ml/¹/₂ pint/1¹/₄ cups water
115g/4oz red grapes, halved lengthways
    and seeded if necessary
salt and freshly ground black pepper
fresh basil leaves, to garnish
rocket (arugula) salad, to serve
serves 4

1 ▲ Heat 30ml/2 tbsp of the oil in a large frying pan, add the chicken breast portions and sauté over a medium heat for about 5 minutes until they have changed colour on all sides. Remove with a slotted spoon and drain on kitchen paper.

Cook's Tip
Use part-boned chicken breast portions, if you can get them, in preference to boneless chicken fillets for this dish as they have a better flavour. Chicken thighs or drumsticks could also be cooked in this way.

2 Cut the onions in half, through the root. Trim off the root, then slice the onion halves lengthways to create thin wedges.

3 ▲ Heat the remaining oil in the pan, add the onion wedges and red pesto and cook gently, stirring constantly, for about 3 minutes until the onion is softened, but not browned.

4 ▲ Add the Chianti and water to the pan and bring to the boil, stirring constantly, then return the chicken portions to the pan and add salt and pepper to taste.

5 Reduce the heat, then cover the pan and simmer gently for about 20 minutes or until the chicken is tender, stirring occasionally.

6 ▲ Add the grapes to the pan and cook over a low to medium heat until heated through, then taste the sauce for seasoning. Serve the chicken hot, garnished with basil and accompanied by the rocket salad.

Variations
Use green pesto instead of red, and substitute a dry white wine such as pinot grigio for the Chianti, then finish with seedless green grapes. A few spoonfuls of mascarpone can be added at the end if you like, to enrich the sauce.

Hunter's Chicken

Pollo alla cacciatora

This traditional dish sometimes has strips of green pepper in the sauce for extra colour and flavour instead of the fresh mushrooms.

Ingredients

15g/¹/₂oz/1 cup dried porcini mushrooms
30ml/2 tbsp olive oil
15g/¹/₂oz/1 tbsp butter
4 chicken pieces, on the bone, skinned
1 large onion, thinly sliced
400g/14oz can chopped tomatoes
150ml/¹/₄ pint/²/₃ cup red wine
1 garlic clove, crushed
leaves of 1 sprig of fresh rosemary,
    finely chopped
115g/4oz/1³/₄ cups fresh field
    (portobello) mushrooms,
    thinly sliced
salt and freshly ground black pepper
fresh rosemary sprigs, to garnish

serves 4

1 ▲ Put the porcini in a bowl, add 250ml/8fl oz/1 cup warm water and soak for 20–30 minutes. Remove from the liquid and squeeze the porcini over the bowl. Strain the liquid and reserve. Finely chop the porcini.

2 ▲ Heat the oil and butter in a large flameproof casserole until foaming. Add the chicken. Sauté over a medium heat for 5 minutes, or until golden. Remove and drain on kitchen paper.

3 ▲ Add the sliced onion and chopped mushrooms to the pan. Cook gently, stirring frequently, for about 3 minutes until the onion has softened but not browned. Stir in the canned chopped tomatoes, wine and the reserved mushroom soaking liquid, then add the crushed garlic and chopped rosemary, along with salt and pepper to taste. Bring to the boil, stirring constantly.

4 ▲ Return the chicken to the pan and coat with the sauce. Cover and simmer gently for 30 minutes.

5 Add the fresh mushrooms and stir well to mix into the sauce. Continue simmering gently for 10 minutes or until the chicken is tender. Taste for seasoning. Serve hot, with creamed potato or polenta, if you like. Garnish with rosemary.

Turkey with Marsala Cream Sauce

Tacchino al marsala

Marsala makes a very rich and tasty sauce. The addition of lemon juice gives it a sharp edge, which helps to offset the richness.

Ingredients
6 turkey breast steaks
45ml/3 tbsp plain (all-purpose) flour
30ml/2 tbsp olive oil
25g/1oz/2 tbsp butter
175ml/6fl oz/ ¾ cup dry Marsala
60ml/4 tbsp lemon juice
175ml/6fl oz/ ¾ cup double (heavy) cream
salt and freshly ground black pepper
lemon wedges, and chopped fresh
    parsley, to garnish
mangetouts (snow peas) and French
    (green) beans, to serve

serves 6

1 ▲ Put each turkey steak between two sheets of clear film (plastic wrap) and pound with a rolling pin to flatten and stretch. Cut each steak in half or into quarters, cutting away and discarding any sinew.

2 ▲ Spread out the flour in a shallow bowl. Season well and coat the meat.

Variations
Try veal or pork escalopes (US scallops) or chicken breast fillets instead of the turkey, and 50g/2oz/¼ cup mascarpone instead of the double cream.

3 ▲ Heat the oil and butter in a wide heavy pan or frying pan until sizzling. Add as many pieces of turkey as the pan will hold and sauté over a medium heat for about 3 minutes on each side until crispy and tender.

4 Transfer to a warmed serving dish with tongs and keep hot. Repeat with the remaining turkey. Lower the heat.

5 ▲ Mix the Marsala and lemon juice in a jug (cup), add to the pan and raise the heat. Bring to the boil, stirring in the sediment, then add the cream. Simmer, stirring, until the sauce is reduced and glossy. Taste for seasoning.

6 Spoon over the turkey, garnish with lemon and parsley and serve with the mangetouts and French beans.

Chicken with Prosciutto and Cheese
Pollo alla valdostana

The name Valdostana is derived from Val d'Aosta, home of the Fontina cheese used here.

Ingredients
2 thin slices of prosciutto
2 thin slices of Fontina cheese
4 part-boned chicken breast portions
4 sprigs of basil
30ml/2 tbsp olive oil
15g/¹/₂oz/1 tbsp butter
120ml/4fl oz/¹/₂ cup dry white wine
salt and freshly ground black pepper
tender young salad leaves, to serve
serves 4

Cook's Tip
There is nothing quite like the buttery texture and nutty flavour of Fontina cheese, and it also has superb melting qualities, but you could use a Swiss or French mountain cheese, such as Gruyère or Emmental. Ask for the cheese to be sliced thinly on the machine slicer, as you will find it difficult to slice it thinly yourself.

1 ▲ Preheat the oven to 200°C/400°F/Gas 6. Lightly oil a baking dish. Cut the prosciutto and Fontina slices in half crossways. Skin the chicken breast portions, open out the slit in the centre of each one, and fill each cavity with half a prosciutto slice and a basil sprig.

2 ▲ Heat the oil and butter in a wide heavy frying pan until foaming. Cook the chicken breast portions over a medium heat for 1-2 minutes on each side until they change colour. Transfer to the baking dish. Add the wine to the pan juices, stir until sizzling, then pour over the chicken and season to taste.

3 Top each chicken breast with a slice of Fontina. Bake for 20 minutes or until the chicken is tender. Serve hot, with tender young salad leaves.

Devilled Chicken
Pollo alla diavola

You can tell this spicy, barbecued chicken dish comes from southern Italy because it has dried red chillies in the marinade. Versions without the chillies are just as good.

Ingredients
120ml/4fl oz/¹/₂ cup olive oil
finely grated rind and juice of
    1 large lemon
2 garlic cloves, finely chopped
10ml/2 tsp finely chopped or crumbled
    dried red chillies
12 skinless, boneless chicken thighs,
    each cut into 3 or 4 pieces
salt and freshly ground black pepper
flat leaf parsley leaves, to garnish
lemon wedges, to serve
serves 4

Cook's Tip
Thread the chicken pieces spiral-fashion on the skewers so they do not fall off during cooking.

1 ▲ Make a marinade by mixing the oil, lemon rind and juice, garlic and chillies in a large, shallow glass or china dish. Add salt and pepper to taste. Whisk well, then add the chicken pieces, turning to coat with the marinade. Cover and marinate in the refrigerator for at least 4 hours, or preferably overnight.

2 ▲ When ready to cook, prepare the barbecue or preheat the grill (broiler) and thread the chicken pieces on to eight oiled metal skewers. Cook on the barbecue or under a hot grill for 6-8 minutes, turning frequently, until tender. Garnish with parsley leaves and serve hot, with lemon wedges for squeezing.

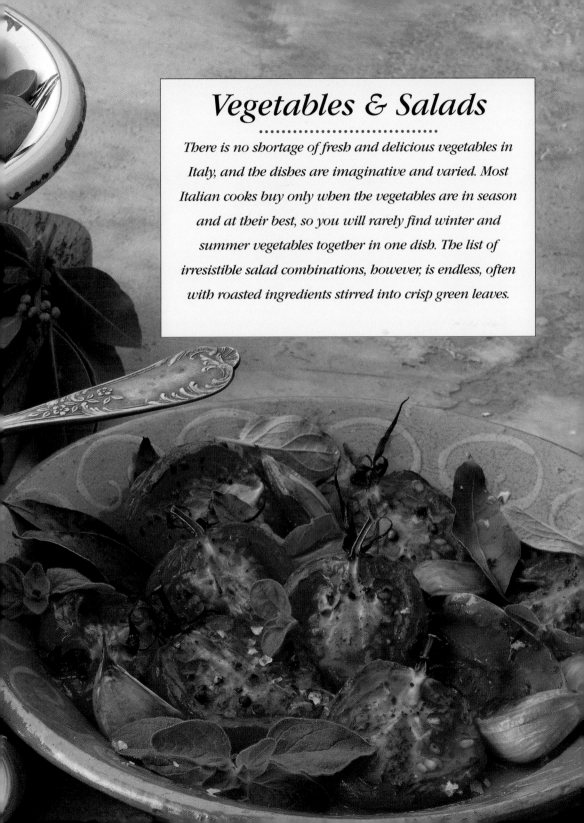

Vegetables & Salads

························

There is no shortage of fresh and delicious vegetables in Italy, and the dishes are imaginative and varied. Most Italian cooks buy only when the vegetables are in season and at their best, so you will rarely find winter and summer vegetables together in one dish. The list of irresistible salad combinations, however, is endless, often with roasted ingredients stirred into crisp green leaves.

Roasted Plum Tomatoes and Garlic

Pomodori al forno

These are so simple to prepare yet taste absolutely wonderful. Use a large, shallow

earthenware dish that will allow the tomatoes to sear and char in a hot oven.

Ingredients
8 plum tomatoes, halved
12 garlic cloves
60ml/4 tbsp extra virgin olive oil
3 bay leaves
salt and freshly ground black pepper
45ml/3 tbsp fresh oregano leaves,
    to garnish
serves 4

Cook's Tip
Use ripe plum tomatoes for this recipe as they keep their shape and do not fall apart when roasted at such a high temperature. Leave the stalks on, if possible.

1 ▲ Preheat the oven to 230°C/450°F/ Gas 8. Select an ovenproof dish that will hold all the tomatoes snugly in a single layer. Place the tomatoes in the dish and push the whole, unpeeled garlic cloves between them.

2 ▲ Brush the tomatoes with the oil, add the bay leaves and sprinkle black pepper over the top. Bake for about 45 minutes until the tomatoes have softened and are sizzling in the pan. They should be charred around the edges. Season with salt and a little more black pepper, if needed. Garnish with oregano and serve.

Green Beans with Tomatoes

Fagiolini al pomodoro

This is a real summer favourite that is ideal for making the most of the best ripe plum tomatoes and French beans when they are in season.

Ingredients

30ml/2 tbsp olive oil
1 large onion, finely sliced
2 garlic cloves, finely chopped
6 large ripe plum tomatoes, peeled,
    seeded and coarsely chopped
150ml/¼ pint/⅔ cup dry white wine
450g/1lb French (green) beans, sliced in
    half lengthways
16 pitted black olives
10ml/2 tsp lemon juice
salt and freshly ground black pepper
serves 4

Cook's Tip

French (green) beans need little preparation and now that they are grown without the string you simply top and tail them.

1 ▲ Heat the oil in a large frying pan. Add the onion and garlic and cook for about 5 minutes until the onion is softened but not brown.

2 ▲ Add the chopped tomatoes, white wine, beans, olives and lemon juice and cook over a gentle heat for a further 20 minutes, until the sauce is thickened and the beans are tender. Season and serve immediately.

Fennel Gratin

Finocchi gratinati

This is one of the best ways to eat fresh fennel. The fennel takes on a delicious, almost creamy, flavour, which contrasts beautifully with the sharp, strong Gruyère.

Ingredients
2 fennel bulbs, about 675g/1½lb
    total weight
300ml/½ pint/1¼ cups milk
15g/½oz/1 tbsp butter, plus extra
    for greasing
15ml/1 tbsp plain (all-purpose) flour
75g/3oz Gruyère cheese, grated
25g/1oz/scant ½ cup dry
    white breadcrumbs
salt and freshly ground black pepper
serves 4

Cook's Tip
Instead of the Gruyère, Parmesan, Pecorino or any other strong cheese would work perfectly.

1 ▲ Preheat the oven to 240°C/475°F/ Gas 9. Discard the stalks and root ends from the fennel. Slice into quarters and place in a large pan. Pour over the milk and simmer for 10–15 minutes until tender. Butter a small baking dish.

2 Remove the fennel pieces with a slotted spoon, reserving the milk and arrange the fennel pieces in the dish.

3 ▲ Melt the butter in a small pan and add the flour, stir well, then gradually whisk in the reserved milk. Stir the sauce until thickened.

4 Pour the sauce over the fennel pieces, sprinkle with the white breadcrumbs and grated Gruyère. Season with salt and black pepper and bake for about 20 minutes, until browned.

Sweet and Sour Onions

Cipolline in agrodolce

Onions are naturally sweet, and when they are cooked at a high temperature the sweetness intensifies. Serve with roasts and meat dishes or as part of an antipasti.

Ingredients
50g/2oz/¼ cup butter
75ml/5 tbsp sugar
120ml/4fl oz/½ cup white wine vinegar
30ml/2 tbsp balsamic vinegar
675g/1½lb small pickling onions, peeled
salt and freshly ground black pepper
serves 4

Cook's Tips
This recipe also looks and tastes delicious when made with either yellow or red onions, which are cut into either thin slices or into chunks. Cooking times will vary, depending on the size of the onion pieces.

1 ▲ Heat the butter in a large pan over a gentle heat. Add the sugar and heat until dissolved, stirring constantly.

2 ▲ Add the vinegars to the pan with the onions and mix together well. Season with salt and pepper and cover and cook over a moderate heat for 20–25 minutes until the onions are a golden colour and soft when pierced with a knife. Serve hot.

Roasted Potatoes with Red Onions

Patate al forno

These mouth-watering potatoes are a fine accompaniment to just about anything. The key is to use small firm potatoes; the smaller they are cut, the quicker they will cook.

Ingredients

675g/1½lb small firm potatoes
25g/1oz/2 tbsp butter
30ml/2 tbsp olive oil
2 red onions, cut into chunks
8 garlic cloves, unpeeled
30ml/2 tbsp chopped fresh rosemary
salt and freshly ground black pepper
serves 4

Cook's Tip

To ensure that the potatoes are crisp, make sure they are completely dry before cooking. Resist the urge to turn the potatoes too often. Allow them to brown on one side before turning. Do not salt the potatoes until the end of cooking – salting beforehand encourages them to give up their liquid, making them limp.

1 ▲ Preheat the oven to 230ºC/450ºF/ Gas 8. Peel and quarter the potatoes, rinse them well and pat thoroughly dry on kitchen paper. Place the butter and oil in a roasting pan and place in the oven to heat.

2 ▲ When the butter has melted and is foaming, add the potatoes, red onions, garlic and rosemary. Toss well then spread out in one layer.

3 Place the pan in the oven and roast for about 25 minutes until the potatoes are golden and tender when tested with a fork. Shake the pan from time to time to redistribute the potatoes. When cooked, season with salt and pepper.

Radicchio and Chicory Gratin

Radicchio e indivia gratinati

Vegetables such as radicchio and chicory take on a different flavour when cooked in this way. The creamy béchamel combines wonderfully with the bitter leaves.

Ingredients

2 heads radicchio, quartered lengthways
2 heads chicory (Belgian endive),
    quartered lengthways
25g/1oz/¹/₂ cup drained sun-dried
    tomatoes in oil, chopped roughly
25g/1oz/2 tbsp butter
15g/¹/₂oz/1 tbsp plain (all-purpose) flour
250ml/8fl oz/1 cup milk
a pinch of grated nutmeg
50g/2oz/¹/₂ cup grated Emmenthal cheese
salt and freshly ground black pepper
chopped fresh parsley, to garnish
serves 4

1 ▲ Preheat the oven to 180°C/350°F/
Gas 4. Grease a 1.2 litre/2 pint/5 cup
baking dish. Trim the radicchio and
chicory and pull away, discarding any
damaged or wilted leaves. Quarter
them lengthways and arrange in the
baking dish. Sprinkle over the sun-
dried tomatoes and brush the leaves
liberally with the oil from the jar.
Season and cover with foil.

2 Bake for 15 minutes, then remove the
foil and bake for a further 10 minutes
until the vegetables are softened.

Cook's Tip

In Italy radicchio and chicory (Belgian
endive) are often grilled (broiled) on
an outside barbecue. To do this,
simply prepare the vegetables as above
and brush with olive oil. Place cut-side
down on the grill (broiler) for 7–10
minutes until browned. Turn and grill
(broil) until the other side is browned,
about 5 minutes longer.

3 ▲ Make the sauce. Place the butter in
a small pan and melt over a moderate
heat. When the butter is foaming, add
the flour and cook for 1 minute, stirring.
Remove from the heat and gradually
add the milk, whisking all the time.

4 Return the pan to the heat and
bring to the boil, then simmer for
2–3 minutes to thicken. Season to
taste and add the nutmeg.

5 Pour the sauce over the vegetables
and sprinkle with the grated cheese.
Bake for about 20 minutes until
golden. Serve immediately, garnished
with parsley.

Potato and Pumpkin Pudding

Tortino di patate e zucca

Serve this savoury pudding with any rich meat dish or simply with a mixed salad.

Ingredients
45ml/3 tbsp olive oil
1 garlic clove, sliced
675g/1½lb pumpkin flesh, cut into
   2cm/¾in chunks
350g/12oz potatoes
25g/1oz/2 tbsp butter
90g/3½oz/scant ½ cup ricotta cheese
50g/2oz/⅔ cup grated
   Parmesan cheese
a pinch of grated nutmeg
4 large (US extra large) eggs, separated
salt and freshly ground black pepper
chopped fresh parsley, to garnish
serves 4

1 Preheat the oven to 200°C/400°F/
Gas 6. Grease a 1.75 litre/3 pint/
7½ cup, shallow, oval baking dish.

Cook's Tip
You may process the vegetables in a
food processor for a few seconds, but
be careful not to over-process, as they
will become very gluey.

2 ▲ Heat the oil in a large, shallow
pan, add the garlic and pumpkin and
cook, stirring often to prevent
sticking, for 15–20 minutes or until
the pumpkin is tender. Meanwhile,
cook the potatoes in boiling salted
water for 20 minutes until tender. Drain,
leave until cool enough to handle, then
peel off the skins. Place the potatoes
and pumpkin in a large bowl and mash
well with the butter.

3 Mash the ricotta with a fork until
smooth and add to the potato and
pumpkin mixture, mixing well.

4 ▲ Stir the Parmesan cheese, nutmeg
and plenty of seasoning into the
ricotta mixture – it should be smooth
and creamy.

5 Add the egg yolks one at a time until
mixed thoroughly.

6 Whisk the egg whites with an
electric whisk until they form stiff
peaks, then fold gently into the
mixture. Spoon into the prepared
baking dish and bake for 30 minutes
until golden and firm. Serve hot,
garnished with parsley.

Fried Spring Greens

Cavolo fritto

This dish can be served as a vegetable accompaniment, or it can be enjoyed simply on its

own, with some warm crusty bread.

Ingredients
30ml/2 tbsp olive oil
25g/1oz/2 tbsp butter
75g/3oz rindless smoked streaky (fatty)
   bacon, chopped
1 large onion, thinly sliced
250ml/8fl oz/1 cup dry white wine
2 garlic cloves, finely chopped
900g/2lb spring greens (collards), shredded
salt and freshly ground black pepper
serves 4

Cook's Tips
This dish would work just as well
using shredded red cabbage and
red wine. Leave to simmer for
10 minutes longer as red cabbage
leaves are slightly tougher than the
spring greens (collards).

1 In a large frying pan, heat the oil
and butter and add the bacon. Fry for
2 minutes, then add the onions and fry
for a further 3 minutes, until the onion
is beginning to soften.

2 Add the wine and simmer vigorously
for 2 minutes to reduce.

3 Reduce the heat and add the spring
greens and salt and pepper. Cook over
a gentle heat for about 15 minutes
until the greens are tender. (Cover the
pan so that the greens retain their
colour.) Serve hot.

Fennel, Orange and Rocket Salad

Insalata di finocchio

This light and refreshing salad is ideal to serve with spicy or rich foods.

Ingredients
2 oranges
1 fennel bulb
115g/4oz rocket (arugula) leaves
50g/2oz/¹/₃ cup black olives

For the dressing
30ml/2 tbsp extra virgin olive oil
15ml/1 tbsp balsamic vinegar
1 small garlic clove, crushed
salt and freshly ground black pepper
serves 4

1 With a vegetable peeler, cut strips of rind from the oranges, leaving the pith behind and cut into thin julienne strips. Cook in boiling water for a few minutes. Drain. Peel the oranges, removing all the white pith. Slice them into thin rounds and discard any seeds.

2 Cut the fennel bulb in half lengthways and slice across the bulb as thinly as possible, preferably in a food processor fitted with a slicing disc or using a mandoline.

3 ▲ Combine the oranges and fennel in a serving bowl and toss with the rocket leaves.

4 ▲ Mix together the oil, vinegar, garlic and seasoning and pour over the salad, toss together well and leave to stand for a few minutes. Sprinkle with the black olives and julienne strips of orange.

Aubergine, Lemon and Caper Salad

Caponata

This cooked vegetable relish is a classic Sicilian dish, which is delicious served as an accompaniment to cold meats, with pasta or simply on its own with some good crusty bread. Make sure the aubergine is cooked until it is meltingly soft.

Ingredients
1 large aubergine (eggplant), about
    675g/1¹/₂lb
60ml/4 tbsp olive oil
grated rind and juice of 1 lemon
30ml/2 tbsp capers, rinsed
12 pitted green olives
30ml/2 tbsp chopped fresh
    flat leaf parsley
salt and freshly ground black pepper
serves 4

Cook's Tips
This will taste even better when made the day before. Serve at room temperature. It will store, covered in the refrigerator, for up to 4 days. To enrich this dish to serve it on its own as a main course, add toasted pine nuts and shavings of Parmesan cheese.

1 ▲ Cut the aubergine into 2.5cm/1in cubes. Heat the olive oil in a large frying pan and cook the aubergine cubes over a medium heat for about 10 minutes, tossing regularly, until golden and softened. You may need to do this in two batches. Drain on kitchen paper and sprinkle with a little salt.

2 ▲ Place the aubergine cubes in a large serving bowl, toss with the lemon rind and juice, capers, olives and chopped parsley and season well with salt and pepper. Serve at room temperature.

Spinach and Roast Garlic Salad   *Insalata di spinaci con aglio arrosto*

Don't worry about the amount of garlic in this salad. During roasting, the garlic becomes

sweet and subtle and loses its pungent taste.

Ingredients
12 garlic cloves, unpeeled
60ml/4 tbsp extra virgin olive oil
450g/1lb baby spinach leaves
50g/2oz/¹/₂ cup pine nuts, lightly toasted
juice of ¹/₂ lemon
salt and freshly ground black pepper
serves 4

Cook's Tip
If spinach is to be served raw in a
salad, the leaves need to be young and
tender. Wash them well, drain and pat
dry with kitchen paper.

1 ▲ Preheat the oven to 190ºC/375ºF/
Gas 5. Place the garlic in a small
roasting pan, toss in 30ml/2 tbsp of
the olive oil and bake for about
15 minutes until the garlic cloves are
slightly charred around the edges.

2 ▲ While still warm, tip the garlic
into a salad bowl. Add the spinach,
pine nuts, lemon juice, remaining
olive oil and a little salt. Toss well and
add black pepper to taste. Serve
immediately, inviting guests to squeeze
the softened garlic purée out of the
skin to eat.

Sweet and Sour Artichoke Salad

Carciofi in salsa agrodolce

Agrodolce is a sweet and sour sauce that works perfectly in this salad. Artichokes are at their best during the summer months.

Ingredients
6 small globe artichokes
juice of 1 lemon
30ml/2 tbsp olive oil
2 medium onions, roughly chopped
175g/6oz/1 cup broad (fava) beans
  (shelled weight)
175g/6oz/1½ cups peas (shelled weight)
salt and freshly ground black pepper
fresh mint leaves, to garnish

For the salsa agrodolce
120ml/4fl oz/½ cup white wine vinegar
15ml/1 tbsp caster (superfine) sugar
handful fresh mint leaves, roughly torn
serves 4

1 ▲ Peel the outer leaves from the artichokes and cut into quarters. Place the artichokes in a bowl of water with the lemon juice.

2 ▲ Heat the oil in a large pan and add the onions. Cook until the onions are golden. Add the beans and stir, then drain the artichokes and add to the pan. Pour in 300ml/½ pint/1¼ cups water and cook, covered, for 10-15 minutes.

3 ▲ Add the peas, season with salt and pepper and cook for a further 5 minutes, stirring from time to time, until the vegetables are tender. Strain through a sieve (strainer) and place all the vegetables in a bowl, leave to cool, then cover and chill.

4 ▲ To make the salsa agrodolce, mix all the ingredients in a pan. Heat gently for 2-3 minutes until the sugar has dissolved. Simmer for 5 minutes, stirring occasionally. Leave to cool. To serve, drizzle the salsa over the vegetables and garnish with mint leaves.

Roasted Pepper and Tomato Salad   *Peperoni arrostiti con pomodori*

This is one of those lovely recipes which brings together perfectly the colours, flavours and textures of southern Italian food. Eat this dish at room temperature with a green salad.

Ingredients
3 red (bell) peppers
6 large plum tomatoes
2.5ml/¹/₂ tsp dried red chilli flakes
1 red onion, finely sliced
3 garlic cloves, finely chopped
grated rind and juice of 1 lemon
45ml/3 tbsp chopped fresh flat
    leaf parsley
30ml/2 tbsp extra virgin olive oil
salt and freshly ground black pepper
black and green olives and extra
    chopped flat leaf parsley,
    to garnish
serves 4

Cook's Tip
(Bell) peppers roasted this way will
keep for several weeks. After peeling
off the skins, place the pepper pieces
in a jar with a tight-fitting lid. Pour
enough olive oil over them to cover
completely. Store in the refrigerator.

1 ▲ Preheat the oven to 220°C/425°F/
Gas 7. Place the peppers on a baking
sheet and roast, turning occasionally,
for 10 minutes or until the skins are
almost blackened. Add the tomatoes
to the baking sheet and bake for
5 minutes more.

2 Place the peppers in a plastic bag,
close the top loosely, trapping in the
steam. Set them aside, with the
tomatoes, until cool enough to handle.

3 ▲ Carefully pull off the skin from
the peppers. Remove the seeds, then
chop the peppers and tomatoes
roughly and place in a mixing bowl.

4 Add the chilli flakes, onion, garlic,
lemon rind and juice. Sprinkle over the
parsley. Mix well, then transfer to a
serving dish. Sprinkle with a little salt,
drizzle over the olive oil and scatter
olives and extra parsley over the top.
Serve at room temperature.

Marinated Courgettes   *Zucchini a scapece*

This is a simple vegetable dish which is prepared all over Italy using the best of the season's courgettes. It can be eaten hot or cold.

Ingredients
4 courgettes (zucchini)
60ml/4 tbsp extra virgin olive oil
30ml/2 tbsp chopped fresh mint,
    plus whole leaves, to garnish
30ml/2 tbsp white wine vinegar
salt and freshly ground black pepper
wholemeal (whole-wheat) Italian bread
    and green olives, to serve
serves 4

Cook's Tip
Carrots, French (green) beans, runner
(green) beans or onions can also be
prepared in this way.

1 ▲ Cut the courgettes into thin
slices. Heat 30ml/2 tbsp of the oil in a
wide heavy pan. Fry the courgettes in
batches, for 4–6 minutes, until tender
and brown around the edges. Transfer
the courgettes to a bowl. Season well.

2 ▲ Heat the remaining oil in the pan,
then add the mint and vinegar and let
it bubble for a few seconds. Pour over
the courgettes. Marinate for 1 hour,
then serve garnished with mint and
accompanied by bread and olives.

Stuffed Aubergines

Melanzane alla liguria

This typical Ligurian dish is spiked with paprika and allspice, a legacy from the days when spices from the East came into northern Italy via the port of Genoa.

Ingredients

2 aubergines (eggplants), about 225g/8oz
each, stalks removed
275g/10oz potatoes, peeled and diced
30ml/2 tbsp olive oil
1 small onion, finely chopped
1 garlic clove, finely chopped
a good pinch each of ground allspice
and paprika
1 egg, beaten
40g/1½oz/½ cup grated Parmesan cheese
15ml/1 tbsp fresh white breadcrumbs
salt and freshly ground black pepper
fresh mint sprigs, to garnish
salad leaves, to serve

serves 4

1 Bring a large pan of lightly salted water to the boil. Add the whole aubergines and cook for 5 minutes, turning frequently. Remove with a slotted spoon and set aside. Add the potatoes to the pan and cook for 20 minutes until soft.

2 ▲ Meanwhile, cut the aubergines in half lengthways and gently scoop out the flesh with a sharp knife and a spoon, leaving 5mm/¼in of the shell intact.

3 Select a baking dish that will hold the aubergine shells snugly in a single layer. Brush it lightly with oil. Put the shells in the baking dish and chop the aubergine flesh roughly.

Cook's Tip

The aubergines (eggplants) can be filled in advance, then covered with foil and kept in the refrigerator. Add the crumb topping just before baking.

4 ▲ Heat the oil in a frying pan, add the onion and cook gently, stirring frequently, until softened. Add the chopped aubergine flesh and the garlic. Cook, stirring often, for 6–8 minutes. Tip into a bowl. Preheat the oven to 190°C/375°F/Gas 5.

5 Drain and mash the potatoes. Add to the aubergine mixture with the spices and beaten egg. Set aside 15ml/1 tbsp of the Parmesan and add the rest to the aubergine mixture, stir in salt and pepper to taste.

6 ▲ Spoon the mixture into the aubergine shells. Mix the breadcrumbs with the reserved Parmesan cheese and sprinkle the breadcrumb mixture over the aubergines.

7 Bake for 40–45 minutes until the topping is crisp. Garnish with mint and serve with salad leaves.

Pepper Gratin

Peperoni gratinati

Serve this simple but delicious dish as an appetizer with a small mixed leaf or peppery salad and some good crusty bread to mop up the juices from the peppers.

Ingredients
2 red (bell) peppers
30ml/2 tbsp extra virgin olive oil
60ml/4 tbsp fresh white breadcrumbs
1 garlic clove, finely chopped
5ml/1 tsp drained bottled capers
8 pitted black olives, roughly chopped
15ml/1 tbsp chopped fresh oregano
15ml/1 tbsp chopped fresh flat
    leaf parsley
salt and freshly ground black pepper
fresh herbs, to garnish
serves 4

1 ▲ Preheat the oven to 200°C/400°F/ Gas 6. Place the peppers under a hot grill (broiler). Turn occasionally until they are blackened and blistered all over. Remove from the heat and place in a plastic bag. Seal and leave to cool.

2 ▲ When cool, peel the peppers. (Don't skin them under the tap as the water would wash away some of the delicious smoky flavour.) Halve and remove the seeds, then cut the flesh into large strips.

3 ▲ Use a little of the olive oil to grease a small baking dish. Arrange the pepper strips in the dish.

4 ▲ Sprinkle the remaining ingredients on top, drizzle with the remaining olive oil and add salt and pepper to taste. Bake for about 20 minutes until the breadcrumbs have browned. Garnish with fresh herbs and serve immediately.

Desserts

••••••••••••••••••••••••••••••••

*An everyday Italian meal usually concludes with
fresh fruit. Desserts are reserved for special
occasions, and are often bought in from the local
pasticceria or gelateria. This is not to say that sweet
things are unpopular, but they are usually eaten
with a cup of espresso coffee at other
times of the day.*

Tiramisu

Tiramisu

The name of this popular dessert translates as 'pick me up', which is said to derive from the

fact that it is so good that it literally makes you swoon when you eat it.

Ingredients
3 eggs, separated
450g/1lb/2 cups mascarpone,
    at room temperature
1 sachet of vanilla sugar
175ml/6fl oz/¾ cup cold, very strong,
    black coffee
120ml/4fl oz/½ cup Kahlúa or other
    coffee-flavoured liqueur
18 savoiardi (Italian sponge fingers)
sifted unsweetened cocoa powder and
    grated dark (bittersweet) chocolate,
    to finish
serves 6–8

1 ▲ Put the egg whites in a grease-free bowl and whisk with an electric mixer until stiff and in peaks.

2 ▲ Mix the mascarpone, vanilla sugar and egg yolks in a separate large bowl and whisk with the electric mixer until evenly combined. Fold in the egg whites, then put a few spoonfuls of the mixture in the bottom of a large serving bowl and spread it out evenly.

3 ▲ Mix the coffee and liqueur together in a shallow dish. Dip a sponge finger in the mixture, turn it quickly so that it becomes saturated but does not disintegrate, and place it on top of the mascarpone in the bowl. Add five more dipped sponge fingers, placing them side by side.

4 ▲ Spoon in about one-third of the remaining mixture and spread it out. Make more layers in the same way, ending with mascarpone. Level the surface, then sift cocoa powder all over. Cover and chill overnight. Before serving, sprinkle with cocoa and grated chocolate.

Stuffed Peaches with Amaretto

Pesche ripiene

Together amaretti and amaretto liqueur have an intense almond flavour, and they make a

natural partner for luscious baked peaches.

Ingredients

4 ripe but firm peaches
50g/2oz amaretti
25g/1oz/2 tbsp butter, softened
25g/1oz/2 tbsp caster (superfine) sugar
1 egg yolk
60ml/4 tbsp amaretto liqueur
250ml/8fl oz/1 cup dry white wine
8 tiny sprigs of basil, to decorate
ice cream or pouring cream, to serve
serves 4

3 ▲ Cream the butter and sugar together in a separate bowl until smooth. Stir in the reserved chopped peach flesh, the egg yolk and half the amaretto liqueur with the amaretti crumbs. Lightly butter a baking dish that is just large enough to hold the peach halves in a single layer.

4 ▲ Spoon the stuffing into the peaches, then stand them in the dish. Mix the remaining liqueur with the wine, pour over the peaches and bake for 25 minutes or until the peaches feel tender when tested with a skewer. Decorate with basil and serve immediately, with ice cream or cream.

1 ▲ Preheat the oven to 180°C/ 350°F/ Gas 4. Following the natural indentation line on each peach, cut in half down to the central stone (pit), then twist the halves in opposite directions to separate them. Remove the peach stones, then cut away a little of the central flesh to make a larger hole for the stuffing. Chop this flesh finely and set aside.

2 ▲ Put the amaretti in a large bowl and crush them finely with the end of a rolling pin.

Zabaglione

Zabaglione

This sumptuous warm dessert is very quick and easy to make, but it does need to be served immediately. For a dinner party, assemble all the ingredients and equipment ahead of time so that all you have to do is quickly mix everything together once the main course is over.

Ingredients
4 egg yolks
65g/2 ¹/₂oz/ ¹/₃ cup caster (superfine) sugar
120ml/4fl oz/ ¹/₂ cup dry Marsala
savoiardi (Italian sponge fingers),
    to serve
serves 6

Cook's Tip
When whisking the egg yolks, make sure that the bottom of the bowl does not touch the water or the egg yolks will scramble.

1 ▲ Half fill a pan with water and bring it to simmering point. Put the egg yolks and sugar in a large heatproof bowl and beat with a hand-held electric mixer until pale and creamy.

2 ▲ Put the bowl over the pan and gradually pour in the Marsala, whisking the mixture until it is very thick and has increased in volume.

3 Remove the bowl from the water and pour the zabaglione into six heatproof, long-stemmed glasses. Serve immediately, with savoiardi.

Lovers' Knots

Cenci

The literal translation of cenci *is 'rags and tatters', but they are often referred to by the more endearing name of lovers' knots. They are eaten at carnival time in February.*

Ingredients
150g/5oz/1 ¹/₄ cups plain (all-purpose) flour
2.5ml/ ¹/₂ tsp baking powder
a pinch of salt
30ml/2 tbsp caster (superfine) sugar,
    plus extra for dusting
1 egg, beaten
about 25ml/1 ¹/₂ tbsp rum
vegetable oil, for deep-frying
makes 24

Cook's Tip
If you do not have a deep-fat fryer with a built-in thermostat, or a deep-fat thermometer, test the temperature of the oil before deep-frying by dropping in a scrap of the dough trimmings – it should turn crisp and golden in about 30 seconds.

1 ▲ Sift the flour, baking powder and salt into a bowl, then stir in the sugar. Add the egg. Stir with a fork until it is evenly mixed with the flour, then add the rum gradually and continue mixing until the dough draws together. Knead the dough on a lightly floured surface until it is smooth. Divide the dough into quarters.

2 ▲ Roll each piece out to a 15 x 7.5cm/ 6 x 3 in rectangle and trim to make them straight. Cut each rectangle lengthways into six strips, 1cm/ ¹/₂in wide, and tie into a simple knot.

3 Heat the oil in a deep-fat fryer to a temperature of 190°C/375°F. Deep-fry the knots in batches for 1–2 minutes, until crisp and golden. Transfer to kitchen paper with a slotted spoon. Serve warm, dusted with sugar.

Fresh Orange Granita

Granita all'arancia

A granita is like a water ice, but coarser and quite grainy in texture, hence its name. It makes a refreshing dessert after a rich main course, or a cooling treat on a hot summer's day.

Ingredients
4 large oranges
1 large lemon
150g/5oz/ ³/₄ cup granulated (white) sugar
475ml/16fl oz/2 cups water
blanched pared strips of orange and
   lemon rind, to decorate
dessert cookies, to serve
serves 6

1 ▲ Thinly pare the rind from the oranges and lemon, taking care to avoid the bitter white pith, and set aside for the decoration. Cut the fruit in half and squeeze the juice into a jug (pitcher). Set aside.

2 Heat the sugar and water in a heavy pan, stirring over a gentle heat until the sugar dissolves. Bring to the boil, then boil without stirring for about 10 minutes, until a syrup forms.

3 ▲ Remove the syrup from the heat, add the pieces of orange and lemon rind and shake the pan. Cover and allow to cool.

4 ▲ Strain the sugar syrup into a shallow freezer container and add the fruit juice. Stir well to mix, then freeze, uncovered, for about 4 hours until slushy.

Cook's Tip
To make the decoration, slice extra orange and lemon rind into thin strips. Blanch for 2 minutes, refresh under cold water and dry before use.

5 ▲ Remove the half-frozen mixture from the freezer and mix with a fork, then return to the freezer and freeze for 4 hours more or until frozen hard.

6 To serve, turn into a bowl and allow to soften for 10 minutes, then break up with a fork again and pile into long-stemmed glasses. Decorate with the strips of orange and lemon rind and serve with dessert cookies.

Apple Cake

Torta di mele

This moist cake is best served warm. It comes from Genoa, home of the whisked sponge.

When whipping the cream, add grated lemon rind – it tastes delicious.

Ingredients

675g/1½lb dessert apples
finely grated rind and juice of
    1 large lemon
4 eggs
150g/5oz/¾ cup caster (superfine) sugar
150g/5oz/1¼ cups plain (all-purpose) flour
5ml/1 tsp baking powder
a pinch of salt
115g/4oz/½ cup butter, melted and
    cooled, plus extra for greasing
1 sachet of vanilla sugar, for sprinkling
very finely pared strips of citrus rind,
    to decorate
whipped cream, to serve
serves 6

3 ▲ Sift half the flour, all the baking powder and the salt over the egg mousse, then fold in gently with a large metal spoon. Slowly drizzle in the butter from the side of the bowl and fold it in gently with the spoon. Sift over the remaining flour, fold it in gently, then add the apples and fold these in equally gently.

4 ▲ Spoon into the prepared tin and level the surface. Bake for 40 minutes or until a skewer comes out clean. Leave to settle in the tin for about 10 minutes, then invert on a wire rack. Turn the cake the right way up and sprinkle the vanilla sugar over the top. Decorate with the citrus rind. Serve warm, with whipped cream.

1 ▲ Preheat the oven to 180°C/350°F/ Gas 4. Brush a 23cm/9in springform tin (pan) with melted butter and line the base with baking parchment. Quarter, core and peel the apples, then slice thinly. Put the slices in a bowl and pour over the lemon juice.

2 ▲ Put the eggs, sugar and lemon rind in a bowl and whisk with a hand-held electric mixture until the mixture is thick and mousse-like. The whisks should leave a trail.

Sicilian Ricotta Cake

Cassata siciliana

The word cassata *is often used to describe a layered ice cream cake. In Sicily, however, it is a traditional cake made of layers of sponge, ricotta cheese and candied peel, imbibed with alcohol, and it looks and tastes truly delicious.*

Ingredients
675g/1½lb/3 cups ricotta cheese
finely grated rind of 1 orange
2 sachets of vanilla sugar
75ml/5 tbsp orange-flavoured liqueur
115g/4oz candied peel
8 trifle sponge cakes
60ml/4 tbsp freshly squeezed
    orange juice
extra candied peel, to decorate
serves 8–10

1 ▲ Push the ricotta cheese through a sieve (strainer) into a bowl, add the orange rind, vanilla sugar and 15ml/ 1 tbsp of the liqueur and beat well to mix. Transfer about one-third of the mixture to another bowl, cover and chill until serving time.

2 ▲ Finely chop the candied peel and beat into the remaining ricotta cheese mixture until evenly mixed. Set aside while you prepare the tin (pan).

3 ▲ Line the base of a 1.2 litre/2 pint/ 5 cup loaf tin with non-stick baking parchment. Cut the trifle sponges in half through their thickness. Arrange four pieces of sponge side by side in the bottom of the loaf tin and sprinkle with 15ml/1 tbsp each of liqueur and orange juice.

4 ▲ Put one-third of the ricotta and fruit mixture in the tin and spread it out evenly. Cover with four more pieces of sponge and sprinkle with another 15ml/1 tbsp each liqueur and orange juice as before.

5 Repeat the alternate layers of ricotta mixture and sponge pieces until all the ingredients are used, soaking the sponge pieces with liqueur and orange juice each time, and ending with soaked sponge. Cover the top of the bowl with a piece of non-stick baking parchment.

6 ▲ Cut a piece of card to fit inside the tin, place on top of the non-stick baking parchment and weight down evenly. Chill for 24 hours.

7 To serve, remove the weights, card and paper and run a metal spatula between the sides of the cassata and the tin. Invert a serving plate on top of the cassata, then invert the two so that the cassata is upside down on the plate. Peel off the lining paper.

8 Spread the chilled ricotta mixture over the cassata to cover it completely, then decorate the top with candied peel, cut into fancy shapes. Serve chilled.

Cook's Tip
Don't worry if the *cassata* has pressed into an uneven shape when turned out. This will be disguised when the cake is covered in the chilled ricotta mixture.

Coffee and Chocolate Bombe

Zuccotto

In Italy the commercial ice cream is so good that no one would dream of making their own

ice cream for this dessert. Assembling the zuccotto *is impressive enough in itself.*

Ingredients
15–18 savoiardi (Italian sponge fingers)
about 175ml/6fl oz/¾ cup
    sweet Marsala
75g/3oz amaretti
about 475ml/16fl oz/2 cups coffee ice
    cream, softened
about 475ml/16fl oz/2 cups vanilla ice
    cream, softened
50g/2oz dark (bittersweet) or plain
    (semisweet) chocolate, grated
chocolate curls and sifted unsweetened
    cocoa powder or icing (confectioners')
    sugar, to decorate
serves 6–8

1 ▲ Line a 1 litre/1¾ pint/4 cup bowl
with a large piece of damp muslin
(cheesecloth), letting it hang over the
top edge. Trim the sponge fingers to
fit the basin, if necessary. Pour the
Marsala into a shallow dish. Dip a
sponge finger in the Marsala, turning it
quickly so that it becomes saturated
but does not disintegrate. Stand it
against the side of the basin, sugared-
side out. Repeat with the remaining
sponge fingers to line the bowl fully.

2 Fill in the base and any gaps around
the side with any trimmings and
savoiardi cut to fit. Chill for about
30 minutes.

Cook's Tip
In Italy there are special dome-shaped
moulds for making this dessert, the
name for which comes from the Italian
word *zucca*, meaning pumpkin. The
shape will not be quite the same when
it is made in a bowl, but it will still
look good and taste delicious.

3 ▲ Put the amaretti in a large bowl
and crush them with a rolling pin.
Add the coffee ice cream and any
remaining Marsala and beat until
mixed. Spoon into the sponge-finger-
lined basin.

4 Press the ice cream against the
sponge to form an even layer with a
hollow. Freeze for 2 hours.

5 Put the vanilla ice cream and grated
chocolate in a bowl and beat together
until evenly mixed. Spoon into the
hollow in the centre of the bowl.
Smooth the top, then cover with the
overhanging muslin. Place in the
freezer overnight.

6 To serve, run a metal spatula
between the muslin and the bowl,
then unfold the top of the muslin.
Invert a chilled serving plate on top of
the *zuccotto*, then invert the two so
that the *zuccotto* is upside down on
the plate. Carefully peel off the muslin.

7 Decorate the *zuccotto* with the
chocolate curls, then sift cocoa
powder or icing sugar over.
Serve immediately.

Ricotta Pudding

This creamy, rich dessert is very easy to make. The combination of ricotta cheese and

candied fruits is very popular in Sicily, where this recipe originated.

Ingredients
225g/8oz/1 cup ricotta cheese
50g/2oz/¹/₃ cup candied fruits
60ml/4 tbsp sweet Marsala
250ml/8fl oz/1 cup double
    (heavy) cream
50g/2oz/¹/₄ cup caster (superfine) sugar,
    plus extra to serve
finely grated rind of 1 orange
350g/12oz/2 cups fresh raspberries
strips of thinly pared orange rind,
    to decorate

serves 4–6

Cook's Tip
Buy candied fruits in large pieces from
a good delicatessen – tubs of chopped
candied peel are too tough to eat raw,
and should only be used in baking.

1 ▲ Press the ricotta through a sieve
(strainer) into a bowl. Finely chop the
candied fruits and stir into the ricotta
with half of the Marsala. Put the
cream, sugar and orange rind in
another bowl and whip until the
cream is standing in soft peaks.

2 ▲ Fold the cream into the ricotta
mixture. Spoon into glass serving
bowls and top with the raspberries.
Chill until serving time. Sprinkle with
the remaining Marsala and dust the top
of each bowl with sugar just before
serving. Decorate with the orange rind.

Chocolate Salami

Salame al cioccolato

This after-dinner sweetmeat resembles a salami in shape, hence its curious name. It is very rich and will serve a lot of people, so is ideal for special occasions. Slice it very thinly and serve with espresso coffee and amaretto liqueur.

Ingredients
24 Petit Beurre biscuits (cookies), broken
350g/12oz dark (bittersweet) or plain
   (semisweet) chocolate, broken
   into squares
225g/8oz/1 cup unsalted butter, softened
60ml/4 tbsp amaretto liqueur
2 egg yolks
50g/2oz/¹/₂ cup flaked (sliced) almonds,
   lightly toasted and thinly
   shredded lengthways
25g/1oz/¹/₄ cup ground almonds
serves 8–12

1 ▲ Place the biscuits in a food processor fitted with a metal blade and process until coarsely crushed.

2 Place the chocolate in a large heatproof bowl. Place the bowl over a pan of barely simmering water, add a small chunk of the butter and all the liqueur and heat until the chocolate melts, stirring occasionally.

Cook's Tip
Take care when melting chocolate that it does not overheat or it will form a hard lump. The base of the bowl containing the chocolate must not touch the water, and the chocolate must be melted very slowly and gently. If you think the water is getting too hot, remove the pan from the heat.

3 ▲ Remove the bowl from the heat, allow the chocolate to cool for a minute or two, then stir in the egg yolks followed by the remaining butter, a little at a time. Tip in most of the crushed biscuits, leaving behind a good handful, and stir well to mix. Stir in the shredded almonds. Leave the mixture in a cold place for about 1 hour until it begins to stiffen.

4 ▲ Process the remaining crushed biscuits in the food processor until they are very finely ground. Tip into a bowl and mix with the ground almonds. Cover and set aside until serving time.

5 ▲ Turn the chocolate and biscuit mixture on to a sheet of lightly oiled greaseproof (waxed) paper, then shape into a 35cm/14in sausage shape with a palette knife or metal spatula, tapering the ends slightly so that the roll looks like a salami. Wrap in the paper and freeze for at least 4 hours until solid.

6 To serve, unwrap the 'salami'. Spread the ground biscuits and almonds out on a clean sheet of greaseproof paper and roll the salami in them until evenly coated. Transfer to a board and leave to stand for about 1 hour before serving in slices.

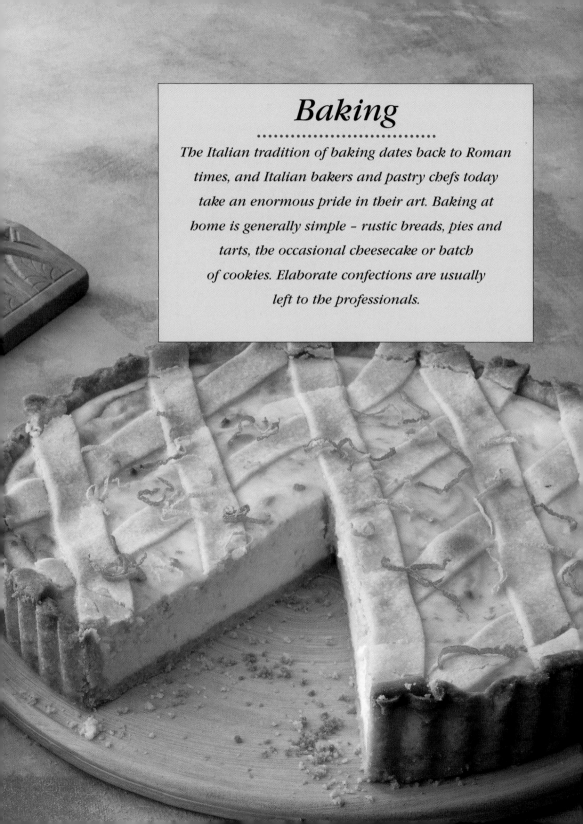

Baking

·······················

The Italian tradition of baking dates back to Roman times, and Italian bakers and pastry chefs today take an enormous pride in their art. Baking at home is generally simple – rustic breads, pies and tarts, the occasional cheesecake or batch of cookies. Elaborate confections are usually left to the professionals.

Sultana and Walnut Bread

Pane di uva con noci

This bread is delicious with soup for a first course, or with salami, cheese and salad for lunch. It also tastes good with jam, and toasts extremely well when it is a day or two old.

Ingredients

300g/11oz/2¾ cups strong white
    bread flour
2.5ml/½ tsp salt
15ml/1 tbsp butter
7.5ml/1½ tsp easy-blend (rapid-rise)
    dried yeast
115g/4oz/scant 1 cup sultanas
    (golden raisins)
75g/3oz/½ cup walnuts, roughly chopped
melted butter, for brushing
makes 1 loaf

1 ▲ Sift the flour and salt into a bowl, cut in the butter, then stir in the yeast.

2 ▲ Gradually add 175ml/6fl oz/¾ cup tepid water to the flour mixture, stirring with a spoon at first, then gathering the dough together with your hands. Turn the dough out on to a floured surface and knead for about 10 minutes until smooth and elastic.

Cook's Tip

Easy-blend (rapid-rise) dried yeast is sold in sachets at most supermarkets. It is a real boon for the busy cook because it cuts out the need to let the dough rise before shaping.

3 ▲ Knead the sultanas and walnuts into the dough until they are evenly distributed. Shape into a rough oval, place on a lightly oiled baking sheet and cover with oiled clear film (plastic wrap). Leave to rise in a warm place for 1–2 hours until doubled in bulk. Preheat the oven to 220°C/425°F/Gas 7.

4 Uncover the loaf and bake for 10 minutes, then reduce the oven temperature to 190°C/375°F/Gas 5 and bake for a further 20–25 minutes.

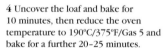

5 ▲ Transfer to a wire rack, brush with melted butter and cover with a dish towel. Cool before slicing.

Chocolate Bread

In Italy it is the custom to serve this dessert bread as a snack with mascarpone or

Gorgonzola cheese and a glass of red wine. It also tastes good spread with butter and jam.

Ingredients
450g/1lb/4 cups strong white
   bread flour
2.5ml/¹/₂ tsp salt
30ml/2 tbsp butter
30ml/2 tbsp caster (superfine) sugar
10ml/2 tsp easy-blend (rapid-rise)
   dried yeast
30ml/2 tbsp unsweetened
   cocoa powder
75g/3oz/¹/₂ cup plain (semisweet)
   chocolate chips
melted butter, for brushing
makes 2 loaves

1 ▲ Sift the flour and salt into a large bowl, cut in the butter with a knife, then stir in the sugar, yeast and cocoa powder.

2 Gradually add 300ml/¹/₂ pint/ 1¹/₄ cups of tepid water to the flour mixture, stirring with a spoon at first, then gathering the dough together with your hands.

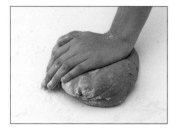

3 ▲ Turn the dough out on to a floured surface and knead for about 10 minutes until it becomes smooth and elastic.

4 ▲ Cut the dough in half and knead half the chocolate chips into each piece of dough until they are evenly distributed. Shape the dough into rounds, place on lightly oiled baking sheets and cover with oiled clear film (plastic wrap). Leave to rise in a warm place for 1–2 hours until the dough has doubled in bulk.

5 Preheat the oven to 220°C/425°F/ Gas 7. Uncover the loaves and bake for 10 minutes, then reduce the oven temperature to 190°C/375°F/Gas 5 and bake for a further 15–20 minutes.

6 ▲ Place the loaves on a wire rack and brush liberally with butter. Cover with a dish towel and leave to cool.

Ricotta Cheesecake

Crostata di ricotta

Low-fat ricotta cheese is excellent for cheesecake fillings because it has a good, firm texture.

Here it is enriched with eggs and cream and enlivened with tangy orange and lemon rind to

make a Sicilian-style dessert.

Ingredients
450g/1lb/2 cups low-fat ricotta cheese
120ml/4fl oz/¹/₂ cup double (heavy) cream
2 eggs
1 egg yolk
75g/3oz/¹/₃ cup caster (superfine) sugar
finely grated rind of 1 orange
finely grated rind of 1 lemon

For the pastry
175g/6oz/1¹/₂ cups plain (all-purpose) flour
45ml/3 tbsp caster (superfine) sugar
a pinch of salt
115g/4oz/8 tbsp chilled butter, diced
1 egg yolk
serves 8

1 ▲ Make the pastry. Sift the flour, sugar and salt on to a cold work surface. Make a well in the centre and put in the diced butter and egg yolk. Gradually work the flour into the diced butter and egg yolk, using your fingertips.

Variations
Add 50–115g/2–4oz/¹/₃–²/₃ cup finely chopped candied peel to the filling in step 3, or 50g/2oz/¹/₃ cup plain (semisweet) chocolate chips. For a really rich dessert, you can add both candied peel and some grated plain chocolate.

2 ▲ Gather the dough together, reserve about a quarter for the lattice, then press the rest into a 23cm/ in fluted tart tin (pan) with a loose base. Chill the pastry case for 30 minutes.

3 ▲ Meanwhile, preheat the oven to 190°C/375°F/Gas 5 and make the filling. Put all the ricotta, cream, eggs, egg yolk, sugar and orange and lemon rinds in a large bowl and beat together until evenly mixed.

4 ▲ Prick the bottom of the pastry case, then line with foil and fill with baking beans. Bake blind for 15 minutes, then transfer to a wire rack, remove the foil and beans and allow the tart shell to cool in the tin.

5 ▲ Spoon the cheese and cream filling into the pastry case and level the surface. Roll out the reserved dough and cut into strips. Arrange the strips on the top of the filling in a lattice pattern, sticking them in place with water.

6 Bake for 30–35 minutes until golden and set. Transfer to a wire rack and leave to cool, then carefully remove the side of the tin, leaving the cheesecake on the tin base.

Pine Nut Tart

Pinolata

Strange though it may seem, this traditional tart is an Italian version of the homely

Bakewell tart from Derbyshire in England.

Ingredients
115g/4oz/8 tbsp butter, softened
115g/4oz/generous ¹/₂ cup caster
(superfine) sugar
1 egg
2 egg yolks
150g/5oz/1¹/₄ cups ground almonds
115g/4oz/1 cup pine nuts
60ml/4 tbsp seedless raspberry jam
icing (confectioners') sugar, for dusting
whipped cream, to serve (optional)

For the pastry
175g/6oz/1¹/₂ cups plain (all-purpose) flour
65g/2¹/₂oz/¹/₃ cup caster (superfine) sugar
1.5ml/¹/₄ tsp baking powder
a pinch of salt
115g/4oz/8 tbsp chilled butter, diced
1 egg yolk
serves 8

3 ▲ Meanwhile, make the filling. Cream the butter and sugar together with an electric mixer until light and fluffy, then beat in the egg and egg yolks a little at a time, alternating them with the ground almonds. Beat in the pine nuts.

Cook's Tip
This pastry is too sticky to roll out, so simply mould it into the bottom and sides of the tin with your fingertips.

4 ▲ Preheat the oven to 160°C/325°F/ Gas 3. Spread the jam over the pastry base, then spoon in the filling. Bake for 30–35 minutes or until a skewer inserted in the centre of the tart comes out clean.

5 Transfer to a wire rack and leave to cool, then carefully remove the side of the tin, leaving the tart on the tin base. Dust with icing sugar and serve with whipped cream, if you like.

1 ▲ Make the pastry. Sift the flour, sugar, baking powder and salt on to a cold work surface. Make a well in the centre and put in the butter and egg yolk. Gradually work the flour into the butter and yolk, using your fingertips.

2 ▲ Gather the dough together, then press it into a 23cm/9in fluted tart tin (pan) with a removable base. Chill for 30 minutes.

Baked Sweet Ravioli

Ravioli dolci al forno

These delicious sweet ravioli are made with a rich pastry flavoured with lemon and filled

with the traditional ingredients used in Sicilian cassata.

Ingredients
225g/8oz/2 cups plain (all-purpose) flour
65g/2¹/₂oz/¹/₃ cup caster (superfine) sugar
90g/3¹/₂oz/¹/₂ cup butter
1 egg
5ml/1 tsp finely grated lemon rind
icing (confectioners') sugar and grated
    chocolate, for sprinkling

For the filling
175g/6oz/³/₄ cup ricotta cheese
50g/2oz/¹/₄ cup caster
    (superfine) sugar
4ml/³/₄ tsp vanilla extract
1 egg yolk
15ml/1 tbsp mixed candied fruits or
    chopped mixed (candied) peel
25g/1oz dark (bittersweet) chocolate,
    finely chopped or grated
1 egg, beaten
serves 4

1 Put the flour and sugar into a food processor and, working on full speed, add the butter in pieces until fully worked into the mixture. With the food processor still running, add the egg and lemon rind. The mixture should form a dough which just holds together.

2 Scrape the dough on to clear film (plastic wrap), cover with another sheet, flatten and chill until needed.

3 ▲ To make the filling, push the ricotta through a sieve (strainer) into a bowl. Stir in the sugar, vanilla extract, egg yolk, candied peel and chocolate until combined.

4 ▲ Remove the pastry from the refrigerator and allow to come to room temperature. Divide the pastry in half and roll each half between sheets of clear film to make strips, measuring 15 x 56cm/6 x 22in. Preheat the oven to 180°C/350°F/Gas 4.

5 Arrange heaped tablespoons of the filling in two rows along one of the pastry strips, ensuring there is at least 2.5cm/1in clear space around each spoonful. Brush the pastry between the dollops of filling with beaten egg. Place the second strip of pastry on top and press down between each mound of filling to seal.

6 Using a 6cm/2¹/₂in plain pastry cutter, cut around each mound of filling to make circular ravioli. Lift each one and, with your fingertips, seal the edges. Place the ravioli on a greased baking sheet and bake for 15 minutes until golden brown. Serve warm sprinkled with icing sugar and grated chocolate.

Spicy Fruit Cake from Siena

Panforte di Siena

This is a delicious flat cake with a wonderful spicy flavour. Panforte is very rich, so should be cut into small wedges – offer a glass of sparkling wine to go with it.

Ingredients
butter for greasing
175g/6oz/1 cup hazelnuts,
    roughly chopped
75g/3oz/¹/₂ cup whole almonds,
    roughly chopped
225g/8oz/1¹/₃ cups mixed candied
    fruits, diced
1.5ml/¹/₄ tsp ground coriander
4ml/ ³/₄ tsp ground cinnamon
1.5ml/¹/₄ tsp ground cloves
1.5ml/¹/₄ tsp grated nutmeg
50g/2oz/¹/₂ cup plain (all-purpose) flour
115g/4oz/¹/₂ cup honey
115g/4oz/generous 1 cup granulated
    (white) sugar
icing (confectioners') sugar,
    for dusting
serves 12–14

1 Preheat the oven to 180°C/350°F/
Gas 4. Grease a 20cm/8in round cake
tin (pan) with the butter. Line the base
with non-stick baking parchment.

2 ▲ Spread the nuts on a baking tray
and place in the oven for about
10 minutes until lightly toasted.
Remove and set aside. Lower the oven
temperature to 150°C/300°F/Gas 2.

3 In a large mixing bowl combine
the candied fruits, all the spices
and the flour and stir together with
a wooden spoon. Add the nuts and
stir in thoroughly.

Cook's Tip
This will store in an airtight container
for up to 2 weeks.

4 ▲ In a small, heavy pan, stir
together the honey and sugar and
bring to the boil. Cook the mixture
until it reaches 138°C/280°F on a
sugar thermometer or when a small
amount forms a hard ball when
pressed between fingertips in iced
water. Take care when doing this and
use a teaspoon to remove a little
mixture out of the pan for testing.

5 ▲ At this stage, immediately
pour the sugar syrup into the dry
ingredients and stir in well until evenly
coated. Pour into the prepared tin.
Dip a spoon into water and use the
back of the spoon to press the mixture
into the tin. Bake in the preheated
oven for 1 hour.

6 When ready, it will still feel quite
soft but will harden as it cools. Cool
completely in the tin and then turn
out on to a serving plate. Dust with
icing sugar before serving.

Hazelnut Bites

Nocciolini

Serve these sweet little nut cookies as petits fours with after-dinner coffee. They will keep for a couple of days in an airtight container and make a lovely gift.

Ingredients
115g/4oz/8 tbsp butter, softened
75g/3oz/¾ cup icing (confectioners')
    sugar, sifted
115g/4oz/1 cup plain (all-purpose) flour
75g/3oz/¾ cup ground hazelnuts
1 egg yolk
blanched whole hazelnuts, to decorate
icing sugar, for dusting
makes about 26

1 ▲ Preheat the oven to 180ºC/350ºF/ Gas 4. Line 3–4 baking sheets with non-stick baking parchment. Cream the butter and sugar together with an electric mixer until light and fluffy.

2 ▲ Beat in the flour, ground hazelnuts and egg yolk until they are evenly mixed.

Cook's Tip
Don't worry that the cookies are still soft at the end of the baking time – they will harden as they cool on the wire rack.

3 ▲ Take a teaspoonful of the mixture at a time and shape it into a round with your fingers. Place the rounds well apart on the baking parchment and press a whole hazelnut into the centre of each one.

4 ▲ Bake the cookies, one tray at a time, for about 10 minutes or until golden brown, then transfer to a wire rack and sift over icing sugar to cover. Leave to cool completely and harden before serving.

Ladies' Kisses
Baci di dama

These old-fashioned Piedmontese cookies make pretty petits fours.

Ingredients
150g/5oz/10 tbsp butter, softened
115g/4oz/¹/₂ cup caster (superfine) sugar
1 egg yolk
2.5ml/¹/₂ tsp almond extract
115g/4oz/1 cup ground almonds
175g/6oz/1¹/₂ cups plain (all-purpose) flour
50g/2oz plain (semisweet) chocolate
makes 20

1 Cream the butter and sugar together with an electric mixer until light and fluffy, then beat in the egg yolk, almond extract, ground almonds and flour until evenly mixed. Chill until firm, for about 2 hours.

2 Preheat the oven to 160°C/325°F/ Gas 3. Line 3–4 baking sheets with non-stick baking parchment.

3 ▲ Break off small pieces of dough and roll them into balls with your hands, making 40 altogether. Place the balls on the baking sheets, spacing them out well as they will spread in the oven.

Cook's Tip
These kisses look extra dainty served in frilly petit four cases.

4 Bake the cookies for 20 minutes or until golden. Remove the baking sheets from the oven, lift off the parchment with the cookies on, then place on wire racks. Leave the kisses to cool on the paper. Repeat with the remaining mixture.

5 ▲ When the kisses are cold, lift them off the paper. Melt the chocolate in a bowl over a pan of hot water. Sandwich the kisses in pairs, with the melted chocolate. Leave to cool and set before serving.

Tea Biscuits
Pastine da the

These cookies are very quick and easy to make. If you don't want to pipe the mixture, simply spoon it on to the baking parchment and press it down with a fork.

Ingredients
150g/5oz/10 tbsp butter, softened
75g/3oz/³/₄ cup icing (confectioners') sugar, sifted
1 egg, beaten
a few drops of almond extract
225g/8oz/2 cups plain (all-purpose) flour
2–3 large pieces of candied peel
makes 20

Variation
Use 10 glacé (candied) cherries instead of the candied peel. Cut them in half and press one half, cut-side down, into the centre of each biscuit.

1 Preheat the oven to 230°C/450°F/ Gas 8. Line two baking sheets with non-stick baking parchment.

2 Cream the butter and sugar with an electric mixer until light and fluffy, then beat in the egg, almond extract and flour until evenly mixed.

3 ▲ Spoon the mixture into a piping bag fitted with a star nozzle and pipe 10 rosette shapes on each of the baking sheets.

4 ▲ Cut the peel into small diamond shapes and press one diamond into the centre of each cookie, to decorate. Bake for 5 minutes or until golden.

5 Transfer the cookies on the baking parchment to a wire rack and leave to cool. Lift the cookies off the paper when cool.

Index

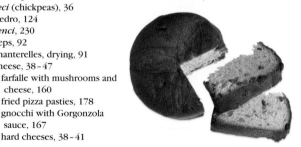

Index

Index

Index

Index

Acknowledgements

All the photographs are by William
Adams-Lingwood and Janine
Hosegood (cut-outs) except the
pictures on pages 6–9, which are by
John Heseltine.

NOTES

NOTES

NOTES

NOTES

NOTES

NOTES

NOTES

NOTES